FAMILY FORMATION IN AN AGE OF NASCENT CAPITALISM

STUDIES IN SOCIAL DISCONTINUITY

Under the Consulting Editorship of:

CHARLES TILLY
University of Michigan

EDWARD SHORTER
University of Toronto

William A. Christian, Jr. Person and God in a Spanish Valley

Joel Samaha. Law and Order in Historical Perspective: The Case of Elizabethan Essex

John W. Cole and Eric R. Wolf. The Hidden Frontier: Ecology and Ethnicity in an Alpine Valley

Immanuel Wallerstein. The Modern World-System: Capitalist Agriculture and the Origins of the European World-Economy in the Sixteenth Century

John R. Gillis. Youth and History: Tradition and Change in European Age Relations 1770 – Present

D. E. H. Russell. Rebellion, Revolution, and Armed Force: A Comparative Study of Fifteen Countries with Special Emphasis on Cuba and South Africa

Kristian Hvidt. Flight to America: The Social Background of 300,000 Danish Emigrants

James Lang. Conquest and Commerce: Spain and England in the Americas

Stanley H. Brandes. Migration, Kinship, and Community: Tradition and Transition in a Spanish Village

Daniel Chirot. Social Change in a Peripheral Society: The Creation of a Balkan Colony

Jane Schneider and Peter Schneider. Culture and Political Economy in Western Sicily

Michael Schwartz. Radical Protest and Social Structure: The Southern Farmers' Alliance and Cotton Tenancy, 1880-1890

Ronald Demos Lee (Ed.). Population Patterns in the Past

David Levine. Family Formations in an Age of Nascent Capitalism

In preparation

Dirk Hoerder. Crowd Action in Revolutionary Massachusetts, 1765-1780

Charles P. Cell. Revolution at Work: Mobilization Campaigns in China

Harry W. Pearson. The Livelihood of Man by Karl Polanyi

FAMILY FORMATION IN AN AGE OF NASCENT CAPITALISM

David Levine

Department of History and Philosophy
The Ontario Institute for Studies in Education
Toronto, Ontario, Canada

Academic Press

New York   San Francisco   London

A Subsidiary of Harcourt Brace Jovanovich, Publishers

ACADEMIC PRESS, INC.
111 Fifth Avenue, New York, New York 10003

United Kingdom Edition published by
ACADEMIC PRESS, INC. (LONDON) LTD.
24/28 Oval Road, London NW1

Library of Congress Cataloging in Publication Data

Levine, David.
    Family formation in an age of nascent capitalism.

    (Studies in social discontinuity)
    Based on the author's thesis, Cambridge University.
    Bibliography: p.
    1.   Family—England—History.   2.   Marriage—England—
History.   3.   Villages—England—Case studies.   4.   Great
Britain—Economic conditions—1760–1860.   I.   Title.
II.   Series
HQ613.L48   1977   301.42'0942   76-50398
ISBN 0–12–445050–4

To Maish

Contents

List of Figures and Tables

Figures

Tables

Acknowledgments

The original research for this book was funded by the generous offices of the Canada Council. At Cambridge I had the privilege to be associated with the Cambridge Group for the History of Population and Social Structure. Roger Schofield, Tony Wrigley, Peter Laslett, Karla Oosterveen, and Richard Wall all showed remarkable tolerance in listening to my inchoate theorizing. Oly Anderson and Ros Davies were of inestimable aid in helping me to solve the practical matters to do with my data. Les Pepper calmed me during those many occasions when the task seemed insurmountable.

While at Cambridge I was fortunate to get to know Keith Wrightson. Our interests in history and social change complemented each other, and I learned a great deal from his careful mastery of source materials, which he combined with an ability to reconstruct sympathetically the often short but rarely simple annals of the poor.

The other person to whom I would like to pay special tribute is Hans Medick. Since our meeting he has always encouraged me to go on with the empirical side of my work while urging me to extend the analysis. Moreover, he has always given me useful advise, freely and graciously. Furthermore, Hans was instrumental in arranging a month-long visit to the Max-Planck-Institut für Geschichte, Göttingen, where his director, Professor Dr. Rudolf Vierhaus, and his colleagues made me welcome and provided me with the kind of oasis in which much of this work was completed.

John Eisenberg, Chad Gaffield, and Bryant Griffiths, colleagues at the Ontario Institute for Studies in Education, have been kind, courteous and willing to provide a forum for discussion. Ian Winchester provided me with the opportunity to complete the manuscript.

My wife Jennifer had almost nothing to do with this book—she had her own work with which to "enjoyce" herself. Together we found that there were other things.

1

INTRODUCTION

The controversy over the growth of population during the English Industrial Revolution provided the starting point for this study, but in the course of my research I found myself, as it were, moving backward in time. This study deals with the impact of early capitalism on the strategies of family formation among four sets of English villagers in the period before the wholesale switch-over to factory industry. Although this era, roughly speaking from 1550 to 1850, has been variously described as "traditional," "preindustrial," and, more recently, "protoindustrial," I prefer to see it as a stage in the transition from feudalism to capitalism—a halfway house.

In Marx's categorical framework the nature of full-blown industrial capitalism is twofold: The worker is not only separated from the ownership of the means of production but also, and perhaps more important, he loses control over the labor process, becoming an extension of the machine that regulates *his* work. It is in the second sense that the industrial activity studied in this volume does not yet fulfill Marx's definition. Rural industrial workers were indeed often reduced to proletarianization, but they almost never lost control over the pace of production. Their skill was valued, not diluted as in later stages of capitalist industrialization. In agriculture, much the same process was under way when the peasantry were first dispossessed of their land and then, later, brought together as wage laborers working the farms of capitalist producers. Gang labor in rural agriculture was not a new phenomenon—slavery is just one age-old variant of this form of labor—and the English rural experience evokes many parallels. But agricultural wage-labor is essentially different from slavery or feudal demesne production in that the laborer sells his labor for a wage determined with reference to distant markets. The important dimension of capitalist agriculture is that unlike other forms of market-oriented, large-scale commercial production it was based on a system of private property, wage labor, and concentrated units of production. This last point is of critical importance in discussing England where the spread of commercial, capitalist agriculture was accompanied by the disappearance of the small farmer.

The demise of the peasantry in England has attracted a great deal of attention from scholars, and a consensus now appears to be emerging that allows for regional, indeed often local, variants but recognizes the later sixteenth and seventeenth centuries as the crucial period in this development.[1] Thereafter, to be sure, small, independent landowners and farmers persisted, but within an economic universe in which the classic triad of landlord, tenant farmer, and wage laborer exercised hegemony.

The impact of these changes—the proletarianization of industrial and agricultural producers—had important demographic implications which have not yet been adequately analyzed. This lack of systematic analysis, employing reliable demographic techniques, implied to me that a great deal of the literature on this subject was of limited value. Theories have played a role out of proportion to the slender evidential basis on which they have been developed. Reacting to this state of affairs, I decided to examine available data and attempt to develop an analysis based on fact but still informed by the contours of the preceding debate. Family reconstitution provided an attractive approach to this problem. Primarily it enabled me to derive precise, verifiable statistics describing the demographic behavior of selected populations. Furthermore, family reconstitution has the advantage of producing comparable results, so that by carefully selecting the populations to be studied it is possible to produce results that might answer many of the questions posed by the original debate. I must admit that I regard family reconstitution as neither a panacea nor a placebo. There are, to be sure, some very real shortcomings with this approach, revolving around the limited, narrowly statistical nature of the information that can be derived by this form of analysis. But in terms of accuracy and precision, the relevance of this approach comes into its own. Important questions concerning nuptiality, fertility, and mortality can be answered only by this method. In the following chapters I

---

[1] See, for example, the panoramic view of E. Kerridge, *The Agricultural Revolution*, and the collection of essays in *The Agrarian History of England and Wales*, ed. J. Thirsk (1967). A very good view of change at the county level is presented in a series of articles by J. A. Yelling focusing on Worcestershire: "Common Land and Enclosure in East Worcestershire, 1540–1870"; "The Combination and Rotation of Crops in East Worcestershire, 1540–1660"; and "Changes in Crop Production in East Worcestershire 1540–1867." Two local studies stand out: W. G. Hoskins, *The Midland Peasant*, and M. Spufford, *Contrasting Communities*. Perhaps the best synoptic review of the whole discussion is by H. J. Habakkuk, "La Disparition du Paysan Anglais."

shall adopt this microanalytical method in studying the four villages that have been selected, but for the remainder of this introduction I prefer to place this study in the context of the larger debate concerning nascent capitalism, early rural industrialization, and the growth of population to which my research is addressed.

The debate over the demographic implications of economic change in early modern times has been carried out largely on a macro-level. Important issues, such as the population rise in the sixteenth century and its apparent stagnation in much of the seventeenth, have been studied on national or regional levels, but little research has been done on the local level. Only by focusing our attention on small units of analysis, however, is it possible to disaggregate the role of the variables and specify the ways in which demographic adjustments were made. For example, a large-scale, aggregative analysis of births (baptisms) and deaths (burials) yields relatively little meaningful data on demographic behavior because, too often, the base population within which these events occurred is not known. Thus, a rising number of births (baptisms) may signify a real increase in the birth rate or it may reflect only a commensurate increase in the base population. Moreover, even if we have relatively reliable information concerning the actual size of the population producing these births (baptisms), we are still some distance from an accurate explanation. This added information enables us to determine whether or not the birth rate was rising, but it does little to explain the mechanism whereby the rise occurred. For instance, a rising birth rate could be caused by any of the following factors, either by itself or in combination with others: lowering of age at marriage, increasing incidence of marriage, rising marital fertility, increasing illegitimacy, improving adult life expectancy, or declining incidence of breast-feeding (which would tend to shorten the intervals between births). This abbreviated list of possible factors can be rendered useful only through the use of a technique which enables the researcher to analyze and study each of the various possibilities. Family reconstitution is such a technique, and the logic behind it is beguilingly simple. One treats a parish register like a giant jigsaw puzzle, the pieces being the particles of information describing births (baptisms), deaths (burials), and marriages. Then one arranges this material into families of origin ("demographic units of production") through a long, laborious but relatively straight-forward process of selection and organization. Once the manual work is completed, it becomes possible to analyze the assembled data according to whatever criteria one wishes. Obtaining detailed information describing such demographic phenomena as the age of mothers at the birth of their last children or the proportion of brides bearing children within eight months of marriage (and, therefore, being pregnant at marriage) becomes a matter of calculation, not guesswork.

Clearly such a method of analysis offers the possibility of testing hypotheses concerning the interplay of demographic behavior and socioeconomic change at the individual level. It is unfortunate, however, that such information is gained only at the expense of hours of toil, so that one cannot study a wide variety of communities but must restrict oneself to a small sample. The vagaries of record survival and, equally important, the wide variations in quality among English parish registers, moreover, further restrict the choices available. For these reasons it was not possible to adopt a random sampling method in designing my research program. It was necessary to approach the problem from the other direction, as it were. The method of selection was, therefore, purposefully carried out in such a way that the communities studied represented distinct socioeconomic types. It was hoped that comparisons, both among villages and across time, would gain further meaning from this approach. The four communities to be discussed in this study represent very different strands in the socioeconomic development of English society in the era of nascent capitalism.

Shepshed, Leicestershire was an unregulated freehold village on the edge of Charnwood forest. Social control there was weak. The inhabitants of Shepshed became involved in the framework knitting industry in the later stages of the seventeenth century, and in the course of the eighteenth century Shepshed became the most intensively industrialized rural community in Leicestershire. By 1812, for example, there were 1000 knitting frames in use within a population of about 3000. During the period under discussion the organization of production underwent a series of shifts from a craft-oriented trade to one where capitalist relations of production held sway. In terms of the typology of capitalist industrialization described by Marx, Shepshed's progress represented a transitional phase during which the workers lost ownership of the means of production at an early stage but never became mere extensions of the machines on which they worked. Although a shift away from household-centered production did occur early in the nineteenth century, these "protofactories" were still dependent upon human-powered production. In fact, the process of production in the incipient factories is more reminiscent of a *Manufaktur* than it is a prediction of the automated labor process of modern industry.[2] The impetus to bring framework knitters together in such "protofactories" arose from entrepreneurs' desires to retain close control over production in order to keep up with the "fantastical folly of fashion."[3] Such a desire was not new. Indeed, when the framework knitting industry began early in the seventeenth century, it was organized on precisely these lines. The move

---

[2] A very interesting essay on the nature of the *modern* factory is provided by S.D. Chapman, "A Textile Factory before Arkwright: A Typology of Factory Development."

[3] On the role of fashion in the early stages of the growth of the hosiery industry see J. Thirsk, "The Fantastical Folly of Fashion: The English Stocking Knitting Industry, 1500–1700."

away from such *Manufaktur* was, at that time, sparked by the capitalists' desire to escape from the countervailing power of the journeymen, who played a decisive role in restricting the capitalists' control over the process of production. And, secondarily, the movement away from London to the east Midlands coincided with a switch to mass production, away from luxury goods made from silk to common goods made from wool and/or cotton. Throughout the whole period of our study, the process of production in Shepshed remained protoindustrial. It was only in the third quarter of the nineteenth century that the switch-over to automated production became widespread.

During the period of the study, 1600–1851, the population of Shepshed grew rapidly—particularly in the period after 1750. Results derived from family reconstitution will be employed to determine the role of different demographic elements in undermining the demographic equilibrium that existed before the onset of rural industrialization. At this point the wider relevance of Shepshed as an example of many similar villages undergoing both economic change and rapid population growth becomes apparent. Because they identify the critical factors causing this disequilibrating behavior, the results of this study affect the wider debate over the impact of nascent capitalism and early industrialization on the family.

The debate over the growth of population during the Industrial Revolution has taken place on confined terrain and employed a narrow conception of the nature of this discontinuity. Attention has been directed almost wholly toward the period of the "classical" Industrial Revolution. This point of view has diverted attention from the continuous demographic discontinuity that followed the proletarianization and wholesale commercialization of agriculture and industry that took place, unevenly to be sure, throughout Western Europe after the advent of the modern capitalist world-system in the sixteenth century.[4] The rise in population after 1750 was unique only in that it continued unabated, for reasons I believe have more to do with technology than with demography. The "modern rise in population" was sustained largely because technological improvements in production and transportation continued to lower the threshold of subsistence while they simultaneously increased the demand for ever more unskilled labor. The evidence from Shepshed supports the argument that the acceleration of economic activity after 1750 was the prime agent breaking down those traditional social controls that previously maintained a demographic equilibrium in which population size was kept in line with resources. Where late age at marriage and, to a lesser extent, restriction of fertility within marriage were once effective methods of demographic regulation, the proletarianization of peasants and craftsman undermined the efficacy of these controls. In the protoindustrial environment of

---

[4] On the wider ramifications of this subject see I. Wallerstein, *The Modern World-System.*

Shepshed, the rising birth rate rather than a falling death rate proved to be of prime importance. The crucial importance of this finding lies in its demonstration that the demographic behavior of these villages was flexible enough to be substantially modified by changing socioeconomic conditions.

The second community I studied was another Leicestershire village, Bottesford, chosen because it stood at the opposite end of the socioeconomic spectrum from Shepshed and yet lay not 15 miles distant. In the seventeenth century both villages were roughly the same size, between 600 and 700, although Bottesford appears to have been the wealthier. The presence of the Manners family, dukes of Rutland and lords of the manor of Bottesford, however, was of crucial importance. Their family seat at Belvoir Castle—overlooking Bottesford from a hilltop position just three miles away—dominated the village—physically, socially, and economically. The duke of Rutland owned 54% of the land in Bottesford. The rector of Bottesford, appointed by the duke, owned a further 14%, and various charitable institutions, controlled by the duke, owned another 11%. Significant relationships between patterns of rural landownership and settlement patterns, village social structure, administration of the poor law, programs of enclosure, and the organization of agricultural production have been found in nineteenth century Leicestershire.[5] In addition, landownership strongly influenced the location of both the rural framework knitting industry and dissenting religious congregations. The dukes of Rutland exercised their uncontested influence in Bottesford and the rest of their domain to keep out rural industry, which they believed would force up the poor rolls and thereby diminish their tenantry's ability to pay their rents.

Bottesford, therefore, presented an experience diametrically opposed to Shepshed. Whereas Shepshed was industrialized and relatively free of direct social supervision, the resident landowners in Bottesford, who were among the wealthiest members of the English nobility, regulated the town closely and maintained its rural character. An anecdote illustrates how the Manners family impinged upon the lives of the inhabitants of Bottesford. In the village church in Bottesford, which also served as the burial place of the Manners family, one whole section is filled with their ostentatious tombs. By the early seventeenth century their monuments had become so enormous that the village church had to be rebuilt to accommodate them.

The interrelationship between Bottesford's agrarian and its demographic history shows how the emergent *national* division of agricultural labor in the seventeenth century affected the most personal decisions of the inhabitants of one village. A different influence of this agrarian capitalism can be found in the third community—Terling, Essex—which

---

[5] D. Mills, "Landownership and Rural Population."

was closely integrated into the London food market from the beginning of the seventeenth century. London's influence in English economic and social history is an acknowledged factor of real significance, and it is interesting to see how, in the case of Terling, it spread into the personal lives of the rural laborers. Terling, like Bottesford, was dominated by its landlord. For this reason the size of the community was regulated by social rather than economic forces. Thus, surplus children who could not find work in their native parish were usually forced out into the wider world. Such emigration usually had one of two destinations—the local town or, suprisingly often, London. E.A. Wrigley has written perceptively of London's role as a center of demographic concentration, anually absorbing up to half the national rate of growth.[6] In the same way, but to a lesser extent, the small cities and towns also consumed the human fodder produced by relatively healthy villages like Terling and Bottesford.

Little is known about the course of the urban death rate in the eighteenth century, but some evidence suggests that the increased use of brick and stone in building may have been of importance in reducing the ravages of the epidemics which killed urban dwellers in startling numbers. It is argued that at some point in the eighteenth century the incidence of such epidemic diseases waned: "It was the peaks rather than the plateau of mortality that was lowered." In other words, the death rate was lowered not so much by a reduction of mortality in *normal* years as by an unmistakable abatement of "great crisis." Epidemic disease ceased to be a great killer.[7] Even more important, perhaps, is the liklihood that there was a change in the age-specific nature of mortality. Children continued to die in great numbers, as any student of the nineteenth century city is aware, but the life expectancy of adults seems to have improved.

As a result of this change in mortality, openings in the urban labor market began to close, and out-migration from rural villages like Terling and Bottesford slowed. From the middle of the eighteenth century, rural villages began to grow, and rural underemployment and unemployment created a great problem. Even in these circumstances the rural birth rate rose. The evidence from the reconstitution studies of Terling and Bottesford shows quite clearly that even in these rural enclaves a rising birth rate was at least as important as a simultaneously falling death rate. This finding was both surprising and significant because in a condition of demographic disequilibrium—such as that initiated by an independently falling death rate—one would expect that the mortality and fertility would move directly, not inversely. But this is precisely what did *not* happen. In this case the demographic scissors opened, and the birth rate rose while the death rate fell.

---

[6] E.A. Wrigley, "A Simple Model of London's Importance in Changing English Society and Economy 1650–1750."

[7] K.F. Helleiner, "The Vital Revolution Reconsidered," p. 85.

The fourth village to be discussed in this study is the touchstone of English historical demography—Colyton, Devon—about which E.A. Wrigley published the first family reconstitution study.[8] Since that time Colyton has assumed an importance out of proportion to its significance: I have included it in this study, however, not to repeat the points Wrigley elucidated but rather to try to understand why this village underwent its peculiar demographic cycle. In doing so I will part company with Wrigley and present an explanation for the phenomenon he has described but not explained.

In the course of my research I discovered that Colyton had a thriving protoindustrial sector in the later sixteenth century, but the reorganization of the woollen trade which occurred in the west of England with the switch-over to the New Draperies in the seventeenth century passed Colyton by. In explaining the dramatic drop in seventeenth century Colyton's rate of reproduction, I shall stress this phase of *deindustrialization*. Essentially, the seventeenth century in Colyton was a period of retrenchment in the face of diminishing economic opportunity, and therein I believe we are able to discover the moving force behind the village's long-term demographic behavior.

The four villages to be discussed in this study present a kind of symmetry. Two—Shepshed and Colyton—were engaged in protoindustry, while the other pair remained agrarian throughout the period of the study. The protoindustrial communities, however, had a substantially different chronology. Colyton's fortunes rose in the later sixteenth century and declined dramatically in the mid-seventeenth, while Shepshed's committment to a nonagrarian way of life began in the later seventeenth century. The town enjoyed a long period of prosperity until the end of the Napoleonic wars when it entered a prolonged moribund period which was ended by introduction of modern, automated production in the third quarter of the nineteenth century. The organization of production in the two villages appears to have been quite different. In Colyton, so far as I can discover, weaving and spinning were largely a by-employment with which poor husbandmen, cottagers, and laborers supplemented the income from their tiny patches of land. In Shepshed the framework knitting industry was, at first, organized as a craft, and the journeymen were able to achieve a position of some independence, buttressed largely by a medieval-style charter of incorporation that prescribed an apprenticeship system and thereby inhibited the spread of wage labor until the middle of the eighteenth century.

---

[8] E.A. Wrigley, "Family Limitation in Pre-Industrial England"; and "Mortality in Pre-Industrial England: The Example of Colyton, Devon, Over Three Centuries." The article, "Family Limitation," first appeared in *Economic History Review*, 2nd series, XIX, (1966) but I prefer to use the reprinted version in the Drake volume cited in the bibliography because it is more accessible. Therefore, all further references to this important essay will refer to that reprinted version.

In the two agricultural villages, similar differences were apparent. Terling was, from the outset, a corn-exporting community with agriculture geared to commercial production. Bottesford, on the other hand, initially produced corn, but its grain production was seriously crippled when villages on the light, sandy soils of southern and eastern England gained a competitive advantage from the spread of convertible husbandry. Thereafter it became first a pastoral and then a dairying center. These shifts in Bottesford's economy were unlike anything experienced by Terling.

At various points in this introduction I have referred to the pullulating nature of economy and population in the era of nascent capitalism. I shall now describe the framework within which these economic and demographic changes occurred. My argument will be presented in simplified and highly stylized terms in order to discuss the themes on which my four examples are variations.

In England the break-up of the feudal economy occurred in the crucible of population decline, popular revolt, declining seigneurial income and authority, and general political anarchy that constituted the later Middle Ages. The sixteenth century saw an initial period of growth in trade, population, and production that reached levels similar to those attained in the high Middle Ages. The early modern economy, however, differed from the feudal in that it was based on capitalist or neocapitalist labor relations. In terms of production potential this distinction was most important because it greatly enhanced the possibility of squeezing surplus value from the mass of laborers and peasants who constituted the bulk of the population. The impact of this exploitation was redoubled by the massive price inflation during the period.

The peasantry had two alternative strategies for coping with not only the difficulties of rising population but also the increased exactions of the capitalist and the state. The first was a form of restricted inheritance whereby family holdings were kept intact and surplus children were forced out into the world. The second was subdividing family holdings among increasing numbers of heirs. In either case the process of proletarianization went forward with astonishing speed in a rural economy capable of only limited absorption. Throughout Europe, the sixteenth century witnessed a proliferation of beggars, vagabonds, and bandits.[9] Cities mushroomed as surplus men and women were forced to leave their native villages.

This proliferation of men and women living marginally on the edges of the agrarian economy was not a new phenomenon. It also occurred in the late thirteenth century, when, as in the sixteenth century, marginal men and women eked out a livelihood any way they could. In the sixteenth century, however, to a surprising extent the marginal men and women

---

[9] Wallerstein, *Modern World-System*, pp. 117–118, 139–143.

were integrated into a larger, extralocal pool of laborers through which bulky, mass-produced goods were transported across the width and breadth of the Western European commercial world.

Long-distance trade controlled by a small group of capitalist merchants was not, of course, a new phenomenon. It could be found at any time and, literally, at any place in medieval Europe. The crucial development was that sixteenth century commerce increasingly involved trade in finished manufactured goods rather than luxury articles.

Finally and—Immanuel Wallerstein would argue—critically, the sixteenth century witnessed the creation of a system of geopolitical states within whose borders production, consumption, and taxation occurred and economic and demographic phenomena played themselves out.[10] The emergent state system thereby created the political forum where the capitalist could vie for power and influence with the aristocratic landowner. The odds, to be sure, favored the traditional elites, but the economic demands of warfare, diplomacy, and corruption gave the capitalist a tool with which to institutionalize his position. Although the new monarchies consistently broke faith with their creditors, their fiscal highhandedness led them nowhere. Stumbling from fiscal crisis to fiscal crisis, the state system evolved the safeguards and the respect for property—liquid as well as landed—that were integral to the survival of merchant capitalism. In this sense, then, the emergence of the state was as important to the development of capitalism as the loans and advances of the bankers and traders were to the survival of the underfinanced, corruption-ridden states. In this sense, the emergence of capitalism was a political phenomenon—the aristocratic rulers recognized that they could not fight and rule without the financial aid of the bourgeoisie, the capitalists that they could have no security without the respect for their property that the state could provide. The formation of nations legitimated, first, the survival and, later, the hegemony of the capitalist system.

Within the context of these wider movements the interaction between demographic and economic movements worked itself out at the individual level. As I have argued, the triumph of the capitalist system was only achieved by dismantling the political, economic, and social structures of the feudal system; but this transition was part of a larger process which proceeded *unevenly* across space and time. Because we cannot stop the historical process and examine its inner workings like those of a clock, we must try to see the system as a whole, and in this way understand the functioning of the individual parts. In this essay I am primarily concerned with the ways in which the nascent capitalist system undermined the demographic bases of the peasant community and substituted a new set of imperatives.

---

[10] Wallerstein, *Modern World-System*, especially Chapter 4, "From Seville to Amsterdam: The Failure of Empire."

One of the characteristics of a demographic analysis is that the information it provides should, in essence, be quite simple. Population can rise only if there are more births or fewer deaths. Thus, to specify what causes population growth, a rising birth rate or a falling death rate, is a question readily answered by family reconstitution. Going beyond this simple answer to the larger, more important question of how and why growth occurs is rather more difficult. An answer to this question must be sought in the context of the wider set of circumstances within which proletarianization occurred.

In any discussion, proletarianization is of prime importance because it removed the strictures and confines from the traditional world of the peasant and craftsman. Nascent capitalism undermined those traditional social controls that maintained a demographic equilibrium in which each generation replaced its predecessor. Insofar as economic independence was a necessary precondition to marriage, age at marriage in the traditional society was kept high by the inelastic demand for labor in the preindustrial economy. Members of each new generation were expected to wait until their fathers retired or died before assuming control over their family farms or workshops. For this reason, peasants and artisans adopted a prudent, calculating approach to marriage. Older brides were often preferred, not only because they had a shorter childbearing period but also because their experience in farmwork and domestic duties were economic assets. Among the poorer members of society it seems that such an approach to marriage was of the greatest importance. The proletarianization of peasants and artisans estranged wide sections of society from the controls which had traditionally operated to maintain an optimum population size. In this way understanding the proletarianization of wide sections of the labor force is of critical importance in understanding the demographically disequilibrating effects of nascent capitalism.

The social dislocation accompanying proletarianization occasioned a fall in the age at marriage—the linchpin of preindustrial demographic equilibrium—in two ways: initially traditional sanctions against early marriage were weakened; subsequently those groups which married early became proportionately more important while those, like peasants and artisans, which married late, became less important. In addition to extending the years of childbearing, the fall in age at marriage also shortened the interval between generations, so that more children were born per unit of time. In this way a declining age at marriage produced a significant rise in the birth rate, even in the absence of any change in fertility. It should be stressed, however, that proletarianization itself did not necessarily lead to a fall in age at marriage—it only removed the disincentive to early marriage. What led to earlier and more frequent marriages was the opportunity for employment offered by protoindustry and capitalist farming. Arthur Young, the eighteenth century English agricultural writer, remarked that "It is employment that creates population: marriages are early and numerous in proportion to the amount of employment." This idea was commonplace among mercantilist social commentators and even received the imprimatur of such later social commentators as Adam Smith and Thomas Malthus who saw the demand for labor as the most important variable in their demographic equation.

In the era of nascent capitalism it became ever more likely that the factors influencing the demand for labor were being determined outside the locale. These exogenous influences on the village-level demand for labor were an important development because they withdrew large segments of the rural population from the relatively self-contained regional economy and integrated them into a national or even worldwide pool of labor. Thus, the well-being of rural proletarians could be determined by trade fluctuations, distant climate conditions or, more ominously, by the vagaries of international diplomacy and its logical extension, war. The demographic importance of this development is obvious—the decision to marry was being determined by conditions beyond a betrothed couple's control and understanding.

The demographic profile of the proletarianized population was characterized by high rates of natural increase: early marriage and a long fertile period combined to produce a substantial rise in the birth rate. This rise was of such a magnitude that it far outstripped the "positive check" afforded by the higher levels of mortality prevailing among the impoverished inhabitants of rural slums. Moreover, the high rates of natural increase had the further effect of altering the population's age distribution by increasing the proportion below childbearing age. A more broadly based age-pyramid meant that each cohort entering the marriage market was substantially larger than its predecessor. In this way, population growth among a proletarianized population developed a self-sustaining impetus.

Because the increase in population forced wages down, it was difficult for a proletarianized family to survive on the husband's earnings alone, and few households included just one wage earner. It was common for the wife and children of the head of the household also to work at production. Such work was essentially different from the contribution women and children traditionally made to the domestic economy. In the peasant household, the wife's duties normally included cleaning, cooking, shopping, and often, gardening and animal minding. Such activity cannot be described as mere housework; it was a critical contribution to the finely balanced household economy. Peasants understood this aspect of their wives' duties and, indeed, often considered domestic skills to be among the most important prerequisites a potential wife could possess. The restructuring of the domestic economy that occurred with the proletarianization of the peasants and craftsmen not only affected the men, but also reordered the division of labor *within* the domestic economy. In addition to her normal chores, the wife of a protoindustrialist or farm laborer was also expected to earn her wages, although, of course, a direct money transfer was not always made. At times the wife's proletarianization was implicit, her work serving as an adjunct to her husband's.

Production was organized in many different ways during the protoindustrial period. In brief, however, two variants stand out. In the first, the household functioned as a self-contained unit, differentiated internally so that each member had a specific task. A good example of this development is protoindustrial textile manufacturing in which different members of the weaver's family carded the wool, spun the yarn, and wove the cloth. In contrast to this "production line," the second protoindustrial variant involved differentiation between households rather than within them. In this variant, each household specialized in one task, be it combing or spinning or weaving, and the article was passed by the merchant capitalist or his agent from one stage in production to the next.

By circumventing the urban workers the merchant capitalist could simultaneously lower his production costs and increase his control over labor, thereby increasing his power enormously. The precise, legal ownership of the tools used in production was not so important as the control over the whole process. Similarly, the fact that the merchant capitalist did not directly supervise the carding, spinning, or weaving is not so important as the fact that he exerted power over the myriad of rural workers by controlling their access to the markets in which their goods were sold. Because the merchant capitalist controlled the marketplace, he was able to force wages down. His success in reducing wages (and thereby massively increasing profits) was abetted by the fact that wage negotiation was carried out individually with rural cottagers who were much less formidable bargainers than urban journeymen. In this sense the success of rural industrialization depended on the de facto proletarianization of the workforce.

The merchant capitalist was primarily concerned with extending his control over labor and thereby reducing costs and increasing his own freedom of action. On the other hand, it should be pointed out that the relocation of industry in a rural setting seems to have had at least as much to do with the needs of the poor peasants and laborers who formed the pool of cheap labor. Rural industries usually located in regions where an impoverished population found it necessary to supplement an inadequate or diminishing agricultural income. Population pressure and a system of divided inheritance together often formed a backdrop to the establishment of industries in the countryside. Initially the peasant laborer cum protoindustrialist usually relied on the advent of industry as a new source of income to stop the gap; but, as I have already outlined, the demographic implications of protoindustry created a completely proletarianized labor force wholly reliant on this source of income.

The transition to this second stage of rural industrialization, in which labor was, in every sense, proletarianized, created what Hans Medick has called "the Janus face of protoindustrialization."[11] For these laborers were the forerunners of the modern factory proletariat—although not in every case because, as I remarked earlier, protoindustrialization was not linear but pullulating. The rural, industrial laborers were both tied to the community and yet, just as surely, rootless. Their affiliations were, in a sense, international, for it was on this larger stage that the vicissitudes of their lives were worked out. Their wages were determined not with reference to local prices but with reference to the international value of their production. This factor is, I believe, of the greatest importance in explaining the pullulating nature of protoindustrialization in which the development and demise of rural industrial regions can be discovered.

Much protoindustrial manufacturing, textiles in particular, could be characterized by the notion Clifford Geertz has dubbed "involution."[12] Economic activity transformed demographic conditions, but equally, there was a reciprocal movement as population growth influenced the organization of production. Not only did the workers replace themselves at a rapid rate, but any sustained period of prosperity occasioned both an increase in the number of marriages and an influx of new recruits. For these reasons, labor costs were kept low. Indeed, it can be stated that in these conditions the "iron law of wages" was axiomatic. As long as labor was both cheap and plentiful, there was little incentive to undertake capital investments to raise productivity. Low wages meant that primitive techniques were most profitable, while this low level was labor intensive, so that cheap labor was of critical importance. At this point the rural worker's condition is intersected by his integration into an extralocal economy. The need on the part of the capitalist to push wages down was determined by the fact that goods in international competition were often cheaper, particularly if they were the work of cottagers who relied on rural by-employment to supplement their agricultural income. For the full time proletarianized rural industrialist such competition was unfair because while he needed to derive *all* his income from his wages, the cottager needed only to gain his margin of subsistence. In these circumstances, the development of one region meant the demise of another. The exit from this blind alley was the introduction of powered machines which replaced human skills with enormous productive capacity. But that is another story.

---

[11] H. Medick, "Haushalt und Familie" and "Strukturen und Funktion der Bevölkerungsentwicklung im proto-industriellen System." These essays are being published in the volume Medick is editing jointly with P. Kriedte and J. Schlumbohm. See also Medick's recent article, "The protoindustrial family economy: The structural function of household and family during the transition from peasant Society to industrial capitalism," *Social History*, 3 (1976): 291–315.

[12] *Agricultural Involution: The Processes of Ecological Change in Indonesia.*

The evidence derived from the four reconstitution studies will show how the ebb and flow in the demand for labour in protoindustry and capitalist agriculture acted as a powerful disequilibrating factor in the demographic equation during the age of nascent capitalism. While proletarianization seems to have been a necessary stage in the breakdown of the preindustrial demographic balance, the transformation of peasants and artisans into wage laborers did not, by itself, necessarily lead to population growth. When employment became available to all who were willing to sell their labor in the marketplace, it became more difficult to maintain the equilibrating mechanism of postponed marriage because men (and women) reached their earning capacity at an early age and no longer had any reason to defer marriage. At this point village-level studies of demographic change must be linked into the development of the regional, national, and international economies of the time. The critical link in the chain was the way pressures from this wider world were mediated through the local demand for labor and thereby influenced strategies of family formation.

2

THE SOCIAL AND ECONOMIC BACKGROUND

In the nineteenth century, Shepshed was the most intensively industrialized village in Leicestershire. As is evident from the occupational
distribution of the adult male population in the two villages at the time of
the 1831 census, presented in Table 2.1, the industrialization of Shepshed
was the significant factor distinguishing it from Bottesford.[1] Although
each village had a similar number of agriculturalists and tradesmen, not
one adult male in Bottesford was engaged in manufacturing.

In this chapter I shall examine the growth and structure of the
framework knitting industry in Shepshed and discuss the social implications of this economic change. At various points references to the social
and economic development of Bottesford will show how that village differed from Shepshed.

The knitting frame, invented by William Lee in 1589, was an impressive
technical innovation, made of over 2000 separate pieces of steel, wood,
and lead. The machine operator could perform more than 1000 stitches per
minute, compared with about 100 stitches a minute that could be made by
hand. But because the earliest machines were expensive, costing £80 each,
their introduction into general use was quite slow. Furthermore, the first
models required two operators, so that labor costs were another factor
limiting the machine's dissemination.[2]

In the first phase of its development, the framework knitting industry

[1] "Enumeration Abstracts, 1831 Census, Vol. I," *P.P.*, 1833, XXXVI, pp. 310–11, 318–19.
[2] J.D. Chambers, "The Worshipful Company of Framework Knitters," pp. 296–312.

TABLE 2.1
Occupational Distribution, 1831

	Bottesford	Shepshed
Agriculture		
Occupiers employing labor	26	27
Occupiers not employing labor	17	25
Agricultural laborers	110	138
Manufacturing, Trade, and Handicraft		
Manufacturing	0	553
Retail trade, handicraft (both masters and workmen)	106	123
Capitalists, bankers, etc.	10	14
Nonagricultural laborers	26	29
"Other" males over 20	24	37
Male servants over 20	3	3
Male servants under 20	3	0
Female servants	57	33

was essentially a London-based trade with a subsidiary center of production in the East Midlands. In 1669, for example, there were only 660 frames in England, of which 400 were in London.[3] At first, production was confined to the manufacture of luxury goods, mainly embroidered silk stockings, which enabled a small group of London merchant-hosiers to dominate the industry by maintaining close contact with changing fashions. In 1663 this London oligarchy secured a royal patent of incorporation as the Worshipful Company of Framework Knitters, empowered to exercise control over the whole industry. Governing powers were vested in a closed, self-perpetuating body of officials who, through the use and abuse of their legal powers, dominated the industry for the next 60 years. The royal patent gave the company the power to fix prices and to exact heavy fines from any member who undercut the established level. By imposing exorbitant fees on journeymen members for the employment of apprentices, the ruling oligarchy put large-scale production beyond the reach of the independent craftsmen. The company also used its authority to protect the interests of the London merchant-hosiers by keeping the provincial masters and men firmly under control.[4]

Between 1680 and 1725, the industry passed into a second phase of development. Substantial technical changes lowered the frame's cost and improved its efficiency by making it possible for one man to operate it. Moreover, changes in fashion favoring plain articles caused labor costs to become a more important consideration, and the provincial hosiers, using

---

[3] "Report of the Commissioners appointed to inquire into the condition of the Frame-work Knitters," *P.P.*, 1845, XV, p. 15.

[4] J.D. Chambers, "Worshipful Company," pp. 296–312.

cheaper country labor, could make these plain stockings for less than London manufacturers. By substituting wool for silk, manufacturers could tap the mass market with fashionable goods sold at a lower price. With the advent of mass production, hosiers demanded a freer hand in their dealings with labor, but this was inhibited by the company's restrictive apprenticeship regulations, although these rules were by no means strictly observed.

In 1710, London journeymen, whose incomes were being threatened by the spread of unapprenticed labor, destroyed nearly 100 frames.[5] The intractability of these journeymen convinced many hosiers that prospects were better elsewhere and thereby precipitated an exodus of men and machines to the Midlands. The movement away from London undermined the company's power and influence. In 1730, at the instigation of the exasperated London journeymen, the company acted against two Nottingham hosiers, Fellows and Cartwright, who were commanded to reduce their number of apprentices from 49 and 23 to three each. When they refused to comply with this ruling, they were fined £400 and £150. When they also refused to pay these fines, the company seized their property as indemnification. Thus provoked, Fellows and Cartwright sued the company for trespass and won. As a result, the company's authority was destroyed, and there were no longer any enforceable regulations controlling labor relations in the industry.[6]

Even earlier, in the later seventeenth century, hosiers were moving from London to the East Midlands in order to enjoy lower labor costs and relative freedom from the interference of the company. The destruction of the frames in 1710 and the 1730 trial merely intensified this trend and further diminished London's importance as a center of production; in 1669 over 60% of the knitting frames were in London, but by 1714 this figure had dropped to 31% and by 1753, 7%. The actual number of frames in the capital had also declined, from 2500 in 1714 to 1000 in 1753.[7]

The expansion of the industry throughout western Leicestershire was extremely rapid. In 1660 there were only 50 frames in the whole county, whereas by 1795 an estimated 43% of the county's population depended on some branch of the trade.[8] In the 1680s there were fewer than a dozen frames in Leicester, but by 1714 there were an estimated 600.[9] In Wigston Magna the industry seems to have been firmly established as early as 1698–1701 when about 16% of the villagers were described in the parish

---

[5] F.A. Wells, *The British Hosiery and Knitwear Industry*, pp. 35–36.

[6] "Commissioners' Report," p. 8. In the Commissioners' report this date is referred to as 1723, but S.D. Chapman has presented evidence which makes it probable that the Commissioners were in error. ("The Genesis of the British Hosiery Industry 1600–1750," p. 15 and footnotes 58 and 59.)

[7] "Commissioners' Report," pp. 15–16.

[8] John Nichols, *The History and Antiquities of Leicestershire*, Vol. 1, part ii, p. 620.

[9] "Commissioners' Report," pp. 15–16.

register as framework knitters.[10] Perhaps Wigston's proximity to Leicester, the distribution center, sparked this precocious growth. In Shepshed, the industry is first mentioned in 1655 when Thomas Trowell, "silkstocking wever," was buried, but the real commitment to industrialization did not come until the beginning of the eighteenth century. From 1701 to 1709 only 4% of the entries in the parish register referred to framework knitters, but within 20 years, in the period 1719 to 1730, this figure jumped to 25%. In all these instances such rapid growth probably coincided with the industry's transition from a journeyman's trade to one in which capitalist relations predominated and cheap labor was a critical factor.

Historians have argued that rural industrialization often became important in areas where an impoverished peasantry was unable to subsist on agricultural income.[11] An examination of inventories from the period from 1660 to 1699 lends support to an argument that the poverty of Shepshed's peasants was an important precondition to its subsequent industrialization. The mean value for 82 Shepshed inventories was £60 12s., the median value was £37 10s. In contrast, the mean value for 100 Bottesford inventories was £109 4s., the median value was £61 2s. Estates valued at less than £25 accounted for only 21% of all Bottesford inventories but for 33% of all estates in Shepshed. On the other hand, estates valued at over £200 accounted for 22% in Bottesford but for just 2.4% in Shepshed. These later seventeenth century inventories describe the relative poverty of the Shepshed yeomen and husbandmen in relation to those in Bottesford. Not only were the Shepshed peasants' estates considerably smaller, but much of their land was also inferior. The land in Shepshed was of very uneven quality; parts lying by the brooks and streams that flowed out of Charnwood Forest and parts on the outer edges of the Soar River's terraces were easily worked and very fertile, but as much as half the village acreage was in Charnwood and was described as "rocky and stony, yeelding fruit not without great labour and expences."[12] With so much land unsuitable for intensive husbandry, the villagers exerted substantial pressure on their fertile land.

Contemporaries noted that there was a close association between the coming of rural industry and a rise in the poor rates. In the villages of Leicestershire there was also a strong correlation between the absence of

---

[10] W.G. Hoskins, *The Midland Peasant*, p. 228.

[11] J. Thirsk, "Industries in the Countryside," pp. 70–88; E.L. Jones, "The Agricultural Origins of Industry," pp. 58–71. Thirsk's study refers primarily to English history while Jones' article looks at this problem in a comparative fashion and has sections which briefly describe rural industrialization in Western Europe, New England, and Japan. In addition to the publications cited in these two studies, see also F.F. Mendels, "Proto-Industrialization: The First Phase of Industrialization."

[12] Quoted in G.E. Fussell, "Four Centuries of Leicestershire Farming," p. 158. In addition, F.M.Auty has noted that in those villages in western Leicestershire that became industrialized the land was less fertile than in other villages which remained agricultural (*The Land of Britain*, pp. 313–25).

domestic industry and the concentration of landownership.[13] In this context, the presence of the Manners family, dukes of Rutland, had enormous significance for the villagers of Bottesford. Not only did the family control almost three-quarters of the village land, but the family seat, Belvoir Castle, three miles away, was the principal customer for the farmers' and craftsmen's wares. It is not surprising that the dukes took advantage of their immense economic power to mould the social structure of the village. Pitt, writing in 1809, described the family's policy: "A numerous and able-bodied peasantry is here supported, no stockingers, or other manufacturers, and care taken there shall be none; poor rents low and rents well paid."[14] The hosiery industry was successfully kept off the Manners' estates in the belief that "the connection between industry and poverty . . . was simple and direct."[15] In Shepshed, property ownership was also heavily concentrated, but the principal landowning family seemed to have been either unwilling or unable to exert rigid control over the villagers. Perhaps the village's proximity to the common lands of Charnwood Forest and the very large number of small landowners combined to frustrate any attempts to dominate parochial affairs.[16]

As long as the trade was confined to the production of luxury articles, the semi-independent journeymen and even the wage laborers enjoyed a moderately high standard of living. As late as Queen Anne's reign, "The average of the hands only worked about four days a week, as meat was 1½d. per pound, and bread 14d. per stone. The earnings throughout the trade were computed to average 10s. a week in the country, and 15s. in London."[17] After the Fellows and Cartwright case in 1730, hosiers were liberated from inhibiting regulations and began to take on apprentices freely in order to lower their production costs.[18] One Nottingham hosier

---

[13] D. Mills, "Landownership and Rural Population," p. 238. All villages with over 240 frames in 1844 were classified as freehold townships as were 15 of 19 villages with between 121 and 240 frames. Conversely, only three villages in all of the county which had no stocking frames were freehold townships, and these were located away from the industrial distribution centers.

[14] W. Pitt, *A General View of Agriculture in the County Leicester* (1809), pp. 15, 324.

[15] Quoted in W.A. Hoskins, *Victoria County History, Leicestershire*, London, Vol. III, p. 239.

[16] In the Land Tax returns for the period from 1780 to 1832, about half of the tax for Shepshed was paid by one owner. The Phillips family had been of local importance in the village since 1683 when they bought the lordship of the manor of Shepshed. They lived at Garrendon Hall within three miles of the village, but do not seem to have wielded the same amount of power as the Dukes of Rutland did in Bottesford. However, apart from the Phillips family there were another 249 landowners in Shepshed in 1832. Many of these people owned tiny parcels of land of less than an acre. Such tiny holdings, and the comparatively high landowner-family ratio (in 1831 there were 769 families of whom roughly one in three owned a piece of land) seem to suggest that partible inheritance was the prevalent way in which land was passed from one generation to the next. J. Thirsk, in her article, "Industries in the Countryside," argues that a system of divided inheritance was an important feature of villages in which rural industry took root.

[17] W. Felkin, *A History of Machine-Wrought Hosiery and Lace Manufactures*, p. 72.

[18] In the hosiery industry there were "the first collective indentures of apprenticeship, by

with a staff of 30 was said to have never employed a single journeyman. It is easy to see how the use of apprentices contributed to the reduction of adult workers' wages.[19]

Once machine operators were reduced to the status of dependent wage laborers, their income was governed by the health of the industry. In good times, when they had all the work they could manage, they prospered, but a trade depression brought suffering and deprivation. The statement quoted earlier mentioned that a country stockinger at the beginning of the eighteenth century could earn 10s. for a four-day week. In an industry dependent on the vagaries of fashion, fluctuations in prosperity were quite usual, but most depressions were short-lived. The American Revolution interrupted a long period of growth and created a severe depression that continued as long as America, the industry's best market, boycotted its goods.[20] Conditions among the operators deteriorated after the outbreak of hostilities, and earnings fell to such an extent that men who earned 2s. 1d. a day 20 years before could make no more than 1s. 7d. even by working many long hours.[21] In an attempt to secure redress of their grievances, the stockingers appealed to Parliament to regulate wages within the industry. Their first attempt failed outright in 1778, and their second, the following year, got lost in committee. In their frustration and anger, the operators resorted to frame smashing as a form of direct, unconditional negotiation with their employers. Although this form of bargaining could wring temporary concessions, conditions improved only after the hostilities ended. The years until the end of the Napoleonic wars were prosperous, and stockingers' earnings seem to have improved. According to Eden, "Stocking-weavers, in general, (earn) from 7s. to 17s. a week; but a few earn £1 1s. a week. . . ."[22]

In the years after 1815 the hosiery industry experienced an almost complete, unrelieved depression resulting from a stagnation in the demand for knitted goods caused by changes in fashion and by the increasing effectiveness of overseas competition.[23] This situation was greatly exacerbated by a continuous rise in the number of workers in the industry which perpetually outstripped the demand for labor. Under these circumstances, both wages and working conditions deteriorated, and many abuses that had always been present became major sources of exploitation. In 1845 a royal commission was appointed to inquire into conditions

---

arrangement between manufacturers and parishes" (P. Mantoux, *The Industrial Revolution in the Eighteenth Century,* p. 193).

[19] "Commissioners' Report," p. 8.
[20] E.B. Schumpeter, *English Overseas Trade Statistics 1697–1808,* pp. 35–37, 69.
[21] Wells, *Hosiery and Knitwear Industry,* pp. 76–77.
[22] F.M. Eden, *The State of the Poor,* Vol. II, p. 374.
[23] Wells, *Hosiery and Knitwear Industry,* p. 110. The depression in the woollen branch, with which about half of Shepshed's production was concerned, was mainly the result of oversupply.

among the framework knitters, and witnesses came forward to testify about their experiences.[24]

During the first decade of the nineteenth century, earnings seem to have averaged between 10s. and 14s. per week, but by 1845 it was not unusual for stockingers to earn as little as 40% of that amount for the same kind of work. John Hucknall, a Whitwick stockinger working for a Shepshed hosier, claimed that he was paid 8s. 6d. per dozen for a type of stocking that brought him a guinea 40 years previously.[25] William Dean, a Loughborough manufacturer, told the commissioners that "as a general principle, 35 years ago we paid double the price we pay now. . . ."[26] Although the price of food fell from its wartime heights, the decline was not sufficient to offset the lower wages prevalent in the 1840s and 1850s.[27] Comparing the wages paid to knitters for standard articles with the official, average wheat price showed that real wages in 1841 stood at about 60% of their 1815 level.[28]

William Felkin, a Nottingham hosier who later wrote an invaluable history of the hosiery industry, told the commissioners that each frame in Shepshed earned a net weekly income of 5s.6d.[29] This estimate was made at a time of full employment. William Cotton, a Shepshed manufacturer, said of the average, net weekly earnings of his 200 workers that "We have frames that will not earn more than 4s.6d. or 5s. and we have some that will earn 10s."[30] William Gibson, manager of another Shepshed firm, believed that during the year preceding the commission, framework knitters "would not earn more than 5s. or 5s. 6d.; because, though some of our men may have been better off, I have seen one-half of them that had

---

[24] The following discussion is based on the evidence presented to the Royal Commission, *P.P.* 1845, xv.

[25] "Minutes of Evidence," Part I, Q. 6078.

[26] "Minutes of Evidence," Part I, Q. 8074.

[27] R. Smith, "The Social Structure of Nottingham and Adjacent Districts in the Mid–Nineteenth Century: An Essay in Quantitative Social History," p. 7.

[28] "Commissioners' Report," p. 38. The figure 60% was derived by dividing the 1841 price (4s. 6d.) for a dozen stockings into the 1815 price (7s. 6d.). The price of wheat was virtually the same at these two dates. However, it is difficult to establish anything like a fixed real wage because of the great fluctuations in the price of wheat from year to year and also from season to season, as well as within the national economy. Thus, if we compared 1851 with 1815, then there would be no noticeable change in real wages as the price of wheat in 1851 was 60% of that prevailing in 1815. This was the method used by Smith ("Social Structure of Nottingham," p. 7) which enabled him to claim that there was no change in the real wages of the framework knitters in the period 1815–51. Moreover, using averages of prices paid for producing quantities of stockings is misleading in another way: as we shall see, the framework knitters were subjected to periods of unemployment as well as to prolonged bouts of very serious underemployment. For this reason, it is unlikely that they earned anything like the stated amount, when we take their overall earnings into consideration. The most that can be said with any real confidence is that, inasmuch as wages deteriorated at a faster rate and more evenly than wheat prices declined after 1815, then it appears that the real wages of framework knitters were lower in the 1840s and 1850s than they were at the earlier date.

[29] "Minutes of Evidence," Part II, Q. 12.

[30] "Minutes of Evidence," Part I, Q. 5783.

not been employed much more than half their time, therefore that reduces their earnings very materially, if you come to make an average."[31] Joseph Ball, a Shepshed stockinger, said that it was unlikely that a man could earn a net wage of 1s. per day.[32] He personally earned a gross weekly wage of 7s. 11d. before deductions. These deductions were so heavy that they often took as much as 40% of a man's gross income. A worker's earnings depended not only on the speed and dexterity of his hands but also on the rate of pay for the type of article on which he was working. Almost all the framework knitters in Shepshed were engaged in the lowest paid branch of the trade, making fully fashioned cotton and worsted hosiery.[33]

Because piece rates were driven to low levels, it was necessary for the stockingers to work long hours; many men claimed that they commonly worked 16 hours a day.[34] This figure is somewhat misleading because it takes no account of the constant interruptions and fluctuations in the demand for labor. Even while they were at work, stockingers were constantly required to make alterations or modifications to their frames in order to meet the specifications of new orders. The major cause of their long working hours lay in the inefficient chain of command between the merchant manufacturers and the individual workmen. Middlemen collected the finished products from the knitters on Friday nights or Saturday mornings, so that most stockingers worked feverishly on Thursdays and Fridays to be sure of meeting their weekly quotas. It was often Monday afternoon before the middlemen distributed the yarn for the following week's orders.[35] Many workingmen could not space their work out over a whole week because the middlemen did not have the financial wherewithal to arrange for yarn to be supplied to them at regular intervals. Thus, the individual knitters were forced to suffer because of the makeshift organization of production.

Apart from their low wages and long, irregular working hours, framework knitters had several more specific grievances pertaining to their treatment by employers. Thomas Briers, who had been a framework knitter in Shepshed for 55 years, told the 1845 royal commission that he had witnessed a considerable deterioration in working conditions during his lifetime.[36] Not coincidentally, the years after 1790 also witnessed the

---

[31] "Minutes of Evidence," Part I, Q. 5824.

[32] "Minutes of Evidence," Part I, Q. 5645.

[33] "Minutes of Evidence," Part II, Q. 12. No one was working the glove, shirt and drawers, and fancy branches of the trade, while just 32 of the 1209 frames were used to make *cutups* which were generally higher-paid articles.

[34] *P.P.*, 1845, XV, Part I, the Index (pp. 503–04) gives a summary of the workmen's statements on their working hours.

[35] P. Head, "Putting Out in the Leicester Hosiery Industry in the Middle of the Nineteenth Century," p. 48. A similar point is made in the Commissioners' Report on the condition of the framework knitters ("Commissioners' Report," pp. 105–06).

[36] "Minutes of Evidence," Part I, Q. 5569.

emergence of middlemen or bag hosiers.[37] Turning work over to middle-men and small masters was in a large merchant manufacturer's interest in that it allowed him to deal with a relatively small number of subcontrac-tors. The dispersion of knitters as far as 10 miles from their employer's warehouse made this division of labor inevitable since "working direct was a notorious time waster, particularly for the knitters. . . ."[38] There were 14 middlemen in Shepshed working for hosiers in Nottingham and Leicester.[39] By turning a blind eye on the impropriety of their subcontrac-tors' dealings with the ordinary workmen, the merchant manufacturers were able to obtain goods very cheaply. Many of the stockingers com-plained that they were subjected to heavy deductions for frame rent, shop charges, and negligent workmanship. These workers had little alternative to accepting their paymasters' decisions because it was both expensive and difficult to change employers. This monopoly of power in the employers' hands led to fraudulence in payments and to the extension of the truck system.

Abuses concerning frame rent, weekly payments for the use of an employer's machine, were the most common sources of grievance. The framework knitters were assessed charges varying between 9d. and 3s. 6d. per week depending on the size of the frame, the employer's avaricious-ness, and peculiar local customs.[40] Even when a workman owned his frame, he still paid frame rent to be sure of getting work.[41] Moreover, full rent had to be paid even if a machine was worn out or in disrepair.[42] Old men and learners were also expected to pay full rent, as were sick or completely unemployed workers.[43] In addition to these forms of direct exploitation, the practice of frame rental was also partly responsible for the oversupply of labor that was at the root of the deteriorating wage rates. It was in an employer's interest to have as large a labor force as possible because he could thereby collect more money in frame rent.[44] For some employers, frame rent was more lucrative than the actual sale of finished products. Lacking even rudimentary methods of collective bargaining, a large, dispersed and hungry labor force presented little real opposition to a concerted effort driving wages down. The prevalence of frame rent also meant that decreases in the demand for goods, rather than causing wholesale unemployment, resulted in widespread underemployment as

---

[37] Head, "Putting Out," p. 48. Wells, *Hosiery and Knitwear Industry*, pp. 72–73.

[38] Head, "Putting Out," p. 48.

[39] *P.P.*, 1854–55, XIV, Select Committee on the Stoppage of Wages (Hosiery), "Minutes of Evidence," QQ. 6271, 6374.

[40] *P.P.*, 1845, XV, Part I, the Index (pp. 488–90) gives an indication of the range of payments made for frame rent.

[41] "Minutes of Evidence," Part I, QQ. 70, 116, 468.

[42] "Minutes of Evidence," Part I, QQ. 267, 4805.

[43] "Minutes of Evidence," Part I, QQ. 116, 250–62, 679, 773, 1226, 1245, 1485, 1727 and many others.

[44] "Minutes of Evidence," Part I, QQ. 41, 635, 2798, 3603.

employers spread available work among as many stockingers as possible to continue collecting frame rents. The effect of this enforced underemployment was exacerbated by the fact that it generally occurred when food prices were highest, stockings and underclothing being articles that poor people economized on or made themselves when the price of necessities was high. It was said to be a maxim of the trade that demand fluctuated inversely with the price of foodstuffs.[45]

Journeymen framework knitters were further afflicted with shop charges levied by the middlemen or by the masters of small workshops where they were employed.[46] Many of these masters controlled fewer than a dozen frames, so that shop charges were an important part of their income. The men who worked these frames had to pay the masters for needles, coals, and candles and make a further payment for "standing in." Middlemen also charged for carrying the raw materials from the warehouse to the shop or to the knitter's residence and for returning the finished products. Men who worked in a master's workshop had further deductions for the winding—performed by young boys who fed yarn onto the machines—and also for the stitching and seaming of the knitted fabric into a finished article. Many of these charges could not be extracted from the man who worked at home aided by his family, so that there was strong incentive for middlemen to force journeymen to work in their shops. It was also claimed that shop charges, like frame rents, were always demanded in full in times of slack demand. Deductions were made before the stockingers received their pay, and as we shall see below, they were in no position to object.

Closely allied to frame rents and shop charges was another abuse resulting from the employers' control over the laborers, the truck system, payment in goods in lieu of money. It was the consensus that this abuse was mainly perpetrated by small-scale masters and middlemen who were thought to be far crueler employers than the large-scale, city-based merchant manufacturers.[47] The truck masters squeezed as much as possible from the workmen they controlled. Not only did they pay their workmen lower wages, they likewise gave them no choice about where they could spend their money, and the truck masters' goods were almost always of lower quality, smaller quantity, and higher price than those of legitimate traders.[48] To bring workmen under their power, some truck masters gave them seemingly easy credit terms, but once in debt, workmen found it almost impossible to get out.[49] Because a workman had to pay interest on a

---

[45] Wells, *Knitwear and Hosiery Industry*, p. 110.

[46] *P.P.*, 1845, XV, Part I, the Index (pp. 488–90) summarizes the amounts paid by various workmen.

[47] "Minutes of Evidence," Part I, QQ. 19, 48, 866, 1824, 3637, 4219–20, 5175.

[48] "Minutes of Evidence," Part I, QQ. 20, 21, 789, 791, 1085 and many others.

[49] "Minutes of Evidence," Part I, QQ. 4893, 5021, 6322.

loan, he was effectively being paid lower wages. In exchange for a further reduction of a workman's level of wages, the truck master would offer to pardon repayment of a part of the outstanding capital sum, but if he refused this offer, then the master would give him less work and ultimately starve him into submission. Truck masters were able to exert such tremendous power over their workers because the men were desperate for whatever work they could find. They also knew that complaining to the magistrates would be of little use because an informal association among the truck masters guaranteed that rebellious men would be hard-pressed to obtain employment again.[50] After a case in Hinckley, for instance, the anti-truck society was obliged to pension its witnesses for a great many weeks while they looked for another employer.[51] Complaining to the magistrates also had little effect because the fines imposed were not stiff enough to deter offenders from repeating their offenses.[52]

The element of deceit employed in truck payments makes it difficult, if not impossible, to separate that system from other forms of fraud in the payment of wages. It was a common complaint that earnings were reduced by masters or middlemen who claimed that the goods were defective or damaged. John Burn, a Shepshed framework knitter, said that "if he finds the least spot upon them he docks you 9d. or 1s. for this bit of dirt, as he pretends to call it."[53] Other ploys used to reduce payments were those of giving the workman less than the contracted price or claiming that his goods did not meet the necessary specifications. Middlemen often cheated their journeymen by claiming that the warehouse price for an article was less than they had actually received and pocketing the difference. John Hucknall, a Whitwick stockinger working for a Shepshed hosier, told the commissioners that he always submitted to deductions even when they were obviously without foundation because "If I didn't submit to them, I must resist them, and then I should lose all my frames and my work." A man like Hucknall, whose family worked eight frames, would be terrified to oppose his employers for fear that he would lose whatever he had. Experience had taught Hucknall to be submissive; for opposing the church rate he was forced to give up the allotment which had provided cheap food for his large family.[54] Under the circumstances it was unlikely that such a man would appeal to the law against his employer for negotiating in bad faith. Such legislation as the Arbitration Act and the Truck Act was irrelevant.

Because wages were so low in the framework knitting industry, it was very difficult for a family to survive on the husband's earnings alone. For

---

[50] "Minutes of Evidence," Part I, QQ. 17, 25, 1817.
[51] "Minutes of Evidence," Part I, Q. 3670.
[52] "Minutes of Evidence," Part I, QQ. 27, 144, 1925–28, 3712, 3837.
[53] "Minutes of Evidence," Part I, Q. 5600.
[54] "Minutes of Evidence," Part I, QQ. 6074 ff.

this reason 80% of knitters' households contained at least two people employed in some branch of the trade, and more than 50% contained three or more. In all instances of what may be called "wage-earning coresidence," this phenomenon was appreciably higher among industrial workers than among agricultural laborers or the trade and craft class. It might also be noted that the availability of employment in the various branches of the framework knitting industry had the effect of increasing the number of "coresident wage earners" among Shepshed's agricultural laborers and artisans. See Table 2.2.

TABLE 2.2
Employed Persons per Household, 1851

	Bottesford				Shepshed				
	Laborers		Craftsmen		Laborers		Craftsmen		Framework knitters
	N	Cumulative frequency	N	Cumulative frequency	N	Cumulative frequency	N	Cumulative frequency	N	Cumulative frequency
1	80	59.7	47	50.5	47	37.0	55	42.3	69	18.1
2	36	86.6	29	81.7	36	65.4	43	75.4	113	47.6
3	12	95.5	10	92.5	17	78.7	20	90.8	69	65.7
4	3	97.8	5	97.8	22	96.1	8	96.9	54	79.8
5	3	100.0	1	98.9	3	98.4	4	100.0	34	88.7
6			0	98.9	1	99.2			25	95.3
7			1	100.0	1	100.0			10	97.9
8									7	99.7
9									0	99.7
10									1	100.0
N	134		95		127		130		382	

The "Commissioner's Report" stated: "Vast numbers of women and children are working side by side with men, often employed in the same description of frames, making the same fabrics, and at the same rate of wages; the only advantage over them which the man possesses being his superior strength, whereby he can undergo the fatigues of labour for longer hours than the weaker physical energies of women and children enable them to bear; and therefore he earns more money, by turning off more work."[55] In addition to actual machine knitting, the trade provided a large amount of other work for the women and children in an operator's family. The winding, seaming, and stitching being part of the knitter's job in producing his wares, he would have to pay for them if no one in his family could do them. By doing such jobs, even young children contributed to the family income and helped to support themselves. Because a

---

[55] "Commissioners' Report," p. 101.

family's framework knitting required all the children's labor, it was most unusual for them to be engaged in another trade. In Shepshed just 4.3% of the employed children were not part of the family production unit.[56]

The 1843 Royal Commission on the Employment of Children reported that 12,924 of the 28,000 people engaged in the framework knitting industry in Leicestershire were under 18.[57] It was quite common for boys to begin working as winders at six, seven, or eight years of age, while girls of a similar age were beginning to work as seamers. These boys had a work day as long as the adult framework knitters', often more than 12 hours, because their presence was of great importance in speeding up production. It was possible for very young boys to add as much as 3s. to the family's weekly income, and their sisters also contributed a couple of shillings. Boys of ten or slightly older began working on the frames and soon were able to make almost as much money as their fathers. For instance, John Burn, a Shepshed stockinger, had a net personal income of 4s. per week. His 13-year-old son also worked on the frame and contributed a similar amount to his family's income.[58] Burn had five other dependent children, so that his son's earnings were of critical importance. The rate of pay for adolescents was, as indicated above, dependent on their stamina not only in making large numbers of stockings but also in avoiding costly errors.

Because children had to work long hours supplementing their fathers' wages, it was uncommon for them to receive any real education. In the Shepshed marriage register for the years from 1837 to 1850 only a third of the framework knitters could sign their names.[59] At Enderby, an industrial village south of Leicester, there was a village free school, but the framework knitters' children did not attend because they had to work.[60] The vicar of Shepshed told the 1845 commission that a similar situation existed in his village and that the only remedy would be to "pay each child an equivalent for the sum he can earn at home."[61] It is not surprising that

---

[56] There were 344 employed children among 333 framework knitters' householders. For 111 laborers' households there were 89 employed children, while in the 101 trade and craft households there were just 50 employed youngsters.

[57] This figure was 46% of the total labor force in the stocking industry. (*P.P.*, 1843, XIV, "Children's Employment Commission; appendix to the second report of the Commissioners (Trades and Manufacturers)." Part 1: Reports and Evidence of the Sub-Commissioners. Manufacture of Hosiery. Report by R.D. Grainger, F13.) In contrast to this figure, it was reported in the 1851 census that just 32% of those employed in the hosiery trade were aged under 19. (*P.P.*, 1852–53, LXXVIII, Part II, pp. 546, 550.)

[58] "Minutes of Evidence," Part I, QQ. 5589–91. The boy was making 10 socks a week at the rate of 3s. per dozen and therefore earned 2s. 6d. per week. From this sum was deducted 9d. per week for frame rent—30% of his earnings.

[59] In contrast, the national level of literacy was about 65% for men. (R.S. Schofield, "Dimensions of Illiteracy, 1750–1850.")

[60] "Minutes of Evidence," Part I, Q. 3407.

[61] "Minutes of Evidence," Part I, Q. 5677.

attendance at school among the industrial population was deemed inadequate. A frequent excuse parents made for not sending their children to school was that they were ashamed to send them without decent or even adequate shoes and clothing. Another deleterious effect of long working hours and undernourishment was that knitters' children were smaller and weaker than those of agricultural laborers.[62] In Shepshed and Loughborough there was great difficulty finding enough able-bodied men to meet the army recruiting quotas.[63] It was a widely held belief that the framework knitters were not strong enough to be employed as heavy manual laborers and "no one would employ them as farm labourers. . . ."[64] Thus, poverty led to poor diet, inadequate education, and familiarity with the framework knitting industry, and insured that these children had no real alternative to following their fathers' occupation.

Women also worked in large numbers to increase their families' incomes. Overall, 49% of the framework knitters' wives were said to be employed at the time of the 1851 census. This phenomenon was most common among young women. Fifty-six percent of wives under 35 were said to be working as either seamers or machine operators. Because they were so poor, it was hard for these young wives to forego working. Only when their children could themselves begin work could stockingers' wives devote their complete attention to domestic duties. Accordingly, only 37% of wives aged 35 to 44 were working, but as their children ceased to be dependent on them and were able to help with either housekeeping or wage earning, it again became common for wives to work. Fifty percent of wives over 45 were contributing directly to the family income. Thus, the employment of women was influenced as much by their life cycle as by the necessity to maintain an adequate *family* income. A contemporary observer noted that the family paid dearly when the wife had to work: "The cleanliness, providence and attention to cooking and mending, must be inevitably neglected when the mother and any daughters capable of working are compelled to toil for bread at a trade. . . ." This situation was said to be so common that "the female population must certainly to some extent be brought up ignorant of the thrifty management of a household."[65] Thus, the framework knitters were caught between the Scylla of absolute want and the Charybdis of secondary poverty.

The successful application of the dukes of Rutland's policy regulating the labor supply within Bottesford resulted in a very low poor rate. In

---

[62] "Minutes of Evidence," Part I, Q. 5859.

[63] "Minutes of Evidence," Part I, QQ. 3058, 7876.

[64] Wells, *Hosiery and Knitwear Industry*, p. 112.

[65] W. Lee, *Report to the General Board of Health on a preliminary inquiry into the sewerage, drainage and supply of water and the sanitary conditions of the inhabitants of the parish of Loughborough*, pp. 18–19.

1847, for example, only 2s. 9½d. per capita were spent on poor relief, a levy of just 6d. in the pound on ratepayers.[66] Although poverty in Bottesford was an inconsequential problem, mainly involving the old and the infirm, in Shepshed it was an overwhelming social evil. Shepshed ratepayers in 1847 paid 3s. 3¾d. in the pound—more than six times as much as those of Bottesford. Richard Hall, the poor law commissioner for Leicestershire, told the Select Committee on the Poor Law Amendment Act that in no part of England had agricultural property been rendered so utterly valueless as in Leicestershire, and especially in the manufacturing villages. He went on to note that in some instances, such as Shepshed, the burden of the paupers had actually exhausted the revenue of the land. In Wigston Magna, another industrial village, land had been rendered wholly unsalable and even put out of cultivation.[67] Per capita expenditure on poor relief in Shepshed was 9s. 4¾d.—more than three times the rate in Bottesford. But the per capita expenditure on poor relief is hardly an accurate guide to the dimension of poverty in the industrial village since the overseers were very mean—each poor law recipient in Shepshed received only about one-half the amount of his counterpart in Bottesford. Indeed, in 1834 the magistrates intervened, forcing the Shepshed overseers to increase the scale of payments to those receiving relief.[68] It seems unlikely that this intervention had lasting effects, for the Shepshed guardians under the New Poor Law continued their efforts to cut costs. In February 1838 the churchwardens in Shepshed were fined for noncompliance with the New Poor Law because they refused to send people to the workhouse, believing that outdoor relief was cheaper.[69] Such resistance at the local level meant that the coming of the New Poor Law was a non-event.

A student of this problem has claimed that "fluctuations in the hosiery trade made a strict application of the (New) Poor Law impossible." The persistence of outdoor relief in Shepshed meant that "market forces" could not determine wage rates for framework knitters. Hosiers were said to rely on the provision of outdoor relief as a "general fund" which the stockingers could call upon to supplement their wages.[70] It is scarcely surprising that their wages were low. Outdoor relief also degraded the independence of these working men in another way. When hosiers laid men off during times of depression, they were usually offered an "inducement" by the

---

[66] These poor law figures for 1847 are quoted from Appendix 6 of D. Mills, "Landownership and Rural Population."

[67] *P.P.*, 1838, XVIII, Part III, "Minutes of Evidence before the Select Committee on the Poor Law Amendment Act," QQ. 16997–17002.

[68] *PP.*, 1834, XXIX, APP. (A), Part II, No. 24, pp. 90–91.

[69] A. Bécherand, "The Poor and the English Poor Laws in the Loughborough Union of Parishes, 1837–1860," pp. 130, 214.

[70] G.A.G. Innocent, "Aspects of the Practical Working of the New Poor Law in Leicester and Leicestershire, 1834–1871," p. 24.

overseers to set the men to work at a reduced rate of pay.[71] Insofar as it did not end the allowance system, which was thought to be the principal cause of pauperization, the New Poor Law was an ineffective instrument of change.

Living with uncertainty and demoralized by the institutional arrangements of society, industrial laborers were not likely to be imbued with regular habits conducive to frugality and self-esteem. It was claimed that in Shepshed the framework knitters were so drunk on Sundays that they were unable to attend religious services.[72] Living in a culture of poverty, they were thought to be so little influenced by rational considerations that "the notion of saving has been scouted as folly."[73] The assistant poor law commissioner complained that the framework knitters in Shepshed believed poor law relief to be a right not a benevolence.[74] Contemporaries argued that they were not only improvident and dissipated but "totally regardless of that sense of shame which is the best prescription of independence."[75] In later chapters I will argue that this ascription of thoughtless behavior appears to be an oversimplification and that the laborers did try to come to terms with their pauperization and destitution. Whether they were able to overcome the anomie and hopelessness caused by their grinding poverty is another question, and one beyond the scope of this book. The strength of Luddism, Chartism, and nonconformity among the population of Shepshed does suggest, however, that they were not altogether passive sufferers.

Shepshed was a center of proletarian unrest for much of the first half of the nineteenth century. In 1811, 1812, 1814, and 1816 special constables were enrolled and regular troops billeted in the village in response to the industrial disturbances associated with Luddism.[76] In this period, frames were destroyed and employers threatened.[77] The workers were said to be "a very proper, and loyal sort of people, in regard to sticking up for wages," but after 1825 they were "beaten down so by the manufacturers. . . ."[78] Still, during the Chartist period, framework knitters in Shepshed were said to be advocates of "physical force" as opposed to "moral force."[79] Support for the People's Charter was forthcoming because it was seen as a form of opposition to "the evils of a stagnating and overcrowded domestic industry as well as being an expression of resistance to the harsh [New] Poor Laws"

---

[71] *P.P.*, 1837–38, XXXVIII, "Second Annual Report of the Poor Law Commissioners, 1836," App. (B), No. 17, p. 397.

[72] "Minutes of Evidence," Part I, Q. 5672.

[73] *P.P.*, 1837–38, XXXVIII, "Second Annual Report," App. (B), No. 17, p. 397.

[74] *P.P.*, 1834, XXIX, App. (A), Part II, No. 24, pp. 83–84.

[75] F.M. Eden, *The State of the Poor*, Vol. II, p. 377.

[76] Bécherand, "The Poor in the Loughborough Union," p. 54.

[77] M. Thomis, *The Luddites*, pp. 178, 182.

[78] "Minutes of Evidence," Part I, QQ. 7479, 7483.

[79] A.T. Paterson, *Radical Leicester*, p. 59.

which threatened unemployed workingmen and their families with the "Bastille."[80]

The pattern of development in the framework knitting industry in Shepshed shows that in many ways protoindustrialization anticipated the onset of full-scale factory industry. In its first stage, the domestic laborers engaged in protoindustrial pursuits as a by-employment to supplement their agricultural income. In a relatively short time, however, the market orientation of production and the comparatively lavish wages paid by this form of work encouraged the creation of full-time wage laborers, proletarians. It must be stressed that these rural workers were not fully integrated into an industrial system insofar as they controlled the pace of their work. In Marx's analysis of the emergence of machine industry this factor was of crucial importance. For Marx it was of greatest significance that when the machine tool replaced the manual tool, the worker, already dispossessed of the means of production, lost control over the labor process.[81] In protoindustry, this boundary was not crossed. In other ways, however, the protoindustrial phase—called *Manufaktur* by Marx—anticipated the coming of modern industry.[82] The worker was divorced from ownership of the means of production, and a complicated division of labor developed which included even the creation of small protofactories.

In the framework knitting industry's initial phase all the stages of production were carried out within the household of the producer. Women spun the yarn, men knit the fashioned article. The "putter-out" supplied the wool to the workers and collected the finished products. In the course of the eighteenth century, particularly after the invention of the spinning machine created an industry, there was a separation of the home and the workplace. The first modern factories in England—those of Arkwright—were specifically designed to supply thread to the hosiery industry. Within a decade of Arkwright's first mill, Shepshed became the site of the first mill to be erected in Leicestershire. Smith Churchill, a

---

[80] Bécherand, "The Poor in the Loughborough Union," p. 54.

[81] K. Marx, *Capital*, Vol. I, p. 510. A similar point has recently been made by S.D. Chapman who sees the triumph of the modern industrial system in the replacement of *batch* production with *flow* production: "flow production means that machines and equipment have been arranged in line sequence to process goods continuously through a sequence of specialized operations. . . ." Such a production process required the use of "semi-automatic machinery [which] was tended by semi-skilled and unskilled workers, with a handful of skilled men to direct the plant and maintain it in smooth running order." Chapman's emphasis is different from Marx's, but both agree that the critical aspect of the *modern* factory, which distinguished it from earlier variants, was that in it workers became tied to the rhythm of the machine. (S.D. Chapman, "A Textile Factory before Arkwright: A Typology of Factory Development," pp. 469–70.)

[82] K. Wolff has attacked the Marxist schema which lumps together premodern industry into one category, that of *Manufaktur*. Wolff argues that the *Verlag* system of putting out should be distinguished from the stage of *Manufaktur* which was more specialized and tended to bring many workers together under the same roof. (K. Wolff, "Stages in Industrial Organization.")

Nottingham hosier, "Moved his business to his native village of Shepshed (near Loughborough) after a mob had demolished his house during the framework knitter's riots in Nottingham in 1779."[83] The advent of machine spinning radically redefined the household division of labor of the framework knitters. It was stated that at this time, the end of the eighteenth century, women first worked on the frames.[84] By 1851, 22.6% (242 of 1071) of the stockingers enumerated in Shepshed were women. Many other women worked as seamers, particularly those who lacked the strength or time to give proper attention to the frames. By the early nineteenth century, workshops had become common. The small masters, the "bag hosiers," brought together a number of machines—up to 40 or 50—in a "frame shop."[85] In this way they could keep their production closely in line with the changing whims of the market. Within such frame shops it became common for the knitted products to be produced in sections rather than "fully fashioned."[86] In Shepshed itself this process was not well developed, although the village's stockingers complained that the prevalence of these cheap, shoddily made *cutups* undermined the reputation of local manufacturers. Such a response was common among artisans in this period whose skill was threatened by the advent of mass production.

As we shall see in a later chapter, protoindustrialization undermined the preindustrial demographic equilibrium. Its extension was accompanied by rapid population growth. The causal arrows, however, did not fly in one direction. There was a reciprocal movement as population growth influenced the organization of production. Not only did workers replace themselves at a rapid rate, but any sustained period of prosperity occasioned both an increase in the number of marriages and an influx of new workers. For these reasons, costs were kept low. As long as labour was both cheap and plentiful, there was little incentive to undertake capital investments to raise productivity. Low wages meant that primitive techniques were most profitable, and yet this low-level technology was labor intensive, so that cheap labour was of critical importance. In effect,

---

[83] S.D. Chapman, *The Early Factory Masters*, p. 73. Smith Churchill was a Unitarian (196), and for this reason neither he nor his family were found in the Anglican parish register.

[84] "Minutes of Evidence," Part I, Q. 5569. The witness, Thomas Briers, had been engaged in the trade as a stockinger for 55 years, since 1789. He noted "as to women, fifty years ago there were very few of them on the frames; but women have been on the increase for a number of years; fifty years ago I knew but one woman in the parish that worked on the frame." Another Shepshed witness, Joseph Ball, remarked that "there may be more women now than formerly. They used to reckon formerly that they went out of the frame when they got married; now I have been witness to seeing them working on the frame with five or six children, and I have seen them working with a baby sucking at their breast." ("Minutes of Evidence," Part I, Q. 5640.)

[85] Wells, *Hosiery and Knitwear Industry*, p. 63. "Minutes of Evidence," Part I, QQ. 3626, 3720.

[86] Wells, *Hosiery and Knitwear Industry*, pp. 80, 82, 84 ff.

these factors created the kind of vicious circle that has been called *involution*.[87]

The severe post-1815 depression created a syndrome I call *industrial involution* which persisted until the second half of the nineteenth century, when the hosiery industry embarked on a period of technical advance as steam power was successfully applied to mechanical knitting. The impulse to switch over to steam-powered production seems to have come from the increasingly strong competition directed against English products in overseas markets. The Germans had already become an important force in the American market, and the threat of foreign encroachment on the home market was becoming clear.[88] It was almost impossible for English manufacturers to lower their wage costs by any significant amount, and yet they were still being undercut by the Germans whose production was still carried out to supplement cottagers' incomes. These Saxon peasants regarded whatever they received for their part-time activity as a bonus. In this way the currents of international trade radically changed the cost advantage of English rural manufacturing—what had previously been low-cost production now, in the face of international competition, became *relatively* high cost. Under these circumstances, the English manufacturers had no alternative to embarking on a capital-intensive program of technological improvement in order to reestablish their competitive advantage. Of course, this transformation did not occur overnight, and the country framework knitters responded to it in a familiar way—they resisted having control over their labor wrested from them. They held on to their "independence." They refused to become an extension of the machine. As long as they remained in competition with each other, Saxon cottagers, and the power-driven machinery, the framework knitters, like the hand-loom weavers of Lancashire and Yorkshire, remained the casualties of progress.

---

[87] C. Geertz, *Agricultural Involution: The Process of Ecological Change in Indonesia*. D.C. Coleman has argued that "the putting-out system, in short, was perhaps the biggest impediment to mechanical innovation the industry ever experienced." (D.C. Coleman, "Textile Growth," p. 5.)

[88] "Minutes of Evidence," Part I, QQ. 871, 872.

3

IMMIGRATION, POPULATION TURNOVER, AND GENERATIONAL REPLACEMENT

In this chapter I shall discuss patterns of immigration, population turnover, and generational replacement in Shepshed and Bottesford. I will present evidence suggesting that protoindustrialization created a stable community in Shepshed by providing more employment than was available in a predominantly agrarian economy such as that of Bottesford.

The population of preindustrial England was highly mobile, a condition resulting from the interaction of three basic characteristics of preindustrial societies: severe underemployment and endemic poverty; tremendous variations in annual mortality; and the small size of individual communities. Thus, in an average-sized community of about 450, the deaths of several adults within a short time would create unexpected vacancies to fill which no suitable candidates from within the community would be available, and immigrants would be attracted from the surrounding villages. This movement tended to be greatest among unmarried adults lacking stable positions. In Cardington, Bedfordshire, in 1782, for example, it was common for young people over 15 to have left home and entered service in a neighboring village.[1] The 1662 Law of Settlement was enacted to inhibit such movement and

---

[1] R.S. Schofield, "Age-Specific Mobility in an Eighteenth Century Rural English Parish."

tie the laborer to his parish of settlement by requiring each parish to assume financial responsibility for the relief of its own poor. When a migrant sought relief in a village where he was not legally settled, it was common for the officials of that village to secure a removal order to return the migrant to his legal settlement and to receive compensation for whatever expenses they incurred in the process. In order to reduce their poor law expenditure and save on removal expenses, however, the officers of the migrant's legal settlement would generally agree to pay the poor law expenses the migrant incurred in his new home. The willingness of village officials to subsidize a laborer's search for employment in this way meant that the Law of Settlement had little practical effect. Within a village community the population turnover could be considerable. Many of the individuals living in a village at one date had been replaced by others 10 or a dozen years later. For example, Clayworth, Nottinghamshire, had 401 inhabitants in 1676 and 412 in 1688 while Cogenhoe, Bedfordshire, had 185 in 1618 and 180 in 1628 despite the fact that "no less than 61.8% of the people living at Clayworth had not been there in 1676, and something like 50 percent of those living in Cogenhoe in 1628 were not there in 1618."[2] Despite such turnovers in population, these villages had nonetheless maintained the fairly constant size dictated by the state of existing agrarian technology.

While mobility in preindustrial England was common, it rarely involved long distances. Settlement certificates and removal orders provide the origins of 239 immigrants to Shepshed and 95 immigrants to Bottesford during the period from 1704 to 1795.[3] These documents show that it was quite unusual for immigrants to journey more than 15 miles to either village. Such long-distance migration accounted for just 5.5% of all cases in Shepshed and only 6.8% in Bottesford.

For the short-distance immigrants, it appears that there was a substantial degree of randomness in their choice of destination, inasmuch as the 226 immigrants to Shepshed came from no fewer than 96 different places while the 89 immigrants to Bottesford came from 49. Furthermore, it appears that distance was not the overriding consideration in this local migration. Only 17.5% of Shepshed's immigrants came from adjoining villages and just 12.5% of Bottesford's. In contrast to the weakness of distance as a factor determining the destination of local migration, rather more than one-third of all nonresident partners in marriages celebrated in the villages' parish churches lived in adjoining communities.

The settlement certificates and removal orders told me that a large proportion of the local immigrants to Shepshed came from other industrial villages in the east Midlands. For instance, 12 came from Barrow-on-Soar,

---

[2] P. Laslett, *The World we have lost*, pp. 146–47.
[3] Leicestershire County Record Office, D.E. 394/38, 39, 40, 42, 43 (Shepshed) D.E. 829/100, 101, 102, 103 (Bottesford).

seven from Whitwick, and another 40 from either Leicester or Nottingham. I found the occupations of 47 immigrants described in these documents; 26 were framework knitters and another five, woolcombers. On the other hand, this brief examination yielded little evidence that the growth of the industrial labor force in Shepshed was significantly aided by the immigration of peasants dispossessed by enclosure for pasture. Indeed, just 12 of the 127 Leicestershire immigrants came from villages in the rural eastern and southern parts of the county.[4]

To gauge the changes in population stability, reconstituted families from Shepshed and Bottesford were arranged into several categories according to their residential status at the time they entered observation. The families were first divided into two groups: those married in the parish and those married elsewhere who moved into observation after their marriage. The parochial marriages were further divided into four subsections according to the residence of each partner prior to marriage: both native; bride native; groom native; and both nonnative. The criterion for separating natives from nonnatives was the record of an individual's birth in the parish register. Since these categories consider only the birthplaces of the partners, it is not unlikely that a significant number of those designated nonnatives had, in fact, lived in the village for a considerable time, immigrating as children or, particularly in Shepshed, as young adults searching for employment. Moreover, underregistration of births could also have contributed to underrepresenting the natives, and, therefore, the degree of endogamy that occurred. The families married elsewhere were subdivided into three categories: native villagers who had married in their bride's parish before returning home; families classified as immigrants who were in observation for at least 10 years or whose burials were recorded in the parish register; and finally all those families who passed through the village but stayed for less than 10 years. In Shepshed 3940 families entered observation after 1600, while in Bottesford 2330 families entered after 1610. In Table 3.1, the figures for Shepshed have been arranged into four separate periods: 1600–1679, the preindustrial village; 1680–1749, the beginnings of protoindustrialization; 1750–1809, full scale industrialization; and 1810–1851, industrial involution. In Table 3.2 the figures for Bottesford have been arranged into three periods in its demographic and economic history: 1610–1669, population growth and arable husbandry; 1670–1789, depopulation and the transition to pastoral farming; and 1790–1851, population growth and dairy farming.

These figures underline the role played by the size of the village community in broadening the choice of likely marriage partners from within

---

[4] The situation in Shepshed was quite unlike that in Wigston Magna. In that village W.G. Hoskins found that many of the immigrants had drifted away from rural parishes in which "contagious enclosure" accompanied the "almost invariable conversion to pasture for large-scale grazing" (W.G. Hoskins, *Midland Peasant*, p. 212).

TABLE 3.1
Population Turnover, Shepshed

| | Parochial Marriages | | | | | | | | | | Marriages Elsewhere | | | | | | | | Total |
| | Both native | | Bride native | | Groom native | | Non-native | | Sub-total | | Husband native | | Immi-grants | | Transients | | Sub-total | | |
	N	%	N	%	N	%	N	%	N	%	N	%	N	%	N	%	N	%	N
1600–1679	32	6.3	62	12.4	42	8.4	94	18.7	230	46.0	89	17.9	138	27.6	45	9.0	272	54.0	500
1680–1749	67	11.5	97	16.6	88	15.1	118	20.2	370	63.5	91	15.5	93	16.0	29	5.0	213	36.5	583
1750–1809	134	10.7	264	21.2	164	13.2	340	27.3	902	72.4	107	8.6	149	11.9	89	7.1	345	27.6	1247
1810–1851	220	13.9	310	19.5	239	15.1	451	28.9	1215	76.9	71	4.5	115	7.3	187	12.3	373	23.1	1588
																			3940

TABLE 3.2
Population Turnover, Bottesford

| | Parochial Marriages | | | | | | | | | | | Marriages Elsewhere | | | | | | | | | Total |
| | Both native | | Bride native | | Groom native | | Non-native | | Sub-total | | Husband native | | Immigrants | | Transients | | Sub-total | | |
	N	%	N	%	N	%	N	%	N	%	N	%	N	%	N	%	N	%	N
1610–1669	51	8.3	62	10.0	101	16.4	146	23.6	360	58.4	105	17.0	107	17.4	45	7.3	257	41.6	617
1670–1789	93	8.7	173	16.3	117	11.0	188	17.9	571	53.9	233	21.9	181	17.1	76	7.1	490	46.1	1016
1790–1851	63	9.5	154	23.2	61	9.2	155	23.4	433	65.4	85	12.8	85	12.8	58	8.8	228	34.6	661
																			2339

the local populace. The number of native men marrying outside the village but returning home to reside seems to be inversely related to the population size. In Shepshed such marriages declined as the villages grew, but in Bottesford between 1670 and 1789 such marriages became more important as the population fell. There also seems to have been a similar inverse relationship between postmarital immigration and the village's population size.

These figures also support an argument linking mobility and marriage with the availability of employment. In preindustrial Shepshed just 46% of the families entering observation had been married in the parish, whereas during protoindustrialization the proportion of parochial marriage rose so that after 1810, 76.9% of all families had been married in the village church. The fact that an increasing proportion of these parochial marriages involved at least one nonnative suggests that migration into the industrial village largely occurred before marriage. The likelihood that immigration after marriage became less common in the period of industrial involution is supported by the concomitant decline in the proportion of families classified as either immigrants or transients.

To determine the extent to which protoindustrialization or commercial agriculture created more stable communities by offering more regular employment, the reconstituted families were reanalyzed by counting the number of families whose children remained in the village as married adults. In this way we were able to create two indexes of generational replacement, presented in Tables 3.3 and 3.4. These tables have been divided into the various periods described above, but they do not go beyond 1809. Because the reconstitution stopped in 1851, it was not possible to include all the marriages of children from post-1810 families. The tabulations have also been adjusted to omit transient families. The first part of each table records the percentage of families whose married children lived in the village; the second part is a reformulation presenting

TABLE 3.3
Generational Replacement, Shepshed

	Part 1: Proportion of all families with married children		Part 2: Of families with married children, number per family	
1600–1679	170 / 457	37.2%	235 / 170	1.38
1680–1749	285 / 554	51.4%	567 / 285	1.99
1750–1809	506 / 1158	43.7%	1181 / 506	2.34

TABLE 3.4
Generational Replacement, Bottesford

	Part 1: Proportion of all families with married children		Part 2: Of families with married children, number per family	
1610–1669	205 572	36.0%	313 205	1.46
1670–1789	372 976	38.1%	609 372	1.64
1790–1809	67 179	37.4%	147 67	2.21

just those families with married children in the village together with the average number of such children per family.

The evidence presented in Table 3.3 concerning generational replacement in Shepshed is contradictory in that the number of families with at least one child living in the village as a married adult declined during industrialization whereas, at the same time, the average number of married children in these families rose substantially. These observations suggest that the benefits of industrial employment were confined to a subsection of the population rather than experienced by all. It appears that some families were successful and proliferated but that a great many others spent just a single generation in the village. The Unwin family provides a classic example of the first type. On July 4, 1796, Thomas Unwin married Mary Wortley and James Unwin married Elizabeth Kiddear; two years later, on August 13, 1798, Isaac Unwin married Elizabeth Start. All three brides were Shepshed natives, but their husbands were immigrants who spent the rest of their lives in their adopted home. The three marriages were fruitful, producing 27 children of whom 23 survived infancy. Of these survivors 17 married in Shepshed and another married elsewhere but returned to his native village shortly afterwards. During the period studied there were many families like the Unwins who multiplied and whose children remained to complete their life cycles in Shepshed.

From the first part of Table 3.4, one is struck by the consistency with which families in Bottesford replaced themselves. During the 200 years analyzed in these calculations just over a third of the families were succeeded by at least one married child. Between 1811 and 1831 the number of families living in the village grew by 47%. The second part of Table 3.4 shows that this temporary relaxation of the social control exerted by the dukes of Rutland over settlement led to a substantial increase in the number of children from families entering observation after 1790 who remained in the village as married adults. This evidence suggests that employment opportunities were critical in regulating population turn-over.

It was argued earlier that the preindustrial village was characterized by a changing population resulting from the interaction of small size, high mortality, and a relatively inelastic demand for and supply of labor. In these conditions the poor were the most mobile, since their lives were governed by the demand for their labor. Insofar as the wealthier yeomen owned their land or enjoyed secure tenure, they displayed far greater residential stability. In Bottesford a core of families persisted throughout continuous change. Only the Bottomley family replaced itself and con-tinued its surname from the 1580s to the middle of the nineteenth century. A further half-dozen families, however, disappeared only in the early nineteenth century, and seven other families persisted well into the eighteenth century. Almost all these families were yeomen or hus-bandmen, except for the Bottomleys who were variously described as laborers, shepherds, cottagers, and shoemakers. When these core families died out or moved away, their positions were filled by others. For exam-ple, the Deweys were last mentioned in 1740, but at this time the Hol-lingsworths first came into observation. Thus it appears that in a rural village like Bottesford the high turnover suggested in Table 3.4 was in some ways illusory since a section of the community provided an element of continuity. This practically immutable core of families probably was critically important to maintaining the village's stable and deferential character. In Shepshed, too, the wealthier peasants provided an element of continuity. Of course, some of the original families disappeared, but the Alts and the Hutchinsons were present from 1538 to the middle of the nineteenth century, while more than a dozen families recorded in the 1851 census could be traced back to the seventeenth century.

In Shepshed most surviving families had members working in some branch of the hosiery industry. At the outset, most framework knitters owned their machines. Before 1725 the stocking trade paid such high wages that a yeoman's younger son would be happy to engage in it. Only after the Worshipful Company of Framework Knitters lost the civil suit brought against it by the provincial hosiers did wage labor become generalized and operators suffer a pronounced decline in status. The Swaine family provides a good example of how industrialization enabled at least one member of a traditional family to continue in the village. Members of this family, which can be traced from the middle of the sixteenth century, were yeomen and bakers during the seventeenth cen-tury. In 1725 Henry Swaine was identified as a framework knitter. Since Henry was a yeoman's second son, it is not unlikely that he would have moved elsewhere if he had not been able to work in the stocking trade. Not only did Henry continue to live in the village, but two of his children married there and the family persisted. These two children were daughters, however, and the family name disappeared in 1779 when Henry's widow was buried.

The Cooks were another family that perpetuated itself in Shepshed by becoming involved in the stocking industry. They appear to have entered the village in 1644 and in the seventeenth century were laborers and shepherds. I argued previously that in preindustrial society members of this class were highly mobile, but the experience of the Cook family demonstrates how industrialization transformed traditional social patterns. In the 1680s and 1690s George and Millicent Cook had eight sons of whom six survived to spend their adult lives in Shepshed. Joseph was a husbandman; Henry a blacksmith; John, Thomas, and George framework knitters; and the sixth brother, William, was not identified by occupation when events concerning him were recorded in the parish register. Between 1700 and 1850 34 more Cooks from succeeding generations resided in the village as married adults, most of them apparently engaged in industry. Ten of the 11 about whom we have occupational information were described as framework knitters. Moreover, these later family members were all descendants of the first three framework knitters.

Industrialization not only changed the lives of those who already lived in Shepshed, it also created new opportunities that attracted many others to the village. The Ing family provides an example of how the availability of employment in Shepshed influenced the residential choices of one young couple and their children. In 1754 William Ing, a nonnative, married Mary Coulson, the daughter of a village slater whose family had then been living in the village for more than a century. From other evidence we learn that the bridegroom's legal place of settlement was Lutterworth, an agricultural village in southern Leicestershire, and that he was a framework knitter. Unfortunately, we do not know how long he lived in Shepshed before his marriage although he was listed as a resident of Shepshed when his marriage was entered in the parish register. William and Mary Ing remained in Shepshed and had 13 children of whom two sons and two daughters also married in the village. Six of their sons' sons also resided in the village as married adults during the first half of the nineteenth century. Those later members of the Ing family for whom occupational information exists were all framework knitters. It appears that the availability of employment that attracted the original William Ing probably influenced the residential choices of his descendants.

So far in this chapter I have looked at population turnover and generational replacement as processes over time—that is, in terms of the experiences of families. It might now be helpful to stop this dynamic process and look at the implications of this information from the perspective of one particular moment in time. The 1851 census provides cross-sectional data for such measurement, for it recorded each individual's birthplace, making it possible to determine not only the rate of persistence among the villagers but also the distance nonnatives had moved to take up residence in either Bottesford or Shepshed. Because the experiences of children were likely to correspond to those of their parents, it was decided to exclude those under 15 from consideration. Fifteen was thought to be a reasonable cutoff because at this age children in traditional society began to leave home to become boarders, lodgers, or servants in households not headed by their parents.

TABLE 3.5
Birthplace, 1851

	Males over 15				Females over 15			
	Bottesford		Shepshed		Bottesford		Shepshed	
	N	Cumulative frequency	N	Cumulative frequency	N	Cumulative frequency	N	Cumulative frequency
Parish	232	53.7	754	64.0	186	44.5	776	66.5
Adjoining	19	58.2	127	74.7	30	51.5	112	76.2
Adjacent	120	86.0	157	87.7	153	88.0	157	90.0
Region	43	96.0	95	96.0	38	97.0	74	96.0
Elsewhere	18	100.0	47	100.0	12	100.0	47	100.0
Number	432		1180		419		1166	

In 1851 the differences in residential choice between the villagers of Bottesford and those of Shepshed are large at the first level—that of the village—but they progressively diminish. Almost 90% of each group of villagers lived in the immediate neighborhood of where they were born. The variations in the intermediate measures—those born in the parish itself or in the first concentric ring of villages around it—had to do with the availability of employment. In Shepshed, a large protoindustrial village which had experienced outmigration for a generation, a preponderance of the adults in 1851 were native born. In Bottesford it was the neighborhood—the two concentric rings of villages surrounding it—which provided employment opportunities. Just as local, nonnative men and women made up a large component of mid–nineteenth century Bottesford so it is likely that young men and women born in Bottesford were scattered throughout the neighborhood because they were unable to find positions in their native village. In Bottesford the preindustrial pattern of extreme volatility at the village level but stability within the slightly larger universe of the neighborhood persisted into an age of commercial agriculture.

4

INDUSTRIAL INVOLUTION AND DOMESTIC ORGANIZATION IN 1851

In England, as early as the sixteenth century, the nuclear family appears to have been the usual form of domestic organization. Households sometimes included servants, but kin and lodgers are rarely mentioned in the documents describing these households. The household containing a stem family seems to have been conspicuous by its absence.[1] In the relatively stagnant preindustrial, semicommercial economy in which the household was the primary unit of production and consumption, controls over nuptiality and, to a somewhat lesser extent, over fertility were of vital importance in keeping population size roughly in line with resources. So long as coresidence (i. e., two or more married couples sharing a single household) remained an unacceptable form of domestic organization, young people had to wait for positions in a village's economy to become vacant before they could marry and set up their own households.[2] Contem-

---

[1] P. Laslett, "Size and Structure of the Household in England Over Three Centuries." This paper has since been revised and extended and has now been included as part of Laslett's two contributions to *Household and Family in Past Times,* which he coedited with Richard Wall. Laslett's two papers are the "Introduction: The history of the family," (pp. 1–89) and "Mean household size in England since the sixteenth century," (pp. 125–58). Laslett's argument that the nuclear family has been the usual form of domestic organization in Western Europe since the sixteenth century has been vigorously criticized by L. Berkner. ("The Stem Family and the Development Cycle of the Peasant Household," and "The Use and Misuse of Census Data for the Historical Analysis of Family Structure."

[2] A recent article by C. Howell has suggested that the emergence of the nuclear family as the predominant type of household organization in England dates from the fifteenth century. In

poraries believed that employment opportunities were of critical importance in regulating the incidence of marriage.

If this explanation, linking economic opportunity to household formation through the mediating mechanism of earlier marriage, is true, then protoindustrialization, by creating sustained growth in employment, should have encouraged people to set up independent households referring primarily to their own needs and aspirations. To the extent that industrial involution, the last phase of protoindustrialization, resulted in the deterioration of adult laborers' wages and living standards, recourse to coresidence rather than a reversion to greater age at marriage might be expected, since laborers were still able to achieve their maximum earnings at a younger age. To begin testing the adequacy of this argument, this chapter will examine the extent to which household structures differed between the industrial and the traditional laboring classes at the time of the 1851 census.

In 1851, the mean household size in Bottesford (4.27) was substantially lower than it was in Shepshed, 4.73. The distribution of its population among households of various sizes confirms the impression that Bottesford's inhabitants had a marked preference for living in smaller units. Mean family size in Shepshed was also larger than it was in Bottesford, 3.82 and 3.41 respectively. The distribution of the population among families of various sizes underlines the differences in conjugal arrangements between the two villages. Whereas 26.8% of the family members in Bottesford lived in groups of more than six, the figure for Shepshed was 36.3%. Apart from the heads' nuclear families, households in both villages included similar numbers of other persons, related or nonrelated. In Bottesford about one household in five included relatives, while one in three had a coresident nonrelative. In Shepshed, on the other hand, resident kin were more common than lodgers or servants; about one-quarter of all households included kin and a rather smaller proportion included lodgers or servants. Information on household composition is presented in Table 4.1.

The main reason for the differences in family size was the larger number of coresident children per family in Shepshed. Children of household heads made up 42% of the population in the protoindustrial village but only 40% in Bottesford. At least one child lived in 74.9% of householders' families in Shepshed but in 67% of those in Bottesford. A more striking difference between the two communities was that 20.2% of Shepshed families contained more than four coresident children but only 14.2% of those in the agricultural village. Moreover, in Shepshed 51% of the chil-

---

the feudal era, Howell claims, the stem family was the usual type of peasant family arrangement. (C. Howell "Stability and Change 1300–1700, The Socio-Economic Context of the Self-Perpetuating Family Farm in England.")

TABLE 4.1
Household Composition, 1851

Agric.   *Indust.*

	Bottesford	Shepshed
Household heads	.98	.98
Wives per family	.73	.77
Children per family	1.70	2.07
Family size	3.41	3.82
Relatives	.34	.48
Nonrelatives	.46	.37
Visitors	.06	.06
Household size	4.27	4.73
Number	302	785

dren lived with at least three siblings while in Bottesford only 42% did so.

These figures give one the misleading impression that whereas more children were born to the villagers in Shepshed, married women in Bottesford lived with a greater number of infant children. The *fertility ratio* (i.e., children under five per 1000 married women ages 15 to 49) was 1040 in Shepshed but 1135 in Bottesford.[3] This disparity between the larger number of infant children and the smaller overall number of coresident children in Bottesford seems to reflect the fact that older children were likely to leave home and become either domestic servants or farm laborers. Among the Shepshed laborers' children whose occupation was recorded in the 1851 census more than two-thirds were engaged in some branch of the hosiery industry. The presence of the framework knitting industry in Shepshed permitted the supply of agricultural labour to stay in line with local demand without recourse to emigration. Easy access to protoindustrial employment absorbed any surplus. In this context, the decision of the dukes of Rutland to keep industry out of Bottesford was of vital importance, for by strictly limiting the demand for labor it forced many of the villagers' children to leave home in search of employment. The small proportion of Bottesford's laboring families with more than four coresident children suggests the plausibility of this explanation.

A larger proportion of the women between 15 and 49 in Shepshed were married than in the agricultural village, 57.9% compared with 56.2% were or had been married at the time of the 1851 census. The evidence also suggests that protoindustrialization enabled women to marry younger; 21.7% of the women under 25 in Shepshed were married but only 15.9% in Bottesford. Among women under 20 this difference was twice as great; 3.8% in the protoindustrial village were married, but only 1.6% in the agricultural. Among older women, however, such differences diminished.

---

[3] This measure is far from being a trustworthy guide as it tells us about *surviving* children rather than about live births. No cognizance is taken of infant mortality, the effect of which, as I will show in later chapters, was quite different in Shepshed and Bottesford.

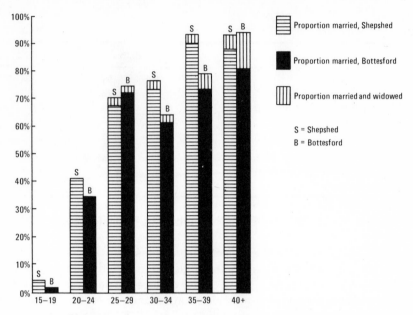

Figure 4.1. Proportion of married women, by age groups.

Indeed, they were reversed. Among women in their 40s, 92.6% in Shepshed were married or widowed while in Bottesford 94.4% were so classified. See Figure 4.1.

Families sharing a house were usually related, and the presence in Shepshed of a larger number of households with resident kin indicates a higher incidence of sharing. Another factor contributing to the prevalence of sharing in Shepshed was the larger number of young married couples in that village. Of married women under 25 in Shepshed 26.9% lived in households not headed by their husbands whereas 17.6% of such women in Bottesford were in similar circumstances.

Very briefly, the differences between the two villages may be summarized as follows: in Shepshed households had a larger average size, were more likely to contain children, were more likely to share the house with relatives or another family; in Bottesford more households were headed by single people and contained servants.

Having seen the ways in which households differed in size and structure between the two communities, let us now consider the extent to which these differences can be linked with the existence of the framework knitting industry in Shepshed. To examine the impact of protoindustrialization upon the domestic organization of the laboring classes, we will analyze the information derived from the 1851 census along occupational lines. The framework knitters will be compared with the laborers and craftsmen of both villages. Insofar as the presence of domestic industry was the vital factor distinguishing the two villages, it will be interesting to see whether household structure and family size among the agricultural laborers and craftsmen in Shepshed were similar to those of their counterparts in Bottesford.[4] If industrialization was as critical as I have assumed it to be, its influence should also have affected some of these other villagers and distinguished them from their counterparts in the agricultural community. Farmers have not been included in any of the following discussions because by the mid–nineteenth century they were amost all employers of labor and, as such, wholly removed from the economic uncertainty that plagued most craftsmen and all laborers and framework knitters.

The information about household size and structure puts into question the assumption that the wealthier groups always had larger, more complex households, Classifying households according to the heads' occupations and then relating household size to the wealth of each group reveal the framework knitters' relatively large households. In fact, although they had larger households than any group except the Shepshed farmers, they were the lowest on the economic scale. To explain this phenomenon we could refer to the contemporary belief that these protoindustrial proletarians had passed a poverty threshold and were no longer controlled by rational considerations. But, on the contrary, it is my argument that the differences in household size and structure that distinguished the framework knitters from the agricultural laborers and village artisans resulted, not from the latters' moral standards but from social and economic factors affecting them all.

From Table 4.2 we can see that the agricultural laborers in both villages had smaller households than the framework knitters. Fewer laborers lived in households of more than six people. The knitters also had larger nuclear families than either group of laborers despite a considerable difference in family size between the two groups of laborers. The Bottesford laborers had fewer coresident children and, therefore, smaller families. This disparity does not seem to have been caused by a difference in fertility (in both villages the fertility ratio of laborers' wives under 30 was about 1800) but by the fact that Bottesford laborers' older children were more likely to leave home. From Table 4.3 we can see that among Bottesford laborers 14% of the households included four or more coresident children of the head whereas in Shepshed the percentage was one and one-half times as great, 21.1%. This difference seems to reflect the fact that the children of

---

[4] It should be noted that the dukes of Rutland's ban on industry in Bottesford did not extend to women. Not only were some of the laborers' and craftsmen's daughters earning extra money as seamers but a few of their wives were too. Nevertheless, their earnings were essentially supplementary insofar as industrial employment was not the mainstay of their budgets, and it was the duke's intention that families in "his" village should not be wholly dependent on manufacturing wages.

TABLE 4.2
Household Composition by Occupation

Mean	Bottesford			Shepshed			
	Farmers	Laborers	Craftsmen	Farmers	Laborers	Craftsmen	Framework knitters
Household heads	1.00	1.00	1.00	1.00	1.00	.99	.99
Wives per family	.41	.88	.79	.74	.85	.80	.87
Children per family	1.12	1.84	2.01	2.54	2.13	2.19	2.21
Family size	2.53	3.72	3.80	4.28	3.98	3.98	4.07
Relatives	.66	.30	.31	.47	.36	.29	.54
Nonrelatives	1.69	.10	.51	1.78	.22	.27	.32
Visitors	.03	.05	.11	.23	.04	.12	.03
Household size	4.91	4.17	4.73	6.76	4.60	4.66	4.96
Number	32	134	93	39	127	130	381

Shepshed laborers more easily found employment outside of their fathers' calling. About two-thirds of the employed children of agricultural laborers in Shepshed worked in the hosiery trade in one role or another. As a result of this availability of alternative employment, although an average of 0.8 employed children lived in each Shepshed laborer's household, in Bottesford the comparable figure was 0.4. Just as employment was more prevalent among the children of Shepshed laborers, it was also more common among their wives. The evidence shows that although 18.1% of the Bottesford laborers' wives had another occupation (besides that of housewife), in Shepshed the corresponding figure was 29.7%.

TABLE 4.3
Distribution of Children, by Occupation

Households	Bottesford				Shepshed					
	Laborers		Craftsmen		Laborers		Craftsmen		Framework knitters	
	N	%	N	%	N	%	N	%	N	%
With at least one child	$\frac{104}{134}$ = 77.5		$\frac{66}{93}$ = 66.7		$\frac{100}{127}$ = 78.7		$\frac{97}{130}$ = 74.5		$\frac{296}{381}$ = 77.7	
With four or more children	$\frac{19}{134}$ = 14.2		$\frac{20}{93}$ = 21.5		$\frac{29}{127}$ = 21.1		$\frac{33}{130}$ = 25.4		$\frac{91}{386}$ = 23.9	
Where children lived with three or more siblings	$\frac{84}{237}$ = 35.4		$\frac{102}{187}$ = 54.5		$\frac{133}{270}$ = 49.3		$\frac{159}{275}$ = 57.8		$\frac{456}{845}$ = 54.0	

While the importance of protoindustrialization in distinguishing domestic arrangements between the two groups of agricultural laborers seems quite clear, the distinctions between the Shepshed laborers and the framework knitters were—taken individually—less pronounced. The framework knitters did have larger families, were more likely to be living with kin or nonrelated people, were more likely to be married, married earlier, had more children living at home, and, in addition, more frequently shared their households with other families. And yet in not one of these individual categories was there a significant difference. Taken together, however, and inasmuch as a larger proportion of framework knitters lived in households of more than six people, these differences became overwhelmingly significant. This clear distinction between the Shepshed agricultural laborers and framework knitters is important. It makes it difficult to argue that it was specifically the dukes of Rutland's policy of barring industry from Bottesford that caused the two laboring classes to be so different, since in Shepshed, where such a policy was not practiced, the differences were still evident.

The tradesmen and craftsmen also differed from the framework knitters in noticeable ways. They had smaller households, and they not only married later but also less often, so that more trade and craft households were headed by unmarried men. These differences were caused by the particular nature of each occupation.

The propensity among framework knitters to marry earlier can be explained by the relatively few obstacles a young man had to overcome before reaching his prime earning capacity. Moreover, there was a significant likelihood that a stockinger's wife would also be employed, so that it was not as difficult for a young couple to establish a household. In Table 4.4 statistics describing the frequency of working wives among the various occupational groups are presented.

Unlike the proletarianized framework knitters, tradesmen and craftsmen generally served an apprenticeship before they began to practice their work. Even then, they did not set out on their own because, being self-employed, they still had to amass sufficient capital to make themselves economically viable. For these reasons they were unlikely to

TABLE 4.4
Working Wives Outside the house.

	Bottesford				Shepshed				
	Laborers		Craftsmen		Laborers		Craftsmen		Framework knitters
	N	%	N	%	N	%	N	%	N	%
	$\frac{23}{127} = 18.1$		$\frac{10}{78} = 12.8$		$\frac{33}{111} = 29.7$		$\frac{19}{101} = 18.9$		$\frac{164}{333} = 49.3$

marry as early as the framework knitters. More households of framework knitters were headed by married men than households of artisans. Furthermore, unmarried framework knitters were unlikely to set up their own households, whereas unmarried craftsmen and tradesmen had a propensity to do so. This type of domestic pattern appears to have largely resulted from the lateness and relative infrequency of marriage among the nonindustrial artisans. In all instances households with nonmarried heads were considerably smaller than those headed by married men. Thus, framework knitters' higher marital frequency meant that, overall, they had larger households than craftsmen. But among those households headed by married men the Shepshed craftsmen and tradesmen had not only larger households but also bigger families than their protoindustrial neighbors. A similar sample of Bottesford craftsmen revealed that their households were exactly the same size as the stockingers' although their families were slightly smaller because fewer of their older children stayed at home. In this context, it is important to note that, as with the agricultural laborers' children, the children of Bottesford's tradesmen and craftsmen were leaving their native village to find employment elsewhere. Whereas in Shepshed the existence of protoindustrial work meant that the children of craftsmen and tradesmen were as likely to be employed as stockingers or seamers as to follow their parents' occupations, in Bottesford this choice did not exist—the labor supply outstripped the carefully regulated demand.

When the household composition of the framework knitters was compared to that of the trade and craft group, some interesting distinctions were found. The stockingers' ties with their kin appear to have been stronger in that they were more likely to be living with relatives or sharing their households with related families. They were also more willing to take in lodgers, while the wealthier tradesmen and craftsmen were more likely to have servants living in their households.

Because the adult framework knitters' wages were lower than either those of the agricultural laborers or those of the tradesmen and craftsmen, it was necessary for them to take measures ensuring that their families were not dependent solely upon their own earnings. For this reason it was common for them to share accommodations with other families in order to have larger numbers of wage earners in their households. The rate of coresidence (i.e., two or more married couples sharing a household) among the traditional laboring classes of the two villages was virtually identical: 4.5% in Bottesford and 4% in Shepshed. Similar levels prevailed among the tradesmen and craftsmen of both villages. Among the framework knitters, in contrast, the level of coresidence was 10.2%, more than twice as high. This phenomenon was only partly caused by the protoindustrialists' precocious nuptiality, since stockingers in their 30s still displayed a marked preference for living in coresidential households.

In Michael Anderson's study of household organization in Preston, Lancashire, he found that the rate of coresidence among married couples was dependent upon the number of children living with them. He considered that family size was of "crucial importance . . . in determining whether or not a couple headed their own household."[5] This predictive framework was a relatively reliable guide to analyzing residential patterns of the framework knitters in Shepshed. The number of coresident children rather than the sharing couple's age was the more important variable. As has been mentioned before, the framework knitters' high incidence of coresidence was not caused only by their predilection for early marriage; even among married couples in which the husband was in his late 30s, 11.1% still lived with kin or as lodgers. See Table 4.5.

When the number of coresident children was used as the independent variable, it was found that whereas 24.5% of the childless couples shared accommodations, this rate was only 5.2% among couples with two or more children. In contrast to the framework knitters, the nonindustrial populations of the two villages do not seem to have displayed any propensity suggesting that family size, rather than age, was the important factor in determining their residential patterns. Only very young couples were found living in other families' households. It seems likely that coresidence among the nonindustrial villagers was caused by parental debility; six of the 10 married couples in Shepshed living in shared households did so with widowed parents who were nominally considered to be those households' heads. The clear distinction between the behavior of the protoindustrial villagers in Shepshed and that of the laborers, tradesmen, and craftsmen of the two villages suggests that Anderson's argument needs to be modified. The residence patterns of married couples in the various occupational groups in terms of the number of coresiding children are set forth in Table 4.6.

A coresiding family was usually found living in a household headed by a parent or parent-in-law of the sharing family's head. This occurred in about two-thirds of the cases for all three occupational groups. There was no difference in the strength of kinship ties among the three groups that could not be accounted for by mere chance fluctuations resulting from the relatively small numbers involved in the calculations. What does stand out is the great strength of ties within the nuclear family, and, since no account has been taken of propinquity of residence between married children and their parents, it seems fair to assume that these figures may even understate the importance of parents to their young, newly married children and children to their elderly, debilitated parents. Distances within Shepshed and Bottesford were very small so that no one lived far from parents or children who also lived in the village. Anderson's study of

---

[5] M. Anderson, *Family Structure in Nineteenth Century Lancashire*, p. 49.

TABLE 4.5
Residence Patterns of Married Couples, by Husband's Age

| | Bottesford | | | Shepshed | | | | | |
| | | | | Nonindustrial | | | Framework knitters | | |
	Head (%)	Sharing (%)	N	Head (%)	Sharing (%)	N	Head (%)	Sharing (%)	N
15–19	—	—	—	—	—	—	50.0	50.0	2
20–24	85.7	14.3	7	73.5	26.5	19	73.5	26.5	34
25–29	86.5	13.5	30	93.2	6.8	29	79.5	20.5	48
30–34	92.9	7.1	28	95.1	4.9	42	89.3	12.7	55
35–39	100.0	—	23	97.1	2.9	35	88.9	11.1	45
40–49	92.2	7.8	51	100.0	—	51	90.5	7.5	40
50–59	100.0	—	46	100.0	—	55	98.9	1.1	81
Over 60	100.0	—	41	97.6	2.4	45	95.5	4.5	46
All	95.1	4.9	226	96.0	4.0	276	89.8	10.2	371

TABLE 4.6
Residence of Married Couples, by Number of Coresident Children

| | Bottesford | | | Shepshed | | | | | |
| | | | | Nonindustrial | | | Framework knitters | | |
	Head (%)	Sharing (%)	N	Head (%)	Sharing (%)	N	Head (%)	Sharing (%)	N
0	95.6	4.4	45	98.9	1.1	83	75.5	24.5	49
1	92.2	7.8	51	92.6	7.4	54	84.4	15.6	90
2+	96.1	3.9	130	96.4	3.6	139	94.8	5.2	232
All	95.1	4.9	226	96.0	4.0	276	89.8	10.2	371

the far larger town of Preston discovered that there was a marked difference in the expected and actual distances between the residences of parents and children. He suggested that "some related [people] did make
positive efforts to live near one another, and to a remarkable extent
succeeded."[6]

If we consider the incidence of sharing in a broader sense and include
families headed by widows, widowers, unmarried mothers, and deserted
wives, the distinction between the protoindustrialists and their neighbors
is still much in evidence. Of households with heads engaged in the hosiery
industry, 13.6% were found to be shared with a broken family. For the
nonindustrial villagers the levels of sharing were 7.8% in Bottesford and
8.4% in Shepshed. Households headed by widows or widowers were
three times more likely to be shared then households headed by married
men. Obviously, sharing his accommodations offered a widowed person
with children many advantages. A widower was provided with help in
housekeeping and childminding, a widow received a vital supplement to
her meager income. A widow unable to share her household with another
family or with unmarried lodgers often had no alternative to entering the
workhouse. Families of unmarried mothers and deserted wives were usually found as sharing families in complex households. In contrast, widows
and widowers were more likely to be heads of households shared with
subsidiary families. Widowed persons were only infrequently heads of
families living in households headed by other persons. Despite these
differences in the strategies of sharing accommodations, the central fact
emerging from this analysis is that a high percentage of widowed persons
and husbandless women lived with other families in single domestic
units. Among such broken families 33.3% in Bottesford, 37.4% among the
nonindustrial population of Shepshed, and 56.9% of the framework knitters did not live in simple, nuclear family households.

The much higher rate of residential complexity among both broken
families and married couples in the protoindustrial population is an indication that their socioeconomic situation was a critical factor distinguishing their domestic arrangements from those of traditional villagers. The
crucial question that must be addressed at this point is whether this
residential complexity was inherent in the household organization of
protoindustrial manufacturing or was a response to recent difficult conditions. Unfortunately the evidence necessary to produce a satisfactory answer to this question is lacking. There is little information describing
household size and structure before 1851. There are none of the informal
censuses Peter Laslett has ingeniously utilized for his study of household
size and structure in preindustrial England. The printed abstracts of the
earlier national censuses are unreliable since it is unclear not only what

---

[6] M. Anderson, *Family Structure*, p. 59.

criteria were used to define a "family" but also whether instructions were consistently followed by the enumerators. In the absence of satisfactory and reliable data from an earlier period it is necessary to reserve final judgment on this important issue. However, a partial, suggestive answer may be forthcoming from a consideration of the evidence presented in this chapter which suggests that the framework knitters' residential complexity was not so much a matter of social custom as one of convenience or necessity. Far from having the irrational, uncalculating behavior contemporaries ascribed to them, the framework knitters were quite conscious of the disastrous consequences that could befall a family in which the number of dependents outstripped the family's earning power. The framework knitters not only had the largest proportion of working wives, but their children also were the most likely to be employed. Therefore, in few framework knitting households was there only one wage earner: it was quite common for three or more household members to engage in the hosiery trade. Living with relatives and lodgers was yet another way in which the number of coresident wage earners could be increased. Thus, the framework knitters' preference for living in large domestic units can be seen as the result of a conscious effort to protect themselves from their unpredictable economic circumstances.

5

THE DEMOGRAPHIC
IMPLICATIONS
OF RURAL INDUSTRIALIZATION

Changing employment opportunities greatly influenced Shepshed's rate of population growth. From the last years of the seventeenth century, industrialization combined with the absence of a dominant landowner to produce employment for the villagers' children and easy settlement for immigrants. During the long period of industrial expansion which lasted until 1815 the villagers made significant demographic adjustments leading to rapid increase in the village population. Slower rates of population growth began after 1815 and absolute retardation occurred in the 1840s, reflecting the fact that the stockingers' living standards were considerably lessened and young people began to emigrate. Indeed, the absolute number of marriages celebrated in Shepshed reached a peak in the 1810s and declined after that. Evidence suggesting that villagers' older, unmarried children began to leave the village in substantial numbers comes from the changes in family size reported in the nineteenth century civil censuses. In 1811 mean family size was 5.52, but by 1851 it had dropped to 3.82. We shall see that this decline was probably not caused by a decline in fertility or a rise in mortality.

In Figure 5.1 I have plotted a nine-year weighted, moving average of baptisms, burials, and marriages occurring in Shepshed between 1600 and 1850. A weighted, moving average was chosen in preference to a single graphic representation of annual changes because it yields a clearer impression of overall, long-run trends while still allowing for the effect of yearly fluctuations.

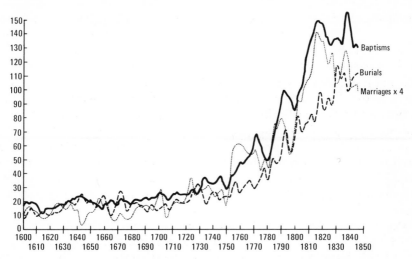

Figure 5.1. A nine-year weighted, moving average of baptisms, burials, and marriages (×4), Shepshed.

During the first three-quarters of the seventeenth century there appear to have been no obvious trends in either the baptismal or the burial curves and their movements seem to have more or less cancelled each other out.[1] After 1680, during the initial period of industrialization, there was a slow rise in the baptismal curve which, except for the later 1720s, produced a small annual surplus. Then, after 1750, there was a radical demographic discontinuity within the industrial population when the baptismal curve was characterized by a wave-like movement with distinct peaks in 1771, 1790, and 1814–15 interrupted by equally distinct troughs in 1779 and 1799. After 1815 the baptismal curve reached a stable level around which it fluctuated until the end of the period under observation. These pronounced oscillations in the post-1750 baptismal curve are of obvious importance in explaining the village population's natural increase. Moreover, when these oscillations are viewed in conjunction with the steadier, upwards movement in the burial curve, it appears that in Shepshed changes in the birth rate provided the dynamic impetus behind population growth.

Looking more closely at this series of moving averages, we can see that these oscillations in the baptismal curve after 1750 were quite similar to the variations in the frequency of marriages. Noting that its response was

---

[1] Seventeenth century ecclesiastical censuses show little change in the size of the village population. The "Liber Cleri," in 1603 reported 392 communicants while in 1676 the "Compton Census" recorded 366 conformists, six papists, and four nonconformists or, in other words, the equivalent of 376 communicants. (*Victoria County History of Leicestershire*, Vol. III, p. 168; W. G. D. Fletcher, "A Religious Census of Leicestershire in 1676," p. 298.)

not always immediate, and considering that no allowance was made for variations in marital fertility, we can see that the baptismal curve's oscillations reflect changes in the frequency of marriages, which can themselves be explained by referring to the changing fortunes of the framework knitting industry on which a large section of the population was dependent. To the extent that demographic behaviour was flexible, fluctuations in prosperity were critically important. Insofar as marriage and immigration were subject to rational control, people attempting to optimize their material conditions would be likely to defer marriage or decide against moving into an adversely affected area during a depression. On the other hand, when industry was booming, marriage would occur more frequently and there would also be heavy immigration of young people in search of work.

The great increase in the number of marriages celebrated in the later 1750s and 1760s coincided with a boom in exports and a period of great technical innovation. The American colonists' embargo on British goods deprived the stocking industry of its largest overseas market, and during the years of the American Revolution the bottom fell out of the export market.[2] In these years there was also a fall in the number of marriages celebrated in Shepshed. The end of hostilities in America and the 1786 treaty with France, which gave British manufacturers the opportunity to sell their goods in this large and lucrative market, ushered in a period of prosperity that lasted until 1815. Moreover, the effects of this heady economic climate were reinforced by the entry of the generation born between 1755 and 1770 into the marriage market. Again, in the 1780s there was a great increase in the number of marriages celebrated in Shepshed. However, the outbreak of the Napoleonic Wars in 1793 and the wholesale mobilization of men into the armed forces caused a shortfall in the number of marriages. But after 1797 the armed forces reached a stable size, and the marriage curve shot upwards, reaching its peak in 1816. In response to the postwar depression in the framework knitting industry there was a decline in the absolute number of marriages. Indeed, the number of marriages celebrated in Shepshed never again reached the level attained in 1816. Since the village should have contained a large proportion of young people of marriageable age as a result of the tremendous number of births in earlier years, it seems likely that a disproportionate number of these young people emigrated from Shepshed to find better prospects elsewhere.

The annual totals of baptisms, burials, and marriages in Shepshed show that demographic behavior in Shepshed responded to variations in material conditions. But although aggregative analysis is a useful method with which to examine large-scale changes in demographic behavior, it is too

---

[2] E. B. Schumpeter, *English Overseas Trade Statistics 1697-1808*, pp. 3, 57, 69.

blunt an instrument to use to study the interplay of economic and demographic forces at the level of the individual family. Aggregate analysis is not capable of determining the exact nature of the modifications in demographic behavior that occurred. In attempting to probe the causes of such changes, the family reconstitution study will be utilized to investigate individuals' experiences rather than the aggregate experiences of the whole population.

The aggregate analysis of population growth in Shepshed suggested that a significant change occurred in the pattern of marriages during the industrialization of this village. Results derived from the family reconstitution study describe this change at an individual level. In Table 5.1, I present statistics describing changes in age at first marriage of both men and women in Shepshed between 1600 and 1849. These figures have been divided into four cohorts: 1600–1699, the preindustrial village; 1700–1749, the transitional period; 1750–1824, full-scale protoindustrialization; and 1825–1851, industrial involution.

Before a discussion of the significance of these figures it should be noted that throughout the 1600–1851 period there was a constant difference between the mean and median measures of central tendency. Because these distributions were all positively skewed, our perception of the intensity of marriage would be disproportionately influenced by later marriages if we looked just at the mean values. Indeed, for some cohorts as many as two-thirds of the members were married by the mean age at marriage. Of particular interest in this regard is the fact that the difference between the mean and median measures was relatively constant throughout the entire period of observation.

The industrialization of Shepshed was accompanied by a substantial deviation from the preindustrial pattern of relatively late marriage for both

TABLE 5.1
Age at First Marriage

	N	Mean	Standard deviation	Lower quartile	Median	Upper quartile	Inter-quartile range
Men							
1600–1699	80	29.4	6.9	24.8	28.0	33.4	8.6
1700–1749	119	28.5	6.3	24.0	27.5	31.4	7.4
1750–1824	500	24.0	5.0	21.0	23.3	27.0	6.0
1825–1851	391	24.1	4.8	21.2	23.3	27.0	5.8
Women							
1600–1699	121	28.1	5.9	23.6	26.8	31.2	7.5
1700–1749	133	27.4	6.1	23.2	26.4	30.3	7.0
1750–1824	420	24.1	5.3	20.6	23.0	26.0	5.4
1825–1851	479	22.6	4.6	20.1	22.1	24.7	4.6

men and women. In the second quarter of the nineteenth century men and women were both marrying about five and one-half years earlier than they had before 1700. In the preindustrial village more than one-quarter of all brides were over 30, but after 1825 just one bride in 11 was over 30. Before 1700 just one bride in 15 was under 20, whereas after 1825 this proportion had risen to one in four. Accompanying this decline in age at marriage was a substantial reduction in the interquartile range of the distribution of marriage ages so that, in the demographer's argot, female nuptiality became not only more precocious but also more intense in the period of full-scale industrialization. The men's age at marriage was quite as flexible as their brides'. Before 1700 the mean age at marriage for men was 29.4, whereas in the second quarter of the nineteenth century rather more than five-sixths of all men had married by this age. Similarly, just 11% of men married after 1825 were over 30 in contrast to more than one-third of all preindustrial bridegrooms. Like their brides, men in Shepshed not only married earlier but the distribution of their marriage ages also featured a marked decline in its interquartile range.

In order to examine this reduction in age at first marriage in more detail, we have divided the period after 1700 into ten-year cohorts. These results have been presented in Table 5.2 and depicted graphically in Figure 5.2.

Both Table 5.2 and Figure 5.2 indicate that whereas before 1760 men still entered marriage at 28 or 29, their age at marriage fell dramatically in the

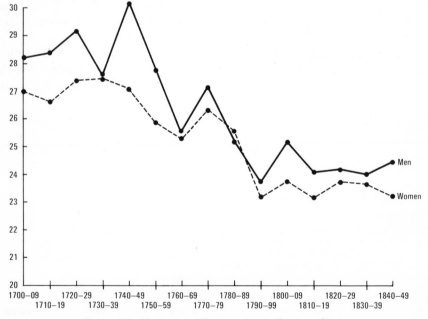

Figure 5.2. Mean age at first marriage, 10-year cohorts.

TABLE 5.2
Mean Age at First Marriage, Ten-Year Cohorts

Men			Women	
N	Age	Date	Age	N
22	28.2	1700–09	27.0	26
21	28.4	1710–19	26.6	19
24	29.2	1720–29	27.4	33
29	27.6	1730–39	27.5	30
23	30.2	1740–49	27.1	25
30	27.8	1750–59	25.9	38
48	25.6	1760–69	25.3	56
44	27.2	1770–79	26.4	59
60	25.2	1780–89	25.6	57
58	23.8	1790–99	23.2	69
69	25.2	1800–09	23.8	91
108	24.1	1810–19	23.2	110
122	24.2	1820–29	23.8	118
119	24.0	1830–39	23.7	147
164	24.5	1840–49	23.2	195

This sample is drawn from a somewhat different group than that described in Table 5.1 since it does *not* include those marriages derived from the "re-reconstitution." The "re-reconstitution" study is described in the Appendix: "The reliability of parochial registration and the representativeness of family reconstitution."

next four decades and reached a new equilibrium after 1790 when it fluctuated around 24. This five-year reduction in the space of less than two generations was not continuous, however, since a rising age at marriage in the 1770s followed a steep fall in the two preceding decades. This temporary reversion to a later age at marriage, of course, occurred during a time when the framework knitting industry was in a depression with its best foreign market embargoed. After the hostilities in America ended, there was a long period of prosperity in the stocking trade. This transition from depression to prosperity is reflected in the statistics on age at marriage: between 1776 and 1785, 44.2% of all bridegrooms (19 of 43) were under 25 in contrast to 65.5% (49 of 76) in the following decade. Moreover, older bridegrooms were twice as common in the depressed years when 18.5% (8 of 43) were over 30, whereas in the buoyant period after 1786 this figure was 9.3% (7 of 76). In terms of average age at marriage, men married more than two years later before 1786 than after, 26.3 as opposed to 23.8. This evidence strongly suggests that in response to deteriorating economic conditions men were deferring marriage. Their brides, however, displayed no such sensitivity to fluctuations in prosperity. Before 1786, brides under 25 were taken in 67.5% (35 of 52) of all marriages as opposed to 69.9% (51 of 73) of marriages after 1786. In both periods older brides, over 30, accounted for 13.5% of all brides (7 of 52; 10 of 73). Furthermore, before 1776 women married later than in the economically depressed years after 1776: in the decade before 1776 their average age at marriage was 26.2—more than one and one-half years later than it was in the following decade when, on average, women married at 24.6. Although the short-term experience of women was quite unlike that of their husbands, in the long term their age at marriage also displayed the same substantial reduction during the course of industrialization. Before 1700 women married about five years later than they did after 1790.

In terms of reproductive capacity, the implications of a five-year reduction in women's age at marriage were most important. The years added to their married life were, from a physiological point of view, their most fecund. Lorimer, in his Hypothetical Fecundity Model, suggests that for each year earlier that a woman marries her completed family size will increase by 0.36 children.[3] Evidence from the reconstitution study of Shepshed agrees broadly with this figure. In Table 5.3 we present the

TABLE 5.3
Completed Family Size, by Age at Marriage

Median age at marriage	Mean	Standard deviation	N
Under 20	7.2	4.2	17
20–24	5.6	3.2	55
25–29	4.5	2.5	51
30–34	3.4	2.4	24
Over 35	1.6	1.0	20

These results are derived from all cohorts, 1600–1849.

results of a cross tabulation showing completed family size as a function of age at marriage. It can be seen from these figures that whereas women who married before 20 had an average completed family of 7.2, those marrying between 30 and 35 had an average of 3.4, 3.8 fewer children than the teen-age brides.

In addition to directly increasing fecundity by lengthening women's childbearing periods, a decline of this magnitude in age at marriage also promoted population growth by reducing the intervals between generations so that more children were born in each unit of time. Even in the absence of changes in fertility, such a reduction in age at marriage would have an important impact on the rate of population growth. In Table 5.4 the figures on age-specific fertility rates for our four cohorts are presented.

These figures describing the fertility of women in Shepshed, like those for age at marriage, show that prior to the onset of full-scale protoindustrialization in the mid–eighteenth century fertility rates were stable. Thereafter a significant rise in marital fertility combined with a substan-

---

[3] F. Lorimer, *Culture and Human Fertility*, pp. 51–54.

TABLE 5.4
Age-Specific Fertility Rates

	Years at risk	Children born	Rate/000
1600–1699			
Under 25	62	22	355
25–29	174	67	385
30–34	224	68	304
35–39	234	61	260
40–44	207	25	121
45–49	177	8	45
1700–1749			
Under 25	111	44	395
25–29	220	81	368
30–34	316	94	297
35–39	282	72	255
40–44	241	25	112
45–49	212	11	52
1750–1824			
Under 25	568	254	447
25–29	765	263	344
30–34	778	245	315
35–39	624	160	256
40–44	482	65	135
45–49	482	10	32
1825–1851			
Under 25	1129	486	430
25–29	1121	396	353
30–34	898	272	303
35–39	562	132	235
40–44	312	38	122
45–49	120	2	17

The data given for women 30–34, 35–39 in the 1825–1851 cohort are somewhat different from those in my article in *Social History*, 2, (1976) because of a typographical error in that text. Thus the "years at risk" in the 30–34 age group were 898 (not 892 as stated in *Social History*) and the "years at risk" for the 35–39 age group were 562 (not 898 as stated in *Social History*).

tially lower age at marriage to produce the acceleration in the rate of population growth that is evident from the graphic representation of the baptismal curve in Figure 5.1. The combined impact of this rise in fertility and the lower age at marriage had the further effect of altering the population's age distribution so that a higher proportion was below childbearing age. This change in age distribution meant that each new cohort entering the marriage market would be significantly larger than its predecessor. In this way population growth developed a self-sustaining impetus. From this perspective the second quarter of the nineteenth century is of particular interest, for at that point the population of Shepshed was confronted with drastically changed economic prospects for which its new demographic profile was most unsuitable. Many young people left the village after 1825, but those who stayed were ill-equipped to reduce the number of children they would inevitably bring into the world. By 1825 it had been the experience of a whole generation that the age at marriage for women was 22.6—1.5 years earlier than in the later eighteenth and early nineteenth centuries. Because both men and women reached their maximum earning capacities at an early age, it was unlikely that a reduction in income would call forth a significant rise in their age at marriage. Indeed, we have already seen that at the time of the 1851 census the framework knitters responded to their adverse economic circumstances by resorting to coresidence in preference to later marriage. Thus, the only option open to those who were to reduce their family size was a limitation on fertility.

The lower fertility rates during later years of married life observed in the 1825–1851 cohort raises the question of whether this phenomenon resulted from conscious attempts to limit fertility. In populations practicing family limitation the age-specific fertility curve tends to be concave to the upper side in the later years of married life.[4] Age-specific fertility rates for higher age groups will be lower than those attained at the same age by a population not practicing family limitation because women who regulate their fertility cease to bear children when they are younger. In such regulated families, fertility is concentrated into the earlier years of marriage, and couples who married earlier begin to restrict their fertility at an age when others, who married later, still have children at more frequent intervals. In Table 5.5 this phenomenon has been compared within the 1750–1824 and 1825–1851 cohorts. Comparison within cohorts should be even more meaningful than comparisons between cohorts, being less likely to be hindered by other intervening variables. The figures presented in Table 5.5 show that although family limitation was practiced on a limited scale by those married during the boom conditions of the later eighteenth and earlier nineteenth centuries, it became both more prevalent and more evident at an earlier age among those married in the depressed conditions after 1825.

Further evidence that there were conscious attempts to restrict fertility by couples married after 1800 is forthcoming if we compare the ages of women at the birth of their last children. From the figures presented in Table 5.6 we can see that women belonging to the last cohort were two and one-half years younger at the birth of their last children than were their predecessors.

---

[4] For an excellent discussion of this phenomenon see E. A. Wrigley, "Family Limitation in Pre-Industrial England." While Wrigley's description of this phenomenon is masterful, his explanation does not seem to me to be convincing. For a revisionist explanation see Chapter 7.

TABLE 5.5
Family Limitation

	30–34		35–39		40–44		45–49	
			Part 1	1750–1824				
Married under 25	147 / 477	308	89 / 371	240	28 / 277	110	3 / 227	13
Married over 25	98 / 300	326	71 / 253	281	37 / 205	180	7 / 164	43
Young brides' fertility in relation to older brides'	0.94		0.85		0.56		0.30	
			Part 2	1825–1851				
Married under 25	182 / 641	284	72 / 367	196	17 / 173	98	1 / 35	28
Married over 25	90 / 257	350	60 / 195	308	21 / 139	151	1 / 85	12
Younger brides' fertility in relation to older brides'	0.81		0.64		0.65		2.3	

In these calculations the numerator represents the total number of birth events, the denominator represents the total number of years that these women were "at risk" in each age group, and the product describes the age-specific fertility rate (per 1000 years lived) of married women in each age group.

Another method of analysis useful in determining the presence of family limitation is an examination of birth intervals. Women restricting their fertility would be expected to space their children's births further apart, particularly in the case of the last child. It is unfortunate, however, that the period between birth and baptism began to lengthen in the later eighteenth century in Shepshed, so that the statistics describing intergenesic intervals for this period cannot be used with any confidence. For this reason a discussion of intervals between births has not been attempted.

Infant and child mortality rates for Shepshed, using infants with "manufactured" birth dates, have been presented in Table 5.7.[5] To illustrate the implications of these mortality rates in terms of life expectancy at birth we have compared each cohort with the Ledermann Mortality Table to which its experience most closely conforms.[6]

---

[5] The use of "manufactured" birth dates is discussed in the Appendix.

[6] S. Ledermann, Nouvelles Tables–Types de Mortalité. These life tables have been chosen in preference to the Princeton "regional" model life tables because they have been based on more heterogenous sources and allow for a wider range of variation. The Princeton tables are drawn almost totally from the experience of modern populations so their relevance to this study is thereby diminished.

TABLE 5.6
Mother's Age at Birth of Last Child

	Age at marriage					
	Under 30		30 or over		All	
1600–99	39.60	(21)	41.75	(15)	40.55	(36)
1700–49	38.65	(34)	41.94	(11)	39.45	(45)
1750–99	38.69	(69)	40.47	(17)	39.04	(86)
1800–49	36.25	(28)	40.92	(2)	36.56	(30)
All	38.35	(152)	41.29	(45)	39.02	(197)

Numbers in brackets refer to sample sizes.

Table 5.7 indicates that whereas infant mortality was comparatively low before 1700, the onset of protoindustrialization was accompanied by a deterioration in the health of infants and children. Furthermore, this deterioration appears to have been accelerated by the decline in living conditions after 1825. The implications of these mortality rates can be seen in the fourth column showing the number of survivors reaching 15 in each cohort. For every 100 children surviving to 15 before 1700 about 94 did so

TABLE 5.7
Infant and Child Mortality (MF)

		Reconstitution			Ledermann		
Cohort	Age	At risk	Dying	Rate per thousand	Survivors	e^0	Rate per thousand	Survivors
1600–1699	0–1	1531	194	126	1000	49.18	126	1000
	1–4	1104	82	74	874	(p. 115)	80	874
	5–9	788	26	33	809		24	804
	10–14	577	9	16	782		15	785
					770			772
1700–1749	0–1	1254	194	155	1000	44.02	158	1000
	1–4	905	85	94	845	(p. 90)	96	842
	5–9	645	21	33	766		28	761
	10–14	493	6	12	741		17	740
					732			727
1750–1824	0–1	4046	639	158	1000	44.02	158	1000
	1–4	2977	281	94	842	(p. 90)	96	842
	5–9	1953	65	33	763		28	761
	10–14	1342	26	19	738		17	740
					724			727
1825–1849	0–1	832	173	208	1000	37.05	207	1000
	1–4	415	63	152	792	(p. 135)	162	793
	5–9	188	13	69	672		41	665
	10–14	64	1	16	625		26	638
					615			621

e^0 means life expectancy at birth.

between 1700 and 1825, but just 80 among the cohort born after 1825. These changes in mortality suggest that life expectancy at birth dropped from about 49 before protoindustrialization to 44 in the 1700–1825 period. In the depressed conditions of the second quarter of the nineteenth century a child born in Shepshed had a life expectancy at birth of 37 years—12 years less than a child born in the village before the coming of industry.

When demographers talk about infant mortality they are careful to distinguish *endogenous* from *exogenous* infant deaths, to separate first-month infant deaths from other infant deaths, because a very high proportion of endogenous infant deaths are caused by congenital defects or are connected with problems arising from the delivery. On the other hand, exogenous infant mortality is held to be the result of external conditions (disease, improper care, malnutrition, etc.). It is therefore interesting to note that while the endogenous mortality rate remained comparatively stable, there was a substantial rise in exogenous mortality among those born after 1825. This information is presented in Table 5.8. The rates of

TABLE 5.8
Endogenous and Exogenous Infant Mortality (MF)

Endogenous				Exogenous		
At risk	Dying	Rate/100		At risk	Dying	Rate/000
1531	117	76	1600–99	1414	77	55
1254	89	71	1700–49	1165	105	90
2498	219	88	1750–99	2281	171	75
1548	137	88	1800–24	1411	112	79
832	67	81	1825–49	765	106	137

exogenous infant mortality suggest that the protoindustrialization of Shepshed and the concomitant rise in population density in the village created a less healthy environment through a deterioration in the external conditions governing the health of infants and children. In the second quarter of the nineteenth century the deleterious effect of these unhealthy conditions appears to have been exacerbated by the framework knitters' declining incomes. Problems created by an unhealthy, unsanitary environment were compounded by the breakdown of these infants' physical defences against infection and disease caused by a less adequate diet.

During protoindustrialization Shepshed became a relatively densely populated village; in 1851 there were 441 residents per square mile. This figure does not really describe the disastrous effects that accompanied the village's "urbanization." The terraced housing had been jerrybuilt to accommodate the mushrooming industrial population: "mean cottages, low and narrow, badly lit, fronting on the street, or around common yards, and often built in odd shapes to squeeze into odd pieces of land.

They were cheaply built and badly maintained."[7] In this squalid environment, inadequate sanitary arrangements made cholera, typhus, and other "urban" diseases common. For example, there was a severe outbreak of cholera from November 1831 to January 1832, while typhus was recorded in July 1839, March 1840, and December 1840. Smallpox was also endemic.

In order to test the hypothesis that urbanization resulted in higher mortality we have compared infant mortality rates in three contrasting areas of mid–nineteenth century Leicestershire—the urban Registration District of Leicester; the rural, protoindustrial Registration District of Loughborough and Barrow; and the rural, agricultural Registration District of Billesdon, Market Harborough, and Melton Mowbray. The population densities of these three registration districts were 8200, 300, and 126 persons per square mile, respectively. The *Eighth Annual Report of the Registrar-General* gives annual totals of births and infant deaths occurring between 1839 and 1844 in each registration district.[8] Dividing infant deaths into births we can produce an approximation of the infant mortality rate in each registration district. These figures, presented in Table 5.9,

TABLE 5.9
Infant Mortality (MF), Three Registration Districts, 1839–1844

	Births	Deaths	Rate/000
Leicester	12,023	2374	197
Loughborough and Barrow	8,594	1521	177
Billesdon, Market Harborough, and Melton Mowbray	7,232	928	128

show that infant mortality was related to population density. The densely populated city of Leicester had a higher rate of infant mortality than the rural, industrial villages which, in turn, had substantially higher mortality rates than the sparsely settled eastern districts of the county.

Another result of relating population density to mortality is the finding that the mortality rates derived from civil registration are in broad agreement with those derived from the reconstitution study. It is significant that the infant mortality rate in the protoindustrial villages was comparable to that in the urban center because, as we have argued, it is unlikely that external conditions in an overgrown industrial village were much different from those in a city like Leicester. This agreement between the reconstituted results and those derived from the registrar-general's figures

---

[7] A. Bécherand, "The Poor and the English Poor Laws in the Loughborough Union of Parishes, 1837–1860," p. 116.

[8] *P.P.*, 1847–48, XXV, 204–05.

also provides some confidence in the reliability and representatives of the reconstituted results.[9]

Arguing that declining levels of mortality were the motor of population growth after 1750, McKeown and Brown claim that "an increase in the birth rate can have relatively little influence on population growth, first, because a high proportion of children die shortly after birth, and, second, because the proportion who die increases as the birth rate increases."[10] Trying to associate higher infant mortality with larger families is a dubious undertaking, as is evident from reconstituted evidence relating infant mortality to each child's birth rank. From these results it appears that a first child was twice as likely to die in infancy as any succeeding child. Moreover, each of the next four children (birth ranks two through five) displayed an improvement in life expectation. Although mortality rates were higher for subsequent children (birth ranks six or higher), these children were still only half as likely to die as the first child. Indeed, the life expectancy of these later birth ranks was about the same as that of the second and third children. See Table 5.10.

TABLE 5.10
Infant Mortality (MF), by Birth Rank

Birth rank	At risk	Dying	Rate/000
1	212	63	297
2	227	35	154
3	225	31	138
4	230	21	91
5	184	13	71
6+	455	61	134
Total	1533	224	146

These results are based on the experiences of completed families which had at least four birth events and, for this reason, are unlikely to include many post-1825 families.

Having seen that protoindustrialization and urbanization in Shepshed were accompanied by a deterioration in the life expectancy of children, let us now examine the impact of these socioeconomic changes on those surviving childhood. In Table 5.11, I have presented figures describing the changes in adult mortality. Since the study ended in 1851, no cognizance was taken of deaths occurring after that date. Because there was too much uncertainty about the size of the population at risk, it was not possible to produce life expectancy figures for adults married after 1800 although figures describing survival rates (for the ages between 25 and 45)

---

[9] These issues are discussed in the Appendix.
[10] T. McKeown and R. G. Brown, "Medical Evidence Related to English Population Changes in the Eighteenth Century," p. 295.

TABLE 5.11
Adult Mortality (MF)

	1600–99	1700–49	1750–74	1775–99	1800–24
		Part 1	Life expectancy at various ages		
25	32.9	36.1	39.4	36.6	
30	29.9	33.3	35.5	32.8	
35	26.4	30.1	31.5	29.3	
40	23.5	26.5	28.2	25.9	
45	21.1	23.2	24.1	22.5	
50	18.1	20.7	20.9	19.4	
55	15.5	17.1	16.6	15.6	
60	13.2	14.2	14.2	12.4	
65	11.0	11.1	10.7	9.2	
70	8.6	8.8	7.8	6.3	
75	6.9	6.6	.6.8	5.4	
80	6.0	5.3	5.5	3.8	
85+	3.7	3.8	3.8	3.3	
		Part 2	Survivors to various ages		
25	1000	1000	1000	1000	1000
30	937	937	971	966	961
35	890	887	943	928	919
40	818	845	893	874	861
45	729	788	863	832	811
50	656	702	809	760	
55	570	652	762	709	
60	470	569	645	616	
65	373	493	569	533	
70	286	373	454	414	
75	186	258	264	236	
80	96	136	143	119	
85+	54	60	67	48	

for the cohort married in the first quarter of the nineteenth century are presented.

Unlike that of their children, the health of adults seems to have improved during the initial period of protoindustrialization. The cohort married between 1750 and 1775 had a life expectancy at 25 more than six years greater than that of the cohort married before 1700. But the deterioration in health conditions in the industrial village that led to a dramatic rise in infant mortality did not leave the adult population unscathed. Adults married after 1775 had a lower expectancy of life at 25 than did the previous cohort—by almost three years. We can see from the survival rates for the next cohort (1800–24) that this decline in life expectancy continued. More of those married after 1800, nevertheless, survived to 45 than of the adult population married before 1750. Thus, in comparison with the dramatic reductions in life expectancy at birth, the rise in adult mortality accompanying Shepshed's urbanization was slight. The environment of the protoindustrial village was far more dangerous for children than for those who survived to adulthood. In the light of these results, Razzell's contention that "income factors were not important in determining rates of mortality because there was little variation in the incidence of adult mortality between occupational groups" is beside the point inasmuch as the mortality experiences of adults and children in an urban environment were quite dissimilar.[11]

In the first section of this chapter I described the demographic changes that occurred in Shepshed between 1600 and 1851. In this section I present a method I developed for analyzing the total effect of the different variables derived from the family reconstitution study. With this method it will be possible to see the extent to which the rising birth rate contributed to the demographic discontinuity that accompanied protoindustrialization.

I will explain the method by which I derived these net rates of reproduction with reference to the 1600-99 cohort. At the end of this discussion Table 5.12 sets forth the results of this procedure for the four cohorts discussed in this study.

The first priority was to approximate the gross rate of reproduction—the average number of births per woman. For this hypothetical seventeenth century family I assumed that the wife married at the (mean) average age, 28.1, and had a fertility experience corresponding to that of the whole cohort. The mean was chosen in preference to the median because it is an arithmetic rather than an ordinal measurement. The mean describes the midpoint of the area of distribution rather than the midpoint of cumulative frequency. This difference is important because of the skewed distribution of marriage ages. Completed family size was derived as follows:

Age	Years married	Age-specific fertility rate	Children
25–29	1.9	385	0.73
30–34	5.0	304	1.52
35–39	5.0	260	1.30
40–44	5.0	121	0.60
45–49	5.0	45	0.23
		Total (GRR)	4.38

The gross rate of reproduction, 4.38, is based on the assumption that both husband and wife lived to the end of the wife's fertile period. Therefore, it had to be revised to take adult mortality into account, quite a complex affair. If it was impossible to make any allowance for remarriage because

[11] P. E. Razzell, "Population Growth and Economic Change in Eighteenth and Early Nineteenth Century England and Ireland," p. 265.

TABLE 5.12
Net Rate of Reproduction

	1600–1699	1700–1749	1750–1824	1825–1851
GRR	4.38	4.54	5.86	6.16
Revised GRR	3.66	3.94	5.53	5.68
Child survival rate	0.714	0.668	0.686	0.583
Surviving children	2.62	2.63	3.79	3.31
Incidence of marriage	0.838	0.852	0.918	0.948
Children marrying	2.20	2.24	3.48	3.14
NRR	1.10	1.12	1.74	1.57
Generation	33.6	33.4	31.8	30.1
Annual rate of growth	0.28%	0.35%	1.74%	1.51%
Years for population to double	250.0	200.6	40.1	46.4

available data describing the length of widowhood or widowerhood were inadequate, I had no idea, on the other hand, of the number of marriages broken for personal or socioeconomic reasons. I accordingly have assumed that the incidence of remarriage was more or less balanced by the effects of marital breakdown. Bearing this caveat in mind, I began to assess the effect of parental mortality on fertility by assuming that the mortality experiences of husbands and wives were identical. The age-specific mortality figures relate to the combined experiences of men and women—it was decided that the creation of mortality rates least susceptible to chance fluctuations was a higher priority than the assessment of differential effects of male and female mortality. Moreover, I also assumed that husband and wife were the same age at marriage—in this case the wife's age. Given that a seventeenth century marriage was intact at 28.1, the average age at marriage, I have been able to determine the pace with which death took its toll. For the 1.9 years remaining in the 25–29 age period the mortality rate was 25 per 1000 (0.025). Since the husband's likelihood of dying was assumed to be independent of his wife's and vice versa, the probability that their marriage would be broken by the death of at least one of them was the product of each individual's chance of dying: $0.975 \times 0.975 = 0.951$. Thus, of every 1000 marriages intact at 28.1 there would be 951 surviving at the end of the 25–29 age period. Since I further assumed that deaths were evenly distributed during the 1.9 years that this hypothetical couple was "at risk" in the 25–29 age period, I was interested in midpoint marital survival. This was easily derived by adding the number of intact marriages at the beginning of the age period to the number surviving at the end and dividing this sum by two. Having established the midpoint frequency of marriages which, for each age group, were unbroken by the death of at least one spouse, I had now to determine the implications of this set of survival rates in terms of the number of children born to each married woman.

The revised figure for legitimate marital fertility, after taking parental mortality into account, is 3.62.[12] I next used the illegitimacy ratio of the seventeenth century cohort, 1.2%, to determine how the relationship between frequency of legitimate births and completed family size should be proportional to the relationship between frequency of both legitimate and illegitimate births and all births per woman. So, the total number of births—both legitimate and illegitimate—was derived as follows:

$$(0.988/3.62 = (1.000/x) \therefore (x = 3.66).$$

The "typical" seventeenth century woman had a total of 3.66 births: 0.04 before marriage and 3.62 afterward.

How many of these 3.66 children themselves survived to the average age at marriage, 28.1? Referring to the Ledermann Mortality Table to which this cohort's infant and child mortality most closely conformed, I found that 714 per 1000 survived to 28.1. Therefore, the number of children per family surviving to the average age at marriage was: $3.66 \times 0.714 = 2.62$.

Of these 2.62 surviving children per family, how many actually married? Demographers have observed that among populations marrying early, marriage is practically universal, but among populations where the average age at marriage is late, as in preindustrial England, a relatively high proportion never marry at all. Bearing this in mind, the incidence of marriage has been calculated on the assumption that marriage was universal at an average age of 20.0 but that for every year later that it occurred 2% never married (of both men and women).[13] In seventeenth century Shepshed, therefore, an average age at marriage of 28.1 suggests that the incidence of marriage was 83.8%. Of the 2.62 children surviving to the average age at marriage in our hypothetical family, $2.62 \times 0.838 = 2.20$ married.

If there were no difference in the sex ratios of the marrying children, then the net rate of reproduction would be $2.20 \div 2 = 1.10$. We divide the number of children marrying by two because we are interested in a net replacement rate.

---

[12] It should be pointed out that for the 33 first marriages in this cohort for which evidence was derived on completed family size (i.e., marriages in which the wife survived her fertile period or in which her death was recorded before the end) the mean average was 3.9.

[13] Support for this set of assumptions was forthcoming from a comparison of the 1825–51 reconstituted cohort with the enumerated population at the time of the 1851 census. Of the 85 women aged 45–49 at the time of the 1851 census, 95.3% were either married or widowed. The reconstituted results suggest an age at marriage for the 1825–51 cohort of 22.6, and according to my assumptions this would mean that its incidence was 94.8%.

The number of seventeenth century villagers increased by 10% per generation. What did this rate of generational replacement mean in terms of annual average rate of population growth? We can find an answer to this question by using the compound interest formula: $A = P(1 + i)^n$. In our case A means the size of the population at the end of a generation where P is the initial size of the population, i is the rate of growth, and n is the length of a generation. We already know that the initial size of the population is 1000 and that after one generation it is 1100, but we do not yet know the length of a generation. To learn this, we started with the assumption that the length of a generation was equivalent to the mean age at childbearing. Given that a woman married at 28.1 and bore 3.62 children during her marriage, how long would it take her to have 1.81 children, the mean point of her childbearing? Mean age at childbearing was chosen in preference to the median because of the long "tail" on the distribution of fertility. At 30 a woman had given birth to 0.71 children. Assuming that within each age group births were distributed evenly, the mean age at childbearing was 33.6. This figure was derived by discovering the period of time that this woman would require to produce a further 1.10 children (1.10 plus 0.71, born before 30, equals 1.81). An age-specific fertility rate of 304 per 1000 means an annual average of 0.304 births. To produce 1.10 children at a rate of 0.304 per year requires 3.6 years. Thus, the length of a generation, defined as mean age at childbearing, was 33.6 years. With this extra bit of information, it is relatively easy to determine the annual compound rate of growth, 0.28%, and also the period in which a population with a net rate of reproduction of 1.10 would double, 250 years.

In Table 5.12 a composite presentation sets forth all the salient information for the four cohorts. It should be pointed out once more that no special claims are made for the accuracy of this method of analysis, but it seems to me that it is a valuable way of measuring the combined effects of the different demographic variables. Moreover, it enables us to isolate each variable and test its contribution to the sum of the parts. In this way we can gain some insight into the relative importance of changes in the various components of the demographic equation.

In the early eighteenth century, during the transition from a purely agricultural economy, age at first marriage was practically unchanged from the preindustrial period. This lack of change can perhaps be explained in terms of the organization of the framework knitting industry which for much of this time was still a journeyman's trade. Only after 1730 did capitalist wage relations gain currency in industrial villages like Shepshed, and even then the effects of the machine operators' proletarianization were cushioned by the buoyant state of trade which insured that profits could be achieved without bleeding the workers. Only in times of trade depression was there widespread suffering and deprivation. Under these circumstances it is not surprising that the traditional, preindustrial pattern of late marriage was only slowly discarded. As we have seen from the graphic representation of annual changes, the 1750s marked a dramatic break with the past. Apart from the period of the American Revolutionary Wars, when the stocking industry's best overseas market was embargoed, the later eighteenth century was a time of prosperity in Shepshed. In response to these conditions, age at marriage fell by about four years and marital fertility rose so that the gross reproduction rate was substantially higher. Good conditions prevailed until the end of the Napoleonic Wars in 1815 when the framework knitting industry entered a period of a stagnation that lasted for the remainder of the time covered by this study. This stagnation affected the demographic behavior of the villagers, and the annual total of births stabilized roughly at the level attained in 1815.

The results derived from the reconstitution have shown us that, on the one hand, the industrialization of Shepshed was accompanied by a falling age at marriage, rising illegitimacy ratios, and variations in the levels of marital fertility. On the other hand, the urbanization of this village led to a dramatic fall in life expectancy at birth but had a less dire effect on adults' health.

The rate of population growth before the onset of full-scale industrialization was quite modest. The seventeenth century population produced a surplus of 10% over the number needed to replace itself each generation, a condition under which a closed village would double its population every 250 years. In the first half of the eighteenth century the net reproduction rate was fractionally higher—a deterioration in the health of infants and children combined with marginally lower fertility rates to produce a depressive effect on the rate of growth that was cancelled out by a somewhat longer childbearing period and a shorter interval between generations. The figures in Table 5.12 show the disequilibrating effects caused by the interaction of a lower age at marriage and higher fertility (both illegitimate and marital) after 1750. At the same time the relative stability in infant and child mortality acted in conjunction with improvements in adult health so that not only were families left unbroken by death for a longer period but a larger number of children survived and married. Acting together, these changes radically transformed the population's rate of generational replacement from one of relative stability to one of very rapid growth.

The moderation of this state of affairs during the period of industrial involution in the second quarter of the nineteenth century resulted from higher mortality and deliberate fertility restriction which counteracted this cohort's lower age at marriage and the shorter interval between generations. The result was a decline in the rate of population growth from

1.74% per year to 1.51%. Still, it remains significant that even during the period of involution the rate of natural increase was more than three times as great as before the onset of full-scale industrialization.

It is apparent from the preceding discussion that the second quarter of the nineteenth century is of particular interest in that the villagers were then confronted with drastically changed circumstances for which their newly acquired demographic profile was most unsuitable. The framework knitting industry, on which about two-thirds of the population was dependent, entered a state of severe depression after 1815. Real wages fell by about 40%. Emigration became a popular response to these conditions, and many young people left Shepshed to seek better prospects elsewhere. A simple index of this phenomenon is provided by the number of marriages celebrated in the village. In both absolute and relative terms 1815–16 marked the high point of the marriage curve (see Figure 5.1). Since the village population contained an increasingly large number of children of marital age as a result of the broadening base of the age pyramid in conditions of very rapid growth, and since the proportion of marriages involving partners who were residents of Shepshed went up, it seems likely that considerable emigration occurred among those of marital age. Moreover, movement appears to have been largely one-way; in comparison with the agricultural areas of the county, the framework knitting villages had far higher rates of stability (i.e., proportion over 15 born in Shepshed) at the time of the 1851 census. There was substantial emigration from industrial villages, like Shepshed, but there was little immigration. The nonnatives (i.e., proportion over 15 born elsewhere) were almost all from neighboring industrial villages.[14] Those who stayed in Shepshed were ill-equipped to reduce the number of children they would bring into the world. Evidence derived from the family reconstitution study demonstrates that women married after 1825 deliberately restricted their fertility as they grew older. But, as we have already seen, this action was insufficient to produce a significant decline in the rate of natural increase although, in conjunction with higher mortality, it did moderate the explosive effects of an even lower age at marriage and shorter interval between generations.

It is apparent that by the time of the 1851 census framework knitters had further responded to their adverse economic circumstances by making adjustments in their household structures.[15] Far from displaying the irrational behavior contemporaries ascribed to them, these industrial workers were apparently quite aware of the disastrous consequences that would occur if a family was dependent upon just one wage earner—in only 18% of their households was this the case. In contrast to the agricultural

---

[14] This subject is discussed in Chapter 3.
[15] This issue is the focus of Chapter 4.

laborers and the village craftsmen and artisans, the framework knitters had not only the largest proportion of working wives but also children most likely to work from an early age. It was quite common for two, three, four, five, or even more household members to be employed in some branch of the hosiery trade. Living with relatives and lodgers was another way framework knitters could increase the number of coresident wage earners. Coresidence, two or more nuclear family units sharing the same household, was significantly higher among the framework knitters where more than one household in eight headed by a married man contained a coresident family. Among the nonindustrial villagers such sharing was unusual—just one such complex household in 20 existed. The framework knitters' preference for living in large domestic units was part of their conscious effort to protect themselves from precarious economic conditions.

By dint of emigration, fertility restriction, child labor, and coresidence, these industrial laborers created a system that enabled them to survive in a situation of industrial involution. But survival merely intensified the pressures. Living in a demographic hothouse, the framework knitters were both educationally and physically stunted by the experience.

Using the method of analyzing the reconstituted data that has already been described I would like to undertake a simple simulation exercise to show how the villagers' attempts to control their fertility within marriage were undermined by the perpetuation of the early age at marriage which had stabilized in the 1790s. Table 5.13 presents three sets of data from which net reproduction rates are derived: the first is merely that provided in Table 5.12, showing the profile of the 1825–51 population, which had

TABLE 5.13
Effects of Fertility Restriction in Shepshed, 1825–1851

	Controlled fertility, early marriage	Uncontrolled fertility, early marriage	Controlled fertility, later marriage
GRR	6.16	6.47	5.57
Revised GRR	5.68	5.83	5.03
Child survival rate	0.583	0.583	0.590
Surviving children	3.31	3.40	2.97
Incidence of marriage	0.948	0.948	0.918
Children marrying	3.14	3.22	2.72
NRR	1.57	1.61	1.36
Generation	30.1	31.1	31.6
Annual rate of growth	1.51%	1.55%	0.91%
Years for population to double	46.4	45.2	76.9
Age at marriage	22.6	22.6	24.1

controlled fertility but married early; the second describes what would have happened if the villagers in the period had not attempted to control marital fertility; the third shows what would have happened if they had both controlled fertility and married at a somewhat later age, 24.1 rather than 22.6. In all three data sets the infant and child mortality schedules of the 1825–51 cohort are utilized.

The figures in Table 5.13 show clearly that the villagers' response to deteriorating conditions was inadequate. Although they slowed down their rate of replacement by adopting a strategy of more controlled fertility, this safeguard was not nearly so effective as a strategy which *combined* control of fertility in the later years of childbearing with a more prudent approach to marriage would have been. Such a combined strategy would have primarily taken the women's most fecund years out of their legitimate childbearing periods and, secondarily, served to lengthen the interval between generations. As things were, however, the fertility of the 1825–51 population was largely concentrated in the earlier years of marriage so that the mean age at childbearing fell and the interval between generations was reduced. It appears, therefore, that the strategy of family limitation the villagers adopted was of little practical help. On the other hand, had they married later *and* regulated their fertility in the later years of marriage, then these restrictions on the birth rate, acting in tandem with the dramatic rise in the infant death rate, would have almost halved their rate of replacement—from 1.74% per year to 0.91%.

Why did these villagers continue to follow a high pressure reproductive strategy? An answer to this question must, I think, be framed in terms of the peculiar demoeconomic conditions of industrial involution. Of prime importance, therefore, is the economics of the family life cycle. For the framework knitter there appears to have been a *positive* incentive to marry early and, in particular, to concentrate marital fertility into the early years of marriage. The nature of the labor process made it inefficient for a machine operator to work alone—he needed help at a number of stages in his work. To do everything by himself meant that the stockinger had to pay for this supplementary work in the currency of his own labor, but such work could be performed cheaply by members of the framework knitter's own family. Moreover, the alternative—working in a frame shop—was notoriously unattractive because of the confiscatory charges demanded from individual knitters. Thus, there was a positive incentive for a framework knitter to set up an independent, family unit of production at an early age. This factor was of no small importance in shaping the protoindustrialists' marital planning and may account for their persistently low age at marriage in the face of deteriorating conditions. Of more importance in determining the fertility strategy displayed by the framework knitters was the consideration that once one married it was economically most sensible to hurry over the stage during which the dependency ratio within the family was most disadvantageous—the first years of a marriage when children contributed nothing to production, consumed the cost of their own support, and, in addition, distracted the wife/mother so that her contribution was reduced. It is not surprising that the analysis of household structure at the time of the 1851 census revealed that a substantial number of families with either no children or just one small child lived in coresidential domestic units. The exigencies of domestic production were not confined to young families, they extended to all married couples whose family labor input was below some optimum level. This seems to be one reason why as many as one family in nine headed by a man in his later thirties was still found to be living in shared accommodations. The domestic economics of production also seems to explain why there was a positive incentive to fertility in the early years of marriage—the sooner children could contribute to the family economy by helping their parents with the simple, supplementary operations, the sooner the family could emerge from the state of semidependency which characterized the first years of marriage. Last, the cost of having an additional child was not commensurate with that of having the previous one. That is to say, having another child created a marginal cost, not equal to the cost of the previous child and, thus, less than the average cost.[16]

Beyond these short-term calculations, another factor may be of some importance in explaining the rise in marital fertility that accompanied the onset of proletarianized protoindustrialization in mid–eighteenth century Shepshed—the consideration of security in old age. By having more children one amassed a kind of retirement fund or pension plan. Since domestic workers had nothing of value except their innate physical skills, their earnings tended to decline as they reached later middle age. In that their children would themselves create individual units of production, workers from the older generation would be provided for in their declining years. They could slot themselves into their children's domestic production units at precisely the time when the younger generation's families were suffering the most adverse dependency ratios. To summarize, then, it appears that the framework knitters' demoeconomic system had two main thrusts: first, to get over the dependency "hump" early in marriage as quickly as possible; and, second, to be sure that at least one child survived to provide for old age.

Within the parameters and exigencies of this demoeconomic system an explanation for the perpetuation of the villagers' high pressure reproduc-

---

[16] F. Mendels has noted the Belgian protoindustrialists' "asymmetrical" response to fluctuations in their income. He has not, however, extended his analysis to include their fertility strategy as well as their nuptiality. (F. Mendels, "Industry and Marriages in Flanders before the Industrial Revolution.") Hans Medick has convinced me that his "demoeconomic" model of the protoindustrial family not only accords with my evidence but also fills in the blanks in Mendels' argument. An English version of Medick's argument has recently been published. (H. Medick, "The proto-industrial family economy: the structural function of household and family during the transition from peasant society to industrial capitalism.")

tion strategy can be developed. In this argument two factors are of paramount importance: first, the serious rise in infant and child mortality after 1825; and, second, the lower age of brides in the post-1825 cohort. These two factors are themselves intertwined, and their real significance will become apparent only in the course of the explanation. If we begin by bearing in mind that it was of the utmost importance to protoindustrialists to be survived by at least one child, we infer that the sudden rise in infant mortality upset a reproductive strategy based on pre-1825 life expectancy. Parents found that beyond the necessity of getting over the dependency "hump," which itself fostered high fertility in the early years of marriage, the rise in infant mortality decreed that at the *presumed* end of this stage, say after six or seven years, there was less likely to be a surviving child. Thus, the dependency state was attenuated because mortality among first and, to a lesser extent, second children was above normal. Even if a couple wanted to limit the overall number of their children, they had to make sure that their first children survived the early years during which the risk of death was so great. A contradiction therefore developed because, given the increased uncertainty of each child's survival, a couple was liable to the great hardship of repeating the whole dependency stage by expecting any individual child to survive. This contradiction was resolved by maintaining high fertility until at least one child was old enough to contribute his or her labor to the family economy. Only at this point could conscious fertility limitation commence.

Evidence supporting this interpretation can be found in Table 5.5 which shows that women who married under 25 actively controlled their fertility five years earlier than contemporaries who married later. This goup of brides, moreover, was far more successful in limiting their fertility after 30 than was a similar set of women who married before 1825. Among the younger women marrying after 1825 fertility restriction not only commenced earlier but was also far more effective. It was not, however, totally effective, and these women continued to bear children, albeit at a reduced rate, even after they had insured the old-age security for themselves and their husbands that was such a strong factor in their earlier high fertility rates.

The second factor contributing to the perpetuation of a high rate of reproduction, the lower age at first marriage for women married after 1825, seems to be a statistical artifact. There appear to be two causes for this phenomenon. First, the cohort groupings blur the fact that by the 1790s something like a consensus regarding age at first marriage seems to have emerged in this protoindustrial community. If we refer to Table 5.2, it is apparent that among women and, to a somewhat lesser extent, among their husbands there was a basic stability in age at first marriage after 1790. It was less likely that these people would begin to marry later in response to deteriorating real wages than that they would try to restrict marital fertility and to develop a greater propensity for life in coresident households. Although it may be obvious to anyone who looks at the dynamics of population growth that these strategies were of only limited value, the view of the individual mid–nineteenth century framework knitter and his wife would be quite different. They were trying to get what advantages they could from their precarious circumstances in the most obvious ways, and since it intensified the exigencies of their household demoeconomic system, the alternative of later marriage did not seem to be a real one. Even if a framework knitter did want to marry later, the initial, unfavorable dependency hump could not be avoided—it was built into the contract, as it were. The second cause of this statistical double vision stems from the bunching of marriages in the post-1825 period. There was a major reduction in the number of (relatively) older women marrying. Both the interquartile range and the standard deviation measure the width of the distribution of marriage ages, and both of these measures grew smaller after 1825 as the distribution became more peaked. The fact that the upper quartile age at marriage was 1.3 years earlier after 1825 while that of the lower quartile fell by just 0.5 year underlines this phenomenon.

The argument developed so far assumes that the evidence derived from the village reconstitution study can be used to explain the behavior of one section of villagers, the framework knitters. Although these protoindustrialists formed by far the largest element in the village's socioeconomic mix, it would be dangerous to infer a direct relationship. Ideally, the way to proceed with the argument would have been by breaking the sample into occupational groups and then comparing and contrasting the variations in demographic behavior both between groups and, within groups, across time. But given the relative sparseness of occupational information for much of the period I studied, this procedure was not possible. For the last period, after 1825, it was. Therefore, let us turn our attention to this material.

Because the primary reason for further examination was to determine the extent to which framework knitters' demographic behavior differed from that of the other members of the community, it was decided to make a simple split in the data. Thus the data present the characteristics of framework knitters and "others"—farmers, laborers, shoemakers, carpenters, millers, bakers, and so on. The proliferation of other occupational groups meant that meaningful information could not be presented for any occupational group, except perhaps agricultural laborers, and even among the laborers, the number of observations was disconcertingly small. So, for the sake of providing at least a straightforward comparison, a degree of sociological precision was sacrificed. Furthermore, the reader should bear in mind that the line of distinction between framework knitters and "others" is not as sharp as might be expected. As we saw in the previous chapter, some laborers and, to a lesser extent, some tradesmen and craftsmen were involved in the stocking trade as knitters or seamers.

The evidence presented describing the two groups' nuptiality (Table 5.14) and age-specific marital fertility (Table 5.15) shows quite clearly that not only were the framework knitters' brides about one year younger than brides of other occupational groups but they also showed significantly lower levels of fertility throughout the most fecund years of their childbearing periods. Earlier in this chapter we presented occupationally undifferentiated results from the family reconstitution showing that villagers who married after 1825, to a greater extent than before, deliberately restricted their fertility as they grew older. The onset of this practice was largely determined by the wife's age at marriage. In a family where the wife married before her twenty-fifth birthday, her fertility rate would be lower, from her later 20s, than that of women marrying later at a comparable age. In this instance it is particularly fortunate that we are able to distinguish the behavior of the protoindustrialists from that of their fellow villagers. See Table 5.16.

Occupational influences on marital fertility strategies are important. This evidence impressively supports the argument advanced earlier to reconcile the apparent contradiction between early marriage and high fertility in the first years of marriage on the one hand and, on the other, deliberate family limitation in the later years. We can now see that this demoeconomic explanation applies only to the behavior of the framework knitters. For the remainder of the villagers the force of circumstances was quite different, as was the pattern of their fertility.

Infant mortality presents similar distinctions between the experience of the protoindustrialists and that of the other members of the community.

TABLE 5.14
Age at First Marriage, by Occupation

	N	Mean	Standard deviation	Lower quartile	Median	Upper quartile	Inter-quartile range
Men							
Framework knitters	268	23.6	4.6	20.9	23.0	26.7	5.8
Others	123	24.9	5.1	21.9	24.2	28.3	6.4
All	391	24.1	4.8	21.2	23.3	27.0	5.8
Women							
Framework knitters	312	22.3	3.6	19.9	21.8	24.3	4.4
Others	167	23.5	5.1	20.2	22.6	25.8	5.6
All	479	22.6	4.6	20.1	22.1	24.7	4.6

TABLE 5.15
Age-Specific Fertility, by Occupation

	Years at risk	Children born	Rate/000
1. Framework knitters			
Under 25	714	290	406
25–29	705	242	343
30–34	561	156	278
35–39	374	81	217
40–44	199	24	121
45–49	88	2	23
2. Others			
Under 25	415	196	472
25–29	416	154	370
30–34	337	116	344
35–39	188	51	271
40–44	113	14	124
45–49	32	0	0
3. All			
Under 25	1129	486	430
25–29	1121	396	350
30–34	898	272	303
35–39	562	132	235
40–44	312	38	122
45–49	120	2	17

TABLE 5.16
Fertility Restriction by Age at Marriage, by Occupation

	Under 25	25–29	30–34	35–39	40–44	45–49
Part 1. Framework knitters						
a. Married Under 25	$\frac{290}{714}$ 406	$\frac{198}{599}$ 331	$\frac{100}{401}$ 249	$\frac{46}{238}$ 193	$\frac{11}{108}$ 102	$\frac{1}{22}$ 45
b. Married Over 25		$\frac{44}{106}$ 415	$\frac{56}{160}$ 350	$\frac{35}{136}$ 257	$\frac{13}{91}$ 143	$\frac{1}{66}$ 15
		.80	.71	.75	.71	3.0
Part 2. Others						
a. Married Under 25	$\frac{196}{415}$ 472	$\frac{136}{365}$ 373	$\frac{82}{240}$ 342	$\frac{26}{129}$ 202	$\frac{6}{65}$ 92	$\frac{0}{13}$ 0
b. Married Over 25		$\frac{21}{51}$ 412	$\frac{34}{97}$ 351	$\frac{25}{59}$ 424	$\frac{8}{48}$ 167	$\frac{0}{19}$ 0
		.91	.97	.48	.55	—

In these calculations the numerator represents the total number of birth events, the denominator represents the total number of years that these women were "at risk" in each age group, and the product describes the age-specific fertility rate (per 1000 years lived) of married women in each age group.

TABLE 5.17
Infant Mortality Rates (MF), by Occupation

Framework knitters				Others		
At risk	Dying	Rate/000		At risk	Dying	Rate/000
1013	161	159	1800–24	535	87	163
606	135	223	1825–49	226	38	168

For this set of calculations we are able to analyze the issue two-dimensionally, both across time and within occupational groups. The data in Table 5.17 show that practically all of the rise in infant mortality in the post-1825 cohort was experienced by the protoindustrialists. In contrast, the traditional occupational groups suffered only a slight increase. Referring to the Ledermann tables and comparing these infant mortality rates with his model mortality tables, we find that the initial life expectancy (i.e., pre-1825) was about 44 years for both groups (p. 90) but that while post-1825 life expectancy at birth of framework knitters fell to below 36 years (p. 135), that of the rest of the community changed but little. The observed mortality experience of the whole community, therefore, marks an important compositional variation.

In calculating the difference between the protoindustrialists' net rate of reproduction and that of the other villagers, several variables had to be assumed to be equal for both groups. It was not possible to determine occupational differences in either adult mortality or illegitimacy ratios, although it is likely that the two groups differed in these regards as well. With these caveats in mind we can look at the results of this procedure. The figures in Table 5.18 show that, largely as a result of their increasing infant death rate, the framework knitters' rate of replacement was substan-

TABLE 5.18
Rate of Reproduction, 1825–1851, by Occupation

	Framework knitters	Others
Gross rate of reproduction	6.02	6.26
Revised GRR	5.59	5.86
Child survival rate	0.571	0.698
Surviving children	3.19	4.09
Incidence of marriage	0.954	.930
Children marrying	3.04	3.80
Net rate of reproduction	1.52	1.90
Generational interval	30.3	31.5
Annual rate of growth	1.28%	2.06%
Years for population to double	54.7	34.0
Mean average age at first marriage for women	22.3	23.5

tially lower than that of the other villagers. Among the agricultural laborers, village artisans, and shopkeepers the tides of economic opportunity
unleashed by the Industrial Revolution undermined the "prudential
check" that had previously enabled them to restrain their level of reproduction. But even after 1825 their rate of reproduction was by no means
exceptional. Indeed, if we compare it with those attained by the villagers
of Bottesford, Colyton, and Terling we can see that it broadly conforms to
an emerging pattern. In this light it was the framework knitters who were
out of step with the prevailing demographic trends. For these protoindustrialists the tides of economic opportunity were ebbing—as was the age of
nascent capitalism.

6

ECONOMIC OPPORTUNITY AND FAMILY FORMATION: THE CASE OF BOTTESFORD

In Chapter 5 we saw that in Shepshed there were substantial adjustments in the villagers' demographic behavior in response to protoindustrialization. In this chapter the population history of Bottesford is described and evidence presented to show that in this rural, agricultural village the rate of population growth was similarly affected by modifications in age at marriage which, in turn, can be linked with changes in the demand for labor.

Figure 6.1 presents a weighted, nine-year, moving average of baptisms, burials, and marriages in Bottesford from 1600 to 1845. Allowing for short-run variations, we see that the baptismal curve was characterized by an annual average of about 30 events in the seventeenth century, a downward drift during the eighteenth century to an annual average of slightly fewer than 25 events after 1750, and then a quite dramatic rise after 1800. These long-run movements can be explained partially in terms of changes in the village's agrarian economy.

In the early seventeenth century the Vale of Belvoir was regarded as "the finest corn land in Europe."[1] The land's fertility was greatly valued and more than compensated for difficulties in cultivation arising from its heavy, wet nature. The massive price inflation of the sixteenth and early seventeenth centuries brought prosperity to the farmers of Bottesford that

---

[1] G.E. Fussell, "Four Centuries of Leicestershire Farming," p. 159.

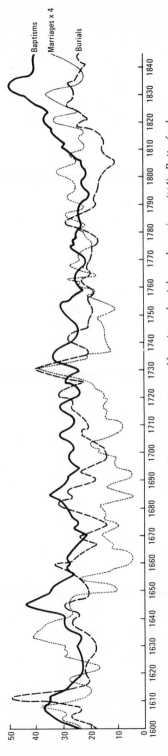

Figure 6.1. A nine-year, weighted, moving average of baptisms, burials, and marriages (×4), Bottesford.

led to a rise in the village's population from about 715 in 1603 to about 870 in 1676.[2] In the second half of the seventeenth century, the development and spread of convertible husbandry, based on nitrogen-fixing legumes, transformed the agricultural economy of England. The heavy clay soils lost their value as premium corn land. In Leicestershire "the movement towards the large-scale grazing received immense impetus from the 1660s onwards," and the eastern sections of the county began to phase out crop farming in favor of pastoral farming.[3] By Defoe's time, the beginning of the eighteenth century, eastern Leicestershire was "a vast magazine of wool for the rest of the nation."[4] Farmers in Bottesford were caught up in these changes: although the surviving inventories for the later seventeenth century show that the wealthiest farmers, those leaving estates valued at more than twice the average, owned more than 90 sheep, by the first half of the eighteenth century members of this class had flocks averaging 140 sheep.[5] This movement to pastoral farming produced a decline in the demand for labor and led to a reduction in the village population from about 870 in 1676 to 772 in 1792.[6]

The Vale of Belvoir was unique among the agricultural parts of Leicestershire in witnessing rapid population growth in the first half of the nineteenth century.[7] In Bottesford the population grew from 804 in 1801 to 1374 in 1851, a rise of 71%. This change can be ascribed to the shift away from fattening and grazing to labor intensive dairy farming, particularly the making of Stilton cheese.[8] The peasant farmer was of no real importance in the nineteenth century village. In the 1851 census, farms of over 100 acres accounted for 77% of the recorded farmland in Bottesford. Thirty men were recorded as farmers and cottagers, working an average of 117.5 acres, the median farm size was 84 acres. This positively skewed distribution indicates that large farms occupied a disproportionate share of the land: 46.2% of the recorded farm land was worked in units of over 200 acres. Farmers working on this scale employed many laborers whose numbers were increased by the switch-over to a more labor intensive form of husbandry. The number of families engaged in agriculture rose swiftly

[2] In 1603 the "Liber Cleri" recorded the number of communicants in each Leicestershire village—there were 477 in Bottesford. (*V.C.H. Leics., III,* 168.) In 1676 the "Compton Census" recorded 581 conformists in the village. (W.G.D. Fletcher, "A Religious Census of Leicestershire," p. 302.) These two figures were then converted into estimates of the total population on the assumption that one-third of the population was under 16 and, therefore, left out of these enumerations.

[3] W.G. Hoskins, *Provincial England,* p. 165.

[4] D. Defoe, *A Tour Through England and Wales,* 1724–26, Vol. II, pp. 89–90.

[5] These figures were derived from an analysis of the surviving probate inventories collected at the Leicestershire County Record Office.

[6] The village population in 1792 is reported in J. Nichols, *The History and Antiquities of Leicestershire,* Vol. II, i, p. 89.

[7] D. Mills, "Landownership and Rural Population," pp. 101–02.

[8] D. Mills, "Landownership and Rural Population," pp. 159, 161.

from 97 in 1811 to 145 in 1831. Moreover, the number of laborers per family also rose. Family size was greatly influenced by the availability of employment which enabled older children to remain at home instead of emigrating to find work elsewhere. In Bottesford, average family size rose from 4.09 in 1792 to 4.49 in 1831. After 1831, however, the old pattern reasserted itself when the dukes of Rutland's policy of keeping the supply of labor in line with local demand was reestablished. Whereas the village population grew by 64% between 1801 and 1831, it grew by only 4% between 1831 and 1851. Average family size fell from 4.49 in 1831 to 4.04 in 1851.

The two outstanding features of the long-run movements in the burial curve in Figure 6.1 are the abatement of extreme variations in mortality levels and the decline in the absolute level of mortality. Both of these phenomena occurred during the middle of the eighteenth century. If we define "crisis mortality" as the occurrence of more than double the annual average of deaths, there was only one such year after 1740 but there were twelve before 1740: 1610, 1642, 1658, 1681, 1684, 1686, 1720, 1727, 1728, 1729, 1730, 1739, and 1784. This curtailment of crisis mortality after 1740 was itself partially responsible for the reduction in the absolute level of annual mortality. The years before 1740 saw an average of 25 burials per year, whereas after 1740 the annual average was under 21. Moreover, mortality fell not only in absolute but also in relative terms, as can be seen by relating the annual average number of burials with rough approximations of the village population. These figures, of course, are not meant to be precise or definitive but are suggested to give an idea of general movements. For 140 years before 1740 village population averaged about 825, so that the mortality rate was roughly 30 per 1000. In the last 60 years of the eighteenth century the village population was about 800 with an average of about 20 burials per year, so that the burial rate was about 25 per 1000. Thus, there was a clear fall in the prevailing level of mortality. The civil censuses enable us to derive mortality rates in which we can have more confidence for each decade of the first half of the nineteenth century. These rates are as follows: 1800s—15 per 1000; 1810s—19 per 1000; 1820s—20 per 1000; 1830s—18 per 1000; and 1840s—16 per 1000. For the whole period the mortality rate (using the average of the five decadal averages) was about 18 per 1000. These roughly drawn figures clearly show a substantial reduction in the rate of mortality in Bottesford from an annual average of 30 per 1000 before 1740 to one of 18 per 1000 after 1800.

In the preceding survey of the population history of Bottesford it is suggested that changes in the demand for labor significantly influenced the movements of the baptismal curve. It is also suggested that there was a marked improvement in life expectancy after 1740. Evidence derived from the family reconstitution study will provide a useful method of testing the adequacy of the suggestions drawn from the aggregated experiences of the villagers by examining their demographic behavior on the individual level.

In the previous chapter I introduced a set of measurements which integrated various demographic parameters—nuptiality, fertility, and mortality—to present a composite picture of population change in different periods. In discussing Bottesford's demographic history, it seems to me that this approach would be useful. Using it, we can see the *systemic* nature of demographic behavior without focusing our attention, unwisely or unwittingly, on the individual contributing measurements.

In the first part of this chapter I suggest that variations in the demand for labor resulting from changing exigencies in the local agrarian economy seem to have affected the birth rate significantly and influenced the rate of population growth. The composite demographic effect of these changes can clearly be seen in the changes in a representative family's rate of reproduction presented in Table 6.1.

The early seventeenth century in Bottesford was a period of relatively slow population growth. Given the reconstituted demographic parameters, I estimate that the villagers were doubling themselves every 70 years. This rate of reproduction, however, was not maintained. The switch from crop farming to pastoral farming markedly affected the villagers' behavior. Age at first marriage for women rose by three-quarters of a year while, at the same time, their fertility—both before and during marriage—fell. As a result, the number of children born to a representative family fell. In addition, the level of mortality among both children and adults rose, so that not only were the years a woman was able to bear children reduced but the number of children surviving to reach the age at marriage also declined. Combined, these phenomena curtailed the rate of population growth, and in the late seventeenth century the village population grew at

TABLE 6.1
Net Rate of Reproduction, Bottesford

	1600–49	1650–99	1700–49	1750–99	1800–49
GRR	5.36	5.08	5.66	4.44	6.37
Revised GRR	4.56	4.10	4.65	4.10	6.08
Child survival rate	.677	.673	.633	.702	.745
Surviving children	3.09	2.76	2.94	2.88	4.53
Incidence of marriage	.886	.872	.850	.870	.902
Children marrying	2.74	2.41	2.50	2.50	4.08
NRR	1.37	1.205	1.25	1.25	2.04
Generation	32.3	32.6	32.0	32.5	32.7
Annual rate of growth	0.98%	0.58%	0.70%	0.69%	2.20%
Years for population to double	71.4	120.7	100.0	101.4	31.8
Age at marriage	25.7	26.4	27.5	26.5	24.9

only 60% of the rate of the pre-1650 cohort. Clearly, the impact of a falling birth rate and rising death rate was significant.

To discover which variable, the falling birth rate or the rising death rate, was the more important contributor to the state of affairs, I again use the simple simulation technique employed in Chapter 6 to derive the data presented in Table 6.2. The results show that the observable adjustment is almost wholly accounted for by a rising age at marriage and lower fertility rates before and during marriage. The long term demographic impact of the increased mortality experienced by children and adults, viewed in group terms, was marginal. Indeed, the impact of a declining illegitimacy ratio was itself significantly more important than that of the higher mortality levels of the seventeenth century.

In reviewing these results, one should bear in mind that they illuminate the behavior of those members of the community who stayed in Bottesford in a time of declining employment opportunity. This context makes their behavior intelligible. In "normal" circumstances, those of demographic equilibrium, a fall in the birth rate would be countered by a fall in the death rate of a similar magnitude. But this seesaw effect was precisely what did not happen. In later seventeenth century Bottesford the villagers actively sought to reduce the number of children by whom they would be survived. They did so because they seemingly knew that any extra children they produced, over and above replacement level, would find no livelihood in the village.

It would be wrong, however, to view this post-1650 adjustment in isolation from the following century's stabilization. As can be seen from Table 6.1, the ways in which the two eighteenth century cohorts achieved

TABLE 6.2
Components of Population Growth in Later Seventeenth Century Bottesford

	1600–1649	Rising death rate	Falling birth rate	Lower illegit- imacy
Gross Rate of Reproduction	5.36	5.36	5.08	5.36
Revised GRR	4.56	4.53	4.13	4.41
Child survival rate	.677	.677	.673	.677
Surviving children	3.09	3.06	2.78	2.98
Incidence of marriage	.886	.886	.872	.886
Children marrying	2.74	2.71	2.43	2.64
Net rate of reproduction	1.37	1.355	1.215	1.32
Generational interval	32.3	32.3	32.7	32.3
Annual rate of growth	0.98%	0.95%	0.60%	0.87%
Years for population to double	71.4	73.7	116.7	80.4
Mean average age at first marriage for women	25.7	25.7	26.4	25.7

almost identical rates of replacement are, I think, both fascinating and significant.

The continued rise in age at first marriage for women after 1700 was more than counteracted by a recovery of fertility to levels exceeding those achieved in the period before 1650. Thus, potential fertility in the early eighteenth century was fully 10% greater than in the later. This rising fertility was necessary, however, to counter a noticeable decline in life expectancy at birth, as just 94% (.633 as opposed to .673) survived to the average age at marriage. Moreover, according to the conventions of my model, a later age at marriage meant that fewer of those who reached marriageable age actually married. Nevertheless, the overall interaction of nuptiality, fertility, and mortality raised the replacement rate only fractionally over that prevailing before 1700.

This stable situation persisted into the later eighteenth century in spite of significantly greater variations in demographic indicators—age at first marriage for women was one year earlier but the rate of marital fertility was considerably lower and a woman bore her last child at an earlier age (see Table 6.3). Together, these factors were balanced by marked improvement in health among both children and adults. In the later eighteenth century 70.2% of children survived to the age at marriage in contrast to 63.3% before 1750. After 1750, 61.7% of marriages remained unbroken at the end of the wives' fertility periods, but before the midcentury the figure was 46.5%. And yet the demographic seesaw remained stable, the rate of generational replacement was precisely what it had been prior to 1750.

The demographic regime of eighteenth century Bottesford illuminates the way in which exogenous influences on the death rate were integrated into the villagers' strategies of family formation. Those people were interested in producing surviving children—survivors who could take up places within their native environment. The facts that fewer of their

TABLE 6.3
Mother's Age at Birth of Last Child, by Age at Marriage, Bottesford

	Under 30		Over 30		All	
1600–1649	39.8	(25)	40.0	(5)	39.8	(30)
1650–1699	38.5	(14)	40.4	(7)	39.2	(21)
1700–1749	41.3	(15)	43.9	(8)	42.2	(23)
1750–1799	37.2	(17)	38.3	(5)	37.4	(22)
1800–1849	35.2	(2)	—		35.2	(2)
All	39.1	(73)	41.0	(25)	39.6	(98)

Numbers in brackets refer to sample sizes.

children were dying during infancy or childhood and that they themselves were surviving with greater frequency made themselves felt in their reproductive calculus, and they adjusted their marital fertility accordingly. The balancing act implicit in eighteenth century Bottesford's population history is a marvellous example of how demographic equilibrium was maintained in response to conditions of economic stabilization. The demand for labor in the village's pastoral economy was relatively unchanging, and the Manners family and its stewards operated the poor laws to keep the village at a constant size throughout the eighteenth century. Inexorably, those surplus to local requirements would be forced out by the operation of the poor law. In these circumstances, it is understandable why the villagers opted for a strategy of family formation that resulted in nearly zero population growth.

After the relative stability of the 1650–1799 period the early nineteenth century villagers replaced themselves three times as fast as their predecessors. The major determinant of this discontinuity was a shift in the local agrarian economy from pastoral farming and grazing to labor intensive dairy farming. This development influenced the Manners family's lordship over Bottesford, and they temporarily loosened their iron grip on settlement. For a few decades many of the villagers' children seem to have been able to settle in Bottesford. The loosening of settlement regulations together with the rising demand for labor seems to have undermined the careful control the eighteenth century villagers exercised over their fertility. After 1800, age at first marriage for women fell by one and one-half years (and by more than two years for their husbands) while marital fertility rose. At the same time the improvement in life expectancy, begun in the later eighteenth century, carried on with even greater momentum. After 1800, life expectancy of children at birth was six years higher than in the later eighteenth century and fully ten years higher than in the earlier eighteenth century. The combined effects of a rising birth rate, and a falling death rate, destabilized the demographic seesaw.

Once again using the basic computation I introduced in Chapter 5, we can disaggregate the components of population growth and, by isolating them, test their relative contribution to this disequilibrium. In Table 6.4, I present a set of figures describing the relative importance of the rising birth rate and falling death rate in the post-1800 population boom in Bottesford.

As with the later seventeenth century slowdown, the dynamic element in this long-term measure of the cohort is the birth rate. The death rate, in comparison, is of little importance. Considered alone, the rising birth rate increased the annual rate of growth from 0.69% to 1.92% while the falling death rate increased it from 0.69% to 0.94%. The impact of the rising birth

TABLE 6.4
Birth and Death Rates in Early Nineteenth Century Bottesford

	Falling death rate	Rising birth rate
Gross rate of reproduction	4.44	6.37
Revised GRR	4.24	5.76
Child survival rate	0.739	0.710
Surviving children	3.13	4.09
Incidence of marriage	0.870	0.902
Children marrying	2.72	3.69
Net rate of reproduction	1.36	1.845
Generational interval	33.5	32.3
Annual rate of growth	0.94%	1.92%
Years for population to double	74.4	36.5
Mean average at first marriage for women	26.5	24.9

rate was more than three times that of the falling death rate. In addition, increased marital fertility and lower age at marriage *each* made a greater contribution to the rate of population growth after 1800 than did lower mortality. Presenting these two components of the birth rate separately, Table 6.5 indicates that they played equal roles in promoting population growth after 1800.

The evidence derived from the Bottesford reconstitution study is of great interest. Not only does it underline the point that the reserve of "prolific power" held in line by a variety of social controls was great indeed, it also reaffirms the point, made above in the analysis of Shepshed's population history and made again below when the demographic experiences of Terling and Colyton are considered, that the impact

TABLE 6.5
Components of a Rising Birth Rate in Early Nineteenth Century Bottesford

	Rising fertility	Falling age at marriage
Gross rate of reproduction	5.68	5.03
Revised GRR	5.06	4.62
Child survival rate	0.703	0.710
Surviving children	3.56	3.28
Incidence of marriage	0.870	0.902
Children marrying	3.09	2.96
Net rate of reproduction	1.545	1.48
Generational interval	33.5	31.8
Annual rate of growth	1.32%	1.25%
Years for population to double	53.0	56.0
Mean average age at first marriage for women	26.5	24.9

TABLE 6.6

Age at First Marriage, Bottesford

	N	Mean	Standard deviation	Lower quartile	Median	Upper quartile	Inter-quartile range
Men							
1600–1649	105	29.2	5.2	25.4	29.0	32.5	7.1
1650–1699	70	27.6	4.8	23.6	27.1	30.5	6.9
1700–1749	81	28.7	5.9	24.7	27.8	31.0	6.3
1750–1799	133	29.0	6.4	24.6	27.3	30.5	5.9
1800–1851	162	26.3	5.4	22.6	24.9	28.7	6.1
Women							
1600–1649	107	25.7	5.2	21.7	24.9	29.1	7.4
1650–1699	71	26.4	5.0	22.8	25.5	30.0	7.2
1700–1749	106	27.5	4.9	24.0	26.9	30.5	6.5
1750–1799	136	26.5	5.4	22.6	25.9	29.1	6.5
1800–1851	192	24.9	9.3	20.7	23.1	27.0	6.3

TABLE 6.7
Age-Specific Fertility, Bottesford

	Years at risk	Children born	Rate/000
1600–1649			
Under 25	100	40	400
25–29	185	68	368
30–34	222	76	342
35–39	191	45	236
40–44	154	25	162
45–49	134	2	15
1650–1699			
Under 25	64	37	579
25–29	104	40	381
30–34	104	33	317
35–39	78	19	244
40–44	74	12	162
45–49	57	1	18
1700–1749			
Under 25	48	20	417
25–29	128	55	430
30–34	184	66	359
35–39	168	56	333
40–44	123	22	179
45–49	88	4	45
1750–1799			
Under 25	60	20	333
25–29	118	43	364
30–34	146	39	269
35–39	124	29	234
40–44	99	13	131
45–49	88	0	0
1800–1851			
Under 25	228	123	540
25–29	258	111	430
30–34	264	89	337
35–39	168	48	304
40–44	83	10	108
45–49	42	4	95

of extralocal influences on the village-level demand for labor had seriously disequilibrating consequences. Even more than the celebrated reduction in mortality, which in Bottesford was not inconsiderable, the rise in fertility promoted rapid population growth.

TABLE 6.8
Infant and Child Mortality (MF), Bottesford

Cohort	Age	Reconstitution				e⁰	Ledermann	
		At risk	Dying	Rate/000	Survivors	e^0	Rate/000	Survivors
1600–1649	0–	1222	196	160	1000	44.02	158	1000
	1–4	865	88	102	840	p. 90	96	842
	5–9	619	27	44	758		28	761
	10–14	469	7	15	725		17	740
					714			727
1650–1699	0–	1176	177	151	1000	44.02	158	1000
	1–4	794	60	75	849	p. 90	96	842
	5–9	542	24	44	748		28	761
	10–14	395	18	45	750		17	740
					716			727
1700–1749	0–	1197	196	164	1000	42.78	168	1000
	1–4	825	89	108	836	p. 134	118	832
	5–9	560	29	52	746		32	734
	10–14	398	8	20	707		21	711
					694			696
1750–1799	0–	999	143	143	1000	46.38	147	1000
	1–4	702	57	81	857	p. 115	82	853
	5–9	518	11	21	787		24	783
	10–14	396	9	23	771		15	764
					758			753
1800–1851	0–	1219	141	115	1000	52.34	125	1000
	1–4	669	51	76	885	p. 196	79	875
	5–9	328	7	21	818		21	806
	10–14	147	2	14	801		14	789
					790			778

e^0 means life expectancy at birth.

99

TABLE 6.9
Adult Mortality (MF), Bottesford

	1600–1649	1650–1699	1700–1749	1750–1799	1800–1824
		Part 1.	Life expectancy at various ages		
25	29.7	30.7	31.1	36.4	
30	26.6	27.1	27.9	32.6	
35	23.0	24.9	24.1	29.0	
40	20.1	21.2	22.1	25.9	
45	17.2	18.0	19.4	22.3	
50	13.9	15.2	16.8	19.2	
55	11.9	13.0	14.4	16.3	
60	10.3	11.2	12.6	13.3	
65	7.6	9.4	10.6	10.4	
70	5.5	7.3	8.2	8.0	
75	4.1	5.7	5.8	6.4	
80	3.5	5.1	3.3	5.1	
85+	3.5	3.4	3.1	3.7	
		Part 2.	Survivors to various ages		
25	1000	1000	1000	1000	1000
30	934	952	937	966	996
35	884	857	896	923	952
40	803	807	786	861	924
45	716	738	705	812	
50	644	646	616	742	
55	508	529	522	658	
60	374	405	412	575	
65	287	298	318	480	
70	184	209	240	360	
75	84	123	163	223	
80	23	51	93	115	
85+	4	22	14	49	

APPENDIX: CRISIS MORTALITY IN BOTTESFORD

The extreme variations in annual mortality levels before 1740 were produced by epidemic mortality or subsistence crises in which a steep rise in the price of bread was accompanied by a dramatic rise in the number of burials combined with a fall in conceptions and marriages. In 1610 the parish clerk recorded that "the dying poisoned many, Th'infection was so great whereat it come it scarce left any." In fact, 125 people died, about one in six, at a time when the annual average was about 25. Of the 11 other crisis years before 1740, we cannot be sure what caused the abnormal mortality, although it appears that the prolonged crisis of 1727–30 resulted from a crisis of subsistence. In the four years after the 1727 harvest there were 197 burials, an annual average of 49.25, about double the level in the

TABLE 6.10
Annual Conceptions, Burials, and Marriages, Bottesford, by Harvest Years

Harvest year	Conceptions	Burials	Marriages
1725	32	17	4
1726	28	16	8
1727	18	45	3
1728	20	66	3
1729	23	39	15
1730	36	47	11
1731	33	29	8
1732	37	19	10
1733	38	22	6
1734	27	24	5
1735	35	17	5

noncrisis years of the 1720s and 1730s. Moreover, the interaction of burials, conceptions, and marriages in those years is exactly what one would
expect to find in a population experiencing a crisis of subsistence. The
annual changes in conceptions, burials, and marriages (according to harvest
years) are presented in Table 6.10 and shown graphically in Figure 6.2.

The burial curve rose dramatically in 1727 and again in 1728. In 1729 and
1730 there continued to be a comparatively high number of burials, and
only in 1731 did the burial curve fall back to the pre-1727 levels. The
conception curve traces a pattern practically the inverse image of the burial

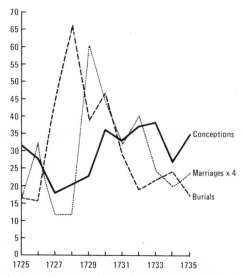

Figure 6.2. Annual conceptions, burials, and marriages, Bottesford, by harvest years.

curve. In 1727 and 1728 there was a sharp drop in conceptions in addition to a decline in the number of marriages celebrated. In 1729 the number of marriages rose spectacularly and persisted at an above normal level through 1732, laying the foundations for a substantial rise in conceptions which also persisted for several years.

The location and economic structure of Bottesford combined to make the villagers peculiarly susceptible to the vagaries of the harvest. Because the village's agrarian economy was heavily committed to pastoral farming, a bad harvest left the population in distress. This problem was compounded by the village's location and the inadequacies of the system of food distribution. The heavy clay soil of the Vale of Belvoir made the roads almost impassable in wet weather after they had been cut up. In addition, Bottesford lay more than 12 miles from navigable water, which made it even more difficult for the villagers to receive adequate food supplies from outside after road communication was obstructed. In these years, 1727–30, the price of wheat rose dramatically and exports dried up—a succession of bad harvests spelled disaster.[9]

---

[9] Similar findings of a local harvest crisis in the West Midlands are reported in A. Gooder, "The Population Crisis of 1727–30 in Warwickshire." Gooder's argument is that national price series often mask important local variations. For Bottesford, unfortunately, no local evidence on the trend of wheat prices is available.

7

COLYTON REVISITED

In his pioneering family reconstitution study of Colyton, Devon, E.A. Wrigley was primarily concerned with showing that significant variations in nuptiality, fertility, and mortality occurred in the period before the Industrial Revolution and the "demographic transition."[1] It is unfortunate that Wrigley did not attempt to relate the substantial shifts in demographic behavior to the socioeconomic environment in which they occurred. This "oversight" can be ascribed to Wrigley's desire to display the results that could be derived from family reconstitution—he wanted to show an unfamiliar and doubting audience that the demography of the preindustrial world was not homogeneous.[2] To explain why such changes occurred was not part of his brief. Such an explanation is, however, central to the present work. Because Wrigley's work on Colyton is so well known and frequently quoted, it proved to be the perfect choice for inclusion in my revisionist study. Moreover, the fact that Wrigley only tangentially related demographic behavior to economic change proved to be a further reason to reconsider this particular study. And, finally, the fact that the hard grind of reconstituting the village population was already completed played no small part in helping me to choose Colyton.

---

[1] E.A. Wrigley, "Family Limitation in Pre-Industrial England"; "Mortality in Pre-Industrial England: The Example of Colyton, Devon, Over Three Centuries."

[2] The "demographic transition" theory posited that a preindustrial regime characterized by high death rates and high birth rates was changed, under the initial impact of economic development on living conditions, to a modern regime characterized by low death rates and fertility restriction. Wrigley's study of deliberate family limitation in the seventeenth century, fully two centuries before the era of the "demographic transition," is of great importance because it has shown that this theory's model of preindustrial demography is too simple.

Before we consider the relationship between economic opportunity and family formation, it might be helpful to review the salient aspects of Colyton's demographic history. Wrigley's choice of Colyton was propitious; the villagers displayed remarkably varying levels of nuptiality, fertility, and mortality.[3] Age at marriage for men remained stable throughout the 300 years of the study, but that for their brides changed dramatically. Of particular interest was the period when women married later, 1647–1719, because it proved to be a time when women also consciously restricted fertility. In his masterful discussion of this phenomenon Wrigley shows that fertility restriction was more stringent among those members of the cohort who married early, which is what we would expect to observe in a population "aiming" at a desired family size. Wrigley devoted most of his space to describing this period because the unexpected finding of deliberate family limitation together with rising age at marriage proved to be of such great interest.

Wrigley gave the years before 1647 and after 1719 relatively short shrift although (or perhaps because) they were characterized by substantially higher levels of reproduction. The central finding of his study of nuptiality and fertility in Colyton was "not only that it was within the powers of preindustrial communities to halt population growth, but also that their powers of growth were very remarkable." In his study Wrigley noted that there was "a well-marked inverse correlation between baptisms and burials until the end of the seventeenth century which can still be detected at times in the eighteenth." Furthermore, "the pattern of change in adult death rates, as with the rates for children, suggests a substantially lower expectation of life at birth in the second half of the seventeenth century than in Elizabethan times or Georgian England." Thus, just as birth rates fluctuated, so death rates varied also.

In interpreting the dramatic demographic discontinuity of the mid-seventeenth century, Wrigley argued that the 1645–46 epidemic of the plague, which carried away perhaps one in five, was understood by the villagers to be a warning—a danger signal against continued rapid growth. The villagers' response was an adjustment of their demographic behavior so as to optimize their real incomes—later marriage and fertility restriction which were (involuntarily) abetted by higher mortality. In opposition to Wrigley's ascription of instinctive prudence, I would argue that this demographic turnabout occurred in response to the *deindustrialization* of Colyton.

In the later sixteenth century Colyton conformed to Joan Thirsk's model of a wood-pasture economy in which the rural textile industry became

---

[3] Detailed tabular information on nuptiality, fertility, and mortality for Colyton can be found at the end of this chapter. The figures used in my work differ from Wrigley's in that I have used somewhat different cohorts. Both sets of figures, however, were derived from the files of the S.S.R.C. Cambridge Group for the History of Population and Social Structure.

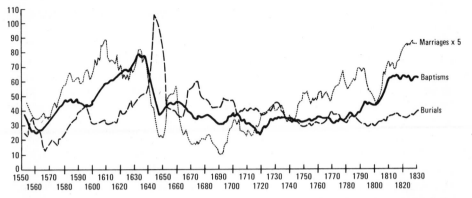

Figure 7.1. A nine-year weighted, moving average of baptisms, burials, and marriages (×5), Colyton.

well established. Small closes made ideal grazing ground on intensively managed pastoral farms. Enclosure of subdivided arable land in east Devon originated in the early middle ages. Most holdings were fragmented, their scattered closes were small and elongated, fossilizing the preenclosure pattern of open-field strips. A survey of the neighboring town of Axminster in 1574 reveals that the manor was dominated by diminutive closes, and flooded meadows were so extensive that only 17% of the land was arable. In the seventeenth century, east Devon surveys show that the average size of a close was less than three acres. In east Devon this pattern was evident as late as 1796.[4]

Given these conditions it was logical for members of the agrarian community to supplement their family incomes through cottage industry. Spinning, weaving, and finishing would be undertaken as subsidiary activities. Although such people would still be engaged in agrarian pursuits to garner a bare subsistence, domestic industry would provide them a margin above subsistence.[5] The productive capacity of an industry organized in this way would be determined largely by the duplication of

---

[4] This paragraph is based on H.S.A. Fox, "The Chronology of Enclosure and Economic Development in Medieval Devon."

[5] For this reason I believe that occupational information found in the parish register would be misleading. People who relied upon by-employment to supplement their agricultural incomes would not be considered in determining the proportion of the population engaged in industry. (For a contrary view, see E.A. Wrigley, "The changing occupational structure of Colyton over two centuries.") For people who lived on the edge of the agrarian system, the marginal addition to their family incomes provided by part-time spinning or weaving was what kept body and soul together. In discussing the precariousness of life among the Chinese peasantry before the Revolution, R.H. Tawney wrote that "There are districts in which the position of the rural population is that of a man standing permanently up to the neck in water, so that even a ripple is sufficient to drown him." (R.H. Tawney, *Land and Labour in China*, p. 77.)

productive units, not by technical efficiency. Available evidence suggests that this situation prevailed in Colyton during the later sixteenth century.[6]

In Elizabethan England the cloth trade boomed and the port of Exeter was a major export center. The trade of Exeter at this time consisted almost wholly of Devon dozens (i.e., kerseys), the traditional broadcloths produced in the region. In the early years of the seventeenth century the dominance of the broadcloths was challenged by the development of a new type of woolens, serges, woven from worsted and never milled. The emergence of the "New Draperies" occurred in a climate of recession and search for new markets.[7] The lighter fabrics produced by the "New Draperies" proved ideal for the export boom in the Mediterranean. "At the turn of the [seventeenth] century the manufacture of serge in Devon had been negligible, in 1624 it was second only to the Devon dozens in Exeter's exports. . . . The remarkable growth of Exeter's serge trade is illustrated beyond all doubt by a comparison of the export figures for the years before and after the Restoration. . . . By 1647 the importance of serge is obvious and by 1666 it had become well established as Exeter's chief export. . . . [Indeed, by] the latter half of the [seventeenth] century all other types of cloth other than serge had become insignificant."[8]

The rapid development of serge manufacturing coincided with a failure of the local wool supply to keep pace with changing demand. An extension of capitalist power brought along its corollary, an increasing class of landless, protoindustrial wage earners. Throughout the seventeenth century there was a steady reorganization of production—the need to import wool from far and near gave the mercantile element the opportunity to wrest control over the production process. W.G. Hoskins, a student of the rise and decline of the serge industry in the southwest, argues that by the beginning of the eighteenth century the reorganization of production was essentially complete:

> the merchant manufacturer at the top of the organization, owning the raw materials and the instruments of production, and controlling the whole process from the buying of the wool to the marketing of the serge on the continent; the large and growing class of workers, landless and dependent entirely on an industrial wage; the diminishing class of small craftsmen struggling in the face of the concentration of industry; and the growing emphasis on the towns in the industrial economy, with their premonition of the factory system in their huddled "courts" and domestic workshops.[9]

---

[6] See, for example, the survey of Colyton conducted in the 1550s (Devonshire Record Office 123/M/E/77) which has several references to fulling mills and to "racks" used for stretching cloth. I owe this reference to the generosity of Dr. H.S.A. Fox who allowed me to view his xerox copy of it.

[7] D.C. Coleman, "An Innovation and Its Diffusion: The 'New Draperies'."

[8] W.B. Stephens, *Seventeenth Century Exeter*, pp. 10, 103, 104.

[9] W.G. Hoskins, "The Rise and Decline of the Serge Industry in the South-West of England, with Special Reference to the Eighteenth Century," p. 4. My discussion of the reorganization of the west-county cloth industry is based on Hoskins' neglected thesis.

Furthermore, the differentiation of roles in production was accompanied by a geographical specialization of function. *Spinning* of Irish wool was confined to the area around the Bristol Channel ports of local wool to areas around Dartmoor, Exmoor, and the Cornish moors. *Weaving* was carried out in the middle Exe valley, the Culm valley, and the lower Creedy valley, the largest area of lowland in Devonshire. Population was heavily concentrated in the rural industrial districts, and in the main weaving areas there were as many as 200 people per square mile—about four times the average population density. *Finishing* was even more concentrated and was carried out largely in Exeter, with a smaller amount of activity in Tiverton.

This specialization of function was largely determined by the Exeter merchants who controlled the importation of raw Irish wool and the export of finished goods. Geography, too, played no small part in determining the structure and location of the various components of production. The logic of this geographical division of labor becomes clear when we realize that it was ideally suited to the capabilities of the existing transportation network. Spinning the raw wool at or near the port of entry insured that the pack trains traversing the north Devon moors carried a product ready for use. Moreover, by having the raw wool spun in isolated areas, the merchants were able to utilize the inexpensive "spare time" of farmers' and fishermen's wives and children. When the semiprocessed yarn was distributed to the weavers, the merchants could reckon on receiving a specified amount of woven fabric. In the weaving areas the workers were brought together into groups that bore a clear resemblance to "incipient factories." This concentration allowed the "agents" or "small masters" to maintain close supervision over production and thereby adjust quickly to changing fashions. Between the main weaving areas and the finishing centers of Exeter and Tiverton communication was easy, making it relatively simple to transport the bulky woven, but as yet unfinished, cloth. The preeminence of Exeter in the finishing process and in mercantile activity can be explained largely by its position at the mouth of the river system running through central Devon.

As a result of this differentiation and stratification in the woolen industry, Colyton soon found itself on the outside, looking in. Hoskins' study of the serge industry is accompanied by two maps clearly showing that the Blackdown Hills cut the Axe Valley off from the main areas of spinning and weaving. A more recent student of the cloth industry in seventeenth century Devon, David Seward, has remarked on the critical role played by communication.

> Devon is noted for its rolling hills and steep valleys, which tend to interrupt communications, particularly from east to west. Because of this, and the rainy climate, Devon roads consisted of steep inclines, bends and mud. Even by early seventeenth century standards Devon roads were bad. . . . . The result of those

poor communications and physical barriers seems to have been to separate the various cloth producing areas in the country, and hinder their development as one economic unit.[10]

In his maps Hoskins notes all the places in Devon involved in the various processes in production of the "New Draperies." Colyton is conspicuous by its absence. It may be suggested that the critical factor in Colyton's demise as an important woolen town was the shift to Irish wool that led to a radical restructuring of the geographical organization of local production. Thereafter, spinning and weaving continued in Colyton, to be sure, but they became vestigial.[11]

The demographic effects of deindustrialization began when a type of employment that offered poor cottagers and husbandmen the chance to supplement their income was lost. Insofar as woolen production was a cornerstone of their household economies, the villagers lost a major source of income. In response to these changing economic conditions, they not only chose older brides but also restricted their family size. Furthermore, this demographic turnabout did not occur overnight, as Wrigley suggests. It was already in train in the first half of the seventeenth century—before the plague epidemic.[12] During that period the woolen industry was already being reorganized, and the impact of this was felt in Colyton.

At this point the question arises of why men in Colyton did not marry at a more advanced age? Why did only their brides marry later? To answer these questions, it is necessary to bear in mind that the later seventeenth century was marked by a dramatic rise in adult mortality. This factor is of great relevance in explaining male age at marriage in a largely peasant community. G. Ohlin has noted that "in a society where death makes room for new families the average age of children at the death of their parents may serve as an index of the age at first marriage."[13] Put another way, in a society where the nuclear family household was preeminent and marriage was dependent upon the acquisition of an independent house-

---

[10] David Seward, "The Devonshire Cloth Industry in the Early Seventeenth Century," pp. 32–33.

[11] In the later eighteenth century, 1765–79, 10% of all occupations listed in the parish register were connected with the cloth industry. Although this figure is not dissimilar to that found in the early seventeenth century, 12%, I would argue that the process of reorganization, stratification, and differentiation which Hoskins described is of essential importance because it removed the widespread reliance on clothworking, as a by-employment, from the domestic economy of the poor members of the peasantry. These eighteenth century descriptions include mention of serge makers, which clashes with Hoskins' map which expressly excludes Colyton from the west-country serge industry (E.A. Wrigley, "Changing occupational structure of Colyton.")

[12] The absolute level of marriages celebrated in the parish church peaked in 1610 and began to decline in the next 30 years, before the 1645–46 epidemic. After a half-century of rapid growth before 1610, this reversal is significant, since one would expect an even larger number of young people to have entered the local marriage market. The fact that these young people were not marrying in their native village is indicative of the tightening local economy.

[13] P.G. Ohlin, "Mortality, Marriage, and Growth in Pre-Industrial Populations."

hold (and occupational position), the age at marriage may be equal to the average expectation of life at the mean age of fatherhood.[14] In this way each generation would succeed the one before. Thus, in Colyton, the decline in adult life expectancy in the later seventeenth century may have offset the reduction in employment opportunities for some men. For others, the reduction in available by-employment must have meant emiration. For those who stayed, the balance of demographic forces allowed them to marry at much the same age as before. According to my argument, male age at marriage held stable as a result of rising adult mortality while, at the same time, men chose older brides in response to deteriorating economic conditions.

My model relating family formation to economic opportunity provides an explanation of the seventeenth century demographic turnabout in Colyton rather different from that proposed by Wrigley. It now remains to show how this model copes with the succeeding period, particularly the years after 1800. As age at marriage for men remained stable while their brides became younger, marital fertility rates rose and mortality became less severe. The demographic scissors opened and rapid growth ensued.

In the sixteenth century the dual, industrial-agricultural economy enabled Colyton's peasants to survive on small holdings. But the reorganization of the west-country cloth industry in the early seventeenth century undermined the viability of these small holdings. By the end of the eighteenth century agricultural writers were remarking on the number of consolidated farms in the district east of the Blackdown Hills. These farms were "applied to the depasturing of dairy cows." The produce of "the prime pastures are found to yield an abundant supply of animal food, to all the large towns situated in the bosom of these enchanting vallies." Locally produced butter was sent as far afield as London.[15] There is no way of knowing how early this latter development occurred, but, insofar as the nature of the road system in the seventeenth century inhibited movement, one expects it to date from the later eighteenth century.

In Bottesford, a similar extension of the urban food market was felt at the individual level. There, age at marriage for men dropped whereas in Colyton it remained stable. The explanation for these contradictory responses probably has to do with the persistence of living-in farm servants in Colyton. Charles Vancouver, the agricultural writer, noted that living-in farm servants were quite common at the beginning of the nineteenth century in this part of Devon. He waxed enthusiastic over their instruction, remarking that servants in the Colyton neighborhood "are formed and instructed in a way perhaps more prevalent in this county than in any

---

[14] R.S. Schofield, "Endogenous and Exogenous Influences on Demographic Structure and Change in Pre-Industrial Societies" (Paper presented to the Sixth International Congress on Economic History, Copenhagen, August 1974, Section B-5-b), p. 2.
[15] C. Vancouver, *A General View of the Agriculture of the County of Devon*, pp. 113, 230.

other of the United Kingdom."[16] In 1851, there were 42 farm servants in Colyton. The demographic importance of this fact becomes clear when we see it in a wider perspective—in mid–nineteenth century England late marriage was correlated with the persistence of servants in agriculture whereas early marriage was linked with wage labor. To be sure, agricultural wage labor did exist in Colyton—in 1851 there were 124 adult male agricultural laborers—but its demographic importance apparently was muted by the coexistence of servants living in with their employers.[17] The lack of alternative by-employment meant that those men who remained in Colyton had to postpone marriage until they inherited a position, became economically independent, and could set up their own households.

To the extent that marriage for men in Colyton was predicated on the inheritance of a vacant position within the local economy, another factor which may go some way toward explaining the maintenance of a relatively late age at marriage for men may be the improvement in adult life expectancy in the eighteenth century. The fact that men lived longer may have postponed the onset of economic independence for their sons. Wrigley's cohort adult mortality rates show that a significant improvement in adult life expectancy occurred among men who married after 1700 in comparison with those who married in the later seventeenth century. Among 50-year-old men, 69% of the seventeenth century cohort survived to their sixtieth birthdays, while for those married after 1700 the figure was 79%, an improvement of 15%. Among 50-year-old men, 44% of those married before 1700 survived until their seventieth birthdays, but 54% did so among those who married after 1700, a 23% improvement.[18] Thus, there was a significant improvement in the parameters of mortality that directly influenced the time at which men could expect to inherit positions. The situation I am positing for the persistence of a comparatively stable age at marriage for eighteenth century Colyton men is, in effect, the reverse of that put forward to explain why later seventeenth century men did not marry later. If we see the demographic determinants of age at marriage within a dynamic system, then we may note the possibility that high adult mortality in the later seventeenth century contributed to relatively early marriage for men while low adult mortality in the eighteenth century held up their age at marriage.

For women the situation was quite different, inasmuch as lacemaking, a rural handicraft using women's and children's labor, had become widespread in east Devon during the course of the eighteenth century. In 1698 there were 353 lacemakers in Colyton.[19] If all these lacemakers were girls

---

[16] C. Vancouver, *General View*, p. 359.

[17] E.A. Wrigley, "Changing Occupational Structure of Colyton," quoting the 1851 census enumeration of the village.

[18] E.A. Wrigley, "Mortality," p. 561. I have used Wrigley's "medium" assumptions.

[19] This reference is from *Case of the Lacemakers in Relation to the Importance of Foreign Lace.*

TABLE 7.1
Net Rate of Reproduction, Colyton

	1538–1599	1600–1649	1650–1699	1700–1749	1750–1799	1800–1849
GRR	6.03	4.25	2.60	3.36	4.29	5.75
Revised GRR	4.91	3.73	2.26	2.87	4.00	5.12
Child survival rate	.704	.650	.626	.647	.701	.723
Children surviving	3.45	2.43	1.46	1.86	2.80	3.70
Incidence of marriage	.860	.858	.808	.826	.874	.912
Children marrying	2.97	2.08	1.18	1.54	2.45	3.37
NRR	1.485	1.04	0.59	0.77	1.225	1.685
Generation	33.9	33.2	34.3	34.4	32.2	32.1
Annual rate of growth/decline	1.18%	0.12%	−1.55%	−0.77%	0.63%	1.65%
Years for population to double (halve)	59.3	583.0	(45.2)	(90.9)	110.0	42.4
Age at marriage	27.0	27.1	29.4	28.3	26.3	24.4

and women, about 60% of all females over 15 were engaged in this activity.[20] Slowly, during the course of the eighteenth century, the demographic influence of this rural handicraft, from which women could make significant contributions to their family income, made itself felt.[21] The ability to supplement family incomes with money earned by making lace provided young women in Colyton with attractive dowries. In this way, the economic *disincentive* to early marriage for women crumbled.

In Table 7.1 I set out the net rate of reproduction for Colyton, using the formula that has been employed previously. From this material we can see the roles played by the various components of the demographic equation.

(1698), Victoria and Albert Museum, Reference: 43 A 2 H. (Quoted by G.F.R. Spenceley, "The Origin of the English Pillow Lace Industry," p. 88.)

[20] In 1695, Gregory King estimated that there were 1554 people living in "Culliton" (Quoted in D.V. Glass, "Two Papers on Gregory King," p. 177). If half of the population was made up of women (777), and three-quarters of these women were over 15 (582), then 60% of all women over 15 (353/582) were engaged in lacemaking. The estimate that three-quarters of the women were over 15 was found in R. Lee, "Estimating Series of Vital Rates and Age Structures from Baptisms and Burials: A New Technique, with Applications to Pre-Industrial England," p. 503.

[21] Spenceley notes that lacemaking was well paid. Lacemakers made as much as, or even more than, female agricultural laborers. ("Origins of the English Pillow Lace Industry," p. 92.) Another investigation of a similar kind of rural handicraft, straw plaiting in Victorian Buckinghamshire and Bedfordshire, discovered that "In the early 1860s a mother and her children working together at straw plait could earn as much as the head of the household, if he were an agricultural labourer on a basic wage rate . . ." (P.L.R. Horn, "Child Workers in the Pillow Lace and Straw Plait Trades of Victorian Buckinghamshire and Bedfordshire," p. 795.) W. Ogle remarked that the women in these regions married early, much earlier than the national average, which he ascribed to their ability to make a supplement to the family income. (W. Ogle, "On Marriage-Rates and Marriage-Ages, with Special Reference to the Growth of Population.") David Sabean suggested to me that this addition to the domestic economy might be regarded as a "constant dowry."

TABLE 7.2
A Falling Birth Rate Compared with a Rising Death Rate, Colyton, Seventeenth Century

	1538–1599	Falling birth rate	Rising death rate
GRR	6.03	2.60	6.03
Revised GRR	4.91	2.19	5.13
Child survival rate	.704	.704	.626
Children surviving	3.45	1.54	3.21
Incidence of marriage	.860	.808	.860
Children marrying	2.97	1.24	2.76
NRR	1.485	0.62	1.38
Generation	33.9	34.1	34.2
Annual rate of growth/decline	1.18%	−1.42%	0.95%
Years for population to double (halve)	59.3	(49.3)	73.7
Age at marriage	27.0	29.4	27.0

The net rate of reproduction shows that the slowdown in population growth was in train well before the plague epidemic of 1645–46. Absolute retardation lasted for a full century, 1650–1749, when the population was not replacing itself. Only gradually thereafter was the later sixteenth century level of growth reattained. A second striking point about these rates is that the birth rate—age at marriage and marital fertility acting in

TABLE 7.3
Rising Birth Rate Compared with a Falling Death Rate, Colyton, Nineteenth Century

	1650–1699	Rising birth rate	Falling death rate
GRR	2.60	5.75	2.60
Revised GRR	2.26	4.81	2.32
Child survival rate	.626	.626	.723
Children surviving	1.46	3.01	1.68
Incidence of marriage	.808	.912	.808
Children marrying	1.18	2.74	1.36
NRR	0.59	1.37	0.68
Generation	34.3	32.0	34.2
Annual rate of growth/decline	−1.55%	0.99%	−1.14%
Years for population to double (halve)	(45.21)	70.7	(61.4)
Age at marriage	29.4	24.4	29.4

tandem—played the major role in dictating the pace of growth. This becomes apparent when we compare the two periods of rapid growth, 1538–99 and 1800–49, with the later seventeenth century.

The data in Tables 7.2 and 7.3 show that the birth rate, *not* the death rate, was the critical variable. A falling birth rate in the later seventeenth century resulted in almost all of the decrease in the net rate of reproduction, and rising mortality was of only marginal importance. Indeed, even given a stable level of mortality, something like 90% of the reduction in the annual rate of growth would still have occurred. The relative unimportance of the death rate in the subsequent recovery of population growth in the early nineteenth century is borne out by the results presented in Table 7.3. Again, the birth rate accounts for almost all of the variation in the net rate of reproduction.

The relative unimportance of the death rate in explaining Colyton's secular demographic trends is, I think, very important. It underlines Wrigley's point "not only that it was within the power of preindustrial communities to halt population growth, but also that their powers of growth were very remarkable." Furthermore, such powers were exercised by the people of Colyton in response to variations in their material world. In Colyton, economic opportunity (or its absence) clearly influenced family formation.

TABLE 7.4
Age at First Marriage, Colyton

	N	Mean	Standard deviation	Lower quartile	Median	Upper quartile	Inter-quartile range
Men							
1550–1599	73	28.1	5.7	23.6	27.8	31.2	7.6
1600–1649	187	26.8	5.6	23.1	25.1	29.4	6.3
1650–1699	76	27.9	5.9	23.6	26.1	31.2	7.6
1700–1749	91	26.8	5.7	22.9	25.5	29.5	6.6
1750–1799	172	27.6	5.9	23.1	26.5	30.6	7.5
1800–1849	146	26.8	6.0	22.3	25.5	29.6	7.3
Women							
1550–1799	126	27.0	6.0	22.0	24.8	28.7	6.7
1600–1649	236	27.1	6.2	22.2	26.0	30.4	8.2
1650–1699	99	29.4	6.7	25.6	28.3	37.2	11.6
1700–1749	84	28.3	7.0	22.7	27.5	32.6	9.9
1750–1799	156	26.3	5.9	21.9	24.5	27.7	5.8
1800–1849	173	24.4	5.2	21.3	23.6	25.9	4.6

TABLE 7.5
Age-Specific Fertility, Colyton

	Years at risk	Children born	Rate/000
1550–99			
Under 25	102	42	412
25–29	188	70	373
30–34	225	85	378
35–39	170	55	324
40–44	148	36	244
45–49	138	5	37
1600–49			
Under 25	155	68	439
25–29	310	105	339
30–34	397	116	293
35–39	367	92	251
40–44	319	35	110
45–49	274	0	0
1650–99			
Under 25	42	14	333
25–29	116	49	423
30–34	137	30	219
35–39	143	26	182
40–44	121	6	50
45–49	99	1	11
1700–49			
Under 25	27	9	333
25–29	74	22	298
30–34	98	21	215
35–39	102	19	187
40–44	97	14	145
45–49	84	1	12
1750–99			
Under 25	107	34	318
25–29	210	64	305
30–34	265	79	299
35–39	229	44	193
40–44	145	13	90
45–49	132	2	16
1800–49			
Under 25	168	76	452
25–29	222	74	334
30–34	141	45	320
35–39	119	29	244
40–44	10	2	200
45–49	1	0	0

TABLE 7.6
Infant and Child Mortality (MF), Colyton

	Reconstitution			Ledermann		
	Age	Rate/000	Survivors	e⁰	Rate/000	Survivors
1538–1600	0–1	120–140	1000	48.37	130	1000
	1–14	124	870	(p. 151)	122	870
			762			764
1600–1649	0–1	126–158	1000	44.19	153	1000
	1–14	176	860	(p. 152)	157	847
			709			714
1650–1699	0–1	118–147	1000	41.86	175	1000
	1–14	200	865	(p. 152)	156	825
			692			696
1700–1749	0–1	162–203	1000	44.19	153	1000
	1–14	124	820	(p. 152)	157	847
			718			714
1750–1837	0–1	122–153	1000	48.37	130	1000
	1–14	119	865	(p. 151)	122	870
			762			764

Based on Wrigley's calculations ("Mortality," p. 571).
e⁰ means life expectancy at birth.

TABLE 7.7
Adult Mortality (MF), Colyton

	1550–1599	1600–1649	1650–1699	1700–1749	1750–1799
Part 1.		Life expectancy at various ages			
25	31.1	31.3	29.1	28.9	30.7
30	27.9	27.8	26.1	26.6	27.0
35	25.6	25.1	22.5	23.8	24.2
40	22.5	22.0	19.7	20.8	21.2
45	19.7	19.5	17.1	18.0	18.4
50	17.0	17.0	15.1	15.1	15.8
55	14.5	13.9	12.4	13.1	13.1
60	11.9	11.8	9.9	10.6	10.8
65	9.5	9.4	7.9	8.1	8.2
70	7.2	7.5	6.5	6.5	6.9
75	4.9	5.5	4.8	5.4	5.2
80+	2.8	3.2	3.6	3.8	3.5
Part 2.		Survivors to various ages			
25	1000	1000	1000	1000	1000
30	942	951	932	909	956
35	852	873	882	831	878
40	786	806	789	761	802
45	707	714	682	681	718
50	624	620	580	598	627
55	534	552	494	481	532
60	445	438	389	384	424
65	350	340	277	289	331
70	249	235	165	180	203
75	162	146	91	95	112
80+	88	78	35	42	50

8

PROLETARIANIZATION AND PAUPERISM: THE CASE OF TERLING

The economic and demographic history of Terling clearly contrasts with that of Colyton. During the early period, especially before 1600, there was a substantial excess of births over deaths, and similarly, during the later period, after 1780, an annual surplus was in evidence. For the intervening years there were generally more births than deaths, to be sure, but not many more. A close inspection of the village's social and economic development between 1538 and 1625 shows that Terling's experience proved to be a precocious variant of the national pattern, anticipating many of the changes normally associated with the eighteenth century. The polarized, hierarchical society of a squire, a few farmers, and a mass of laborers was created.

Terling is located in central Essex about 35 miles from London. The rolling countryside of central Essex was largely enclosed by the time of the accession of Elizabeth I. Even in the late sixteenth century the land was worked in large units. Felix Hull, who studied the agricultural economy of Essex during this period, found that in a sample of 13 Essex manors 8.7% of the tenants, those with holdings of over 50 acres, worked 60.9% of the land. On the other hand, nearly 40% of these manorial tenants held fewer than five acres, and they almost certainly had to work for wages (for some time during the year) to supplement the inadequate produce of their farms. Moreover, these figures leave out of consideration the landless laborers who made up a not inconsiderable proportion of the rural population. In concluding his discussion of late sixteenth and early seventeenth century agricultural society in Essex, Hull remarks that the precocious

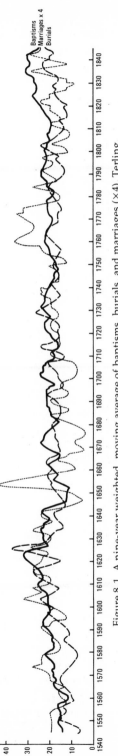

Figure 8.1. A nine-year weighted, moving average of baptisms, burials, and marriages (×4), Terling.

modernity of the county's rural economy was to be found "in the arrangement of farms and holdings [rather] than in actual methods of tillage or crops grown."[1]

In the half-century following the Restoration the polarization already evident in this rural community became even more solidly entrenched. In the upper reaches, among the nobility and squirearchy, the personnel changed with startling rapidity, but the structure went from strength to strength.[2] Farm size grew as did the proportion of the population dependent upon wage labor. By the end of the eighteenth century the average size of a tenanted holding (excluding those of fewer than 10 acres) was 136 acres.[3] Farms of this size employed wage labor, often on a considerable scale.

Recent work in agrarian history has pointed out the rapid diffusion of technical innovation among farmers in the 1650–1750 period. Essex was not untouched by these developments. The heavy clay soil made convertible husbandry based on a rotation utilizing such nitrogen fixing legumes as turnips impractical. In Essex the new husbandry was based on clover and other "foreign grasses" and "where once improved pasture had been established . . . the agrarian pattern so determined has persisted until the present day."[4]

In Essex the disappearance of the peasantry and their replacement by a few large tenant farmers employing wage laborers was essentially a sixteenth century phenomenon. In Terling the countywide pattern repeated itself without deviation. The 1524 subsidy depicts a village community composed mainly of middling peasants with a smaller number of laborers and landless men. Of particular importance, however, is that those at the bottom seem to have been the younger sons and brothers of the middling peasantry. Thus, in the early sixteenth century, landlessness and poverty appear to have been a phase in some life cycles rather than a permanent

---

[1] F. Hull, "Agriculture and Rural Society in Essex, 1560–1640," pp. 81–82, 518.

[2] C. Shrimpton, "Landed Society and the Farming Community in Essex in the Late 18th and Early 19th Centuries." Shrimpton notes that "So frequent had been the changes among the landowners of Essex in the seventeenth century and the first half of the eighteenth that by the time of the War of American Independence only a handful of families remained who had been established landowners before the century commenced" (p. 49). The Strutts of Terling, the present lords of the manor, date their rise from the middle of the eighteenth century. Another Cambridge doctoral dissertation, by C. Clay, describes the way in which two families clawed their way into the position of wealthy, secure landowners through marriage and astute purchases. (C. Clay, "Two Families and their Estates: the Grimstons and the Cowpers from c.1670 to c.1815.") The success of these families was all the more remarkable because it occurred in a period of concentration of landownership during which the smaller gentry "suffered badly from the adverse agricultural conditions that occupied much of the century 1660–1760, and from the heavy taxation levied during the wars against Louis XLV" (p. 455).

[3] C. Shrimpton, "Landed Society and the Farming Community," pp. 363–364.

[4] K.H Burley, "The Economic Development of Essex in the Later Seventeenth and Early Eighteenth Centuries," p. 24.

condition.[5] As already mentioned, the village population appears to have grown rapidly during the later sixteenth century. As a consequence of this phenomenon the bottom of the social pyramid filled up, and the traditional pattern of generational social mobility and self-improvement received a mortal blow from the agrarian crisis of the later 1590s. The smaller peasants, husbandmen, and cottagers found it increasingly difficult to pay their rents—their wills show severe indebtedness. A 1597 survey of the main manor of Terling shows unmistakably that the process of farm consolidation was well advanced.[6] One social consequence of this economic polarization was the emergence of a self-conscious and self-righteous yeoman elite which attacked the traditional cultural and recreational activities. Alehouses were severely regulated, feasting and gaming were proscribed, and church attendance was scrupulously enforced. The forces of puritanism and agrarian capitalism vigorously rooted out all traces of idolatry and sloth.[7]

> The puritan doctrine of thrift, self-denial, and trust in providence met the psychological needs of the small householder struggling against proletarianization. At the same time, puritanism offered a program of social reform, through the suppression of idleness and debauchery, and the provision of systematic relief for the impotent poor. The Essex sources suggest that puritan measures were largely responsible for the development of parochial machinery of poor relief.[8]

In Terling, through the use (and abuse) of parochial and charitable funds, the village elite extended their control over the lives of the villagers. "Badging" the poor was initially practiced in Terling as early as 1626 in accordance with the terms of a charity set up by a village yeoman who expressly provided that its funds should be disbursed only to the obedient and subservient. All those who frequented alehouses, blasphemed notoriously, or regularly broke the sabbath were formally excluded from consideration. Thus, the increasing rigidity of village social structure found expression in ever stricter regulation of the behavior of village laborers. In a face-to-face community the economic masters and social superiors extended their hegemony over both the work and the leisure of their poorer, subservient neighbors.

The emergence of a form of economic and social stability was largely completed by 1636, and the Ship Money assessment for that year shows

---

[5] A similar situation for sixteenth century Cambridgeshire was reported by Margaret Spufford in her recent book, *Contrasting Communities* (1975).

[6] A photograph of this survey is held at the Essex Record Office. The original is in private hands. The village's yeomen farmers were involved in the bulk supply of both local and distant markets. (Essex Record Office, Assize Calendar, Asz 35/17/2/55; Q/SR 304/157, 322/106.)

[7] This issue is discussed at some length in K. Wrightson and D. Levine, "The Social Context of Illegitimacy in Early Modern England."

[8] W.A. Hunt, "The Godly and the Vulgar: Puritanism and Social Change in Seventeenth Century Essex, England," pp. 3–4.

that roughly half the villagers were excused from payment on account of their poverty.[9] It is an interesting result of this social stabilization that an increased proportion of the men entering observation in the family reconstitution study after 1625 were natives of Terling. Before 1625, the proportion of natives was just below one in six, but after 1625 it hovered around the level of one in four. This new rate of persistence continued until the end of the eighteenth century when it rose dramatically from 27.5% before 1775 to 43.3% afterwards. For women there was also a long-term movement toward higher rates of persistence. This development, however, was not nearly so pronounced, and the bulk of the observable rise was confined to the period after 1775. Indeed, during the later seventeenth century the women of Terling were more, not less, likely to be nonnative.

Terling's precocious modernity, then, was fully evident by the early seventeenth century. How were these economic and social developments reflected in the demographic behavior of the villagers? In a review of the descriptive statistics on nuptiality, fertility, and mortality, the most striking information to emerge from the family reconstitution study concerns the relative youth at which men and women married. (See Tables 8.2, 8.3, 8.4, and 8.5 at the end of this chapter.) Compounding the importance of this finding is the fact that throughout the whole period under observation age at first marriage for both men and women remained comparatively stable. In Terling, women and men marrying after 1775 were about two years younger than their Elizabethan and early Stuart predecessors. The trend in the intervening years was toward earlier marriage. I did not find a rise in age at marriage of any appreciable dimensions in either the later seventeenth century or the first three-quarters of the eighteenth century. Thus, the marriage pattern in Terling was quite different from those of Bottesford and Colyton where the age of brides rose after 1650. I argue above that the rising age at marriage in these villages can be explained in terms of the nature of the local demand for labor. The proletarianization of the peasantry in Terling, however, and the increasing integration of the village's agricultural economy into the London food market had quite different repercussions. There was no need to postpone marriage in order to amass the capital needed to stock a peasant farm because the possibility of doing so became increasingly remote. In these circumstances early marriage was "rational" since one reached prime earning capacity at an early age. Equally, an incentive to restrict fertility would be undermined because the problem of succession and inheritance became a nonissue.

Another factor leading to early marriage in Terling was the high level of adult mortality prevailing before 1775. In a small, closed community the supply of labor would be relatively stable, particularly if, as in Terling, life

---

[9] The 1636 Ship Money Assessment is reprinted in C.A. Barton, *Historical Notes and Records of the Parish of Terling, Essex* (1953) Appendix III.

expectancy at the mean age at child bearing was roughly equal to age at marriage. If, as I am positing, there was a "replacement phenomenon" in this proletarianized community, each generation succeeding its predecessor and waiting to marry until a vacancy occurred, the crucial factor in establishing a demographic regime would be the role played by the Settlement Laws which artificially controlled the local supply of labor. The parish officers were empowered to strike their own balance between, on the one hand, a large supply and high poor rates and, on the other, a restricted supply and low poor rates. Under the second alternative, surplus laborers would be forced out, either to look for settlements elsewhere in their native locale or to drift toward the urban centers, particularly London whose appetite for new immigrants was insatiable.[10] It could be argued that the increasing stability in the number of the adult male villagers found in the study goes some way toward supporting this hypothesis.

Why, then, did the age at marriage for men and women not rise in the period after 1775 when the life expectancy of adults showed signs of significant improvement? An answer to this question may lie in the increase in the local supply of labor suggested by the increasing number of resident families found between 1801 and 1851. This increased labor supply was itself occasioned by a rising demand for foodstuffs generally, improvements in agrarian technology that made farming more labor intensive, and improvements in the transportation system that resulted from such endeavors as building canals and turnpikes and facilitated the movement of bulky goods. In effect, the demand curve moved to the right and, as a result, the point at which it intersected the supply curve rose. Temporarily, between 1780 and 1850, Terling and many other villages in rural England experienced substantial population growth. This boom came to an end in the middle years of the nineteenth century when the adoption of labor-saving devices improved the efficiency of agricultural laborers to such an extent that demand first became stable and then began to contract. Terling, like many other villages in rural England, had a larger population in the middle of the nineteenth century than at any other time before or after.

If, as I have argued, a calculating approach to reproductive behavior in Terling was undermined by the proletarianization of the populace, then we should expect to find the later sixteenth century rate of growth carried over into the following era, albeit with rather different results after the size of the village community came under the control of parish officials.

If we use an interaction formula like the one I have proposed, we can see how village populations effectively controlled their reproductive powers

---

[10] E.A. Wrigley, "A Simple Model of London's Importance in Changing English Society and Economy 1650–1750."

with explicit reference to their life expectancies. During the first three periods under review (1550–1624, 1625–1699, and 1770–1774), there was a substantially lower level of reproduction and generational replacement in Terling than in the last period (1775–1851). The fact that the actual size of Terling remained stable for the century and a half between 1625 and 1775 underlines the roles played by the Settlement Laws and the parochial officials in restricting the village labor supply. The picture derived from the reconstituted data is rather different from that yielded by the aggregate statistics. In particular, the convergence of the annual totals of baptisms and burials in the early seventeenth century is cast in a different light. This difference arises because the two forms of measurement are considering dissimilar phenomena. The reconstituted data yield statistics based on the cumulative experience of individuals, but the aggregate figures tell us what happened at the village level, but in undifferentiated terms. The added precision gained from the reconstitution study enables us to modify or extend the hypotheses advanced from a consideration of the simple annual totals of births and deaths. The demographic stabilization of early seventeenth century can now be seen as a nonoccurrence. Instead of regarding this phenomenon in purely demographic terms, we see clearly that the crucial factor was the willingness of parochial officials to use their power to control the local supply of labor. Abetted by the Settlement Laws and the parochial machinery of poor relief, local officials controlled the village size in such a way that surviving children in excess of the replacement level had to find their niches elsewhere, and immigration became more difficult. Social stabilization, not a demographic turnabout, explains the convergence of the annual totals of baptisms and burials in early seventeenth century Terling.

TABLE 8.1
Net Rate of Reproduction, Terling

	1550–1624	1625–1699	1700–1774	1775–1851
GRR	5.09	4.88	5.58	6.73
Revised GRR	4.11	3.76	4.27	5.95
Child survival rate	.701	.705	.715	.710
Children surviving	2.88	2.65	3.05	4.22
Incidence of marriage	.910	.924	.920	.940
Children marrying	2.62	2.45	2.81	3.97
NRR	1.31	1.225	1.405	1.985
Generation	31.9	30.4	30.7	31.5
Annual rate of growth	0.86%	0.67%	1.12%	2.20%
Years for population to double	81.4	104.5	62.5	31.8
Age at marriage	24.5	23.8	24.0	23.0

TABLE 8.2
Age at First Marriage, Terling

	N	Mean	Standard deviation	Lower quartile	Median	Upper quartile	Inter-quartile range
Men							
1550–1624	42	25.9	3.9	23.2	25.0	28.8	5.6
1625–1699	56	25.2	5.4	22.0	24.4	27.3	5.3
1700–1774	78	24.7	4.4	21.0	24.0	27.5	6.0
1775–1851	159	25.7	6.3	21.5	23.9	26.9	5.4
Women							
1550–1624	88	24.5	4.3	21.5	23.8	26.9	5.4
1625–1699	66	23.8	4.9	19.7	23.0	27.2	7.5
1700–1774	113	24.0	4.8	20.5	23.1	27.0	6.5
1775–1851	179	23.0	5.0	19.4	21.9	25.0	5.6

From the calculations of the net rate of reproduction in Terling it is clear
that the period after 1775 marks a distinct break with the past. Age at
marriage fell and fertility rose while infant and child mortality levels
remained stable. An explanation for this phenomenon can be discovered
in the workings of the Old Poor Law which granted families aid in relation
to their numbers of dependents. In this way the incentive to restrict
fertility was undermined. Evidence supporting this argument can be
found in the family reconstitution study. Although age at first marriage for
women was a full year earlier for the post-1775 cohort, these women had
significantly higher rates of fertility in their 40s than did the pre-1775

TABLE 8.3
Age-Specific Fertility, Terling

	Years at risk	Children born	Rate/000
1550–1624			
Under 25	82	35	427
25–29	110	35	318
30–34	121	32	267
35–39	98	25	258
40–44	81	11	136
45–49	60	0	0
1625–1699			
Under 25	106	40	377
25–29	130	40	305
30–34	139	39	281
35–39	121	27	223
40–44	92	7	76
45–49	55	0	0
1700–1744			
Under 25	172	71	413
25–29	193	70	363
30–34	176	53	299
35–39	156	41	263
40–44	110	12	109
45–49	94	0	0
1775–1851			
Under 25	380	156	411
25–29	436	164	376
30–34	403	130	323
35–39	350	97	277
40–44	298	53	178
45–49	246	7	28

cohort. Moreover, the improvement in adult life expectancy meant that after 1775 there were even more women conforming to this pattern of unregulated fertility. In conditions of demographic equilibrium a lowering of the age at first marriage should, *ceteris paribus*, be balanced by a decline in marital fertility. In later eighteenth and early nineteenth century Terling such a balance was not achieved. The pauperization of the labor force undermined the rationale for deliberate fertility control. In summary, then, the reconstituted information from my study of Terling lends impressive support to the Malthusian argument by showing the great reserve of "prolific power" that was unleashed when traditional social norms, prudential checks on reproduction, were rendered obsolete.

TABLE 8.4
Infant and Child Mortality (MF), Terling

Cohort	Age	Reconstitution				Ledermann		
		At risk	Dying	Rate/000	Survivors	e^0	Rate/000	Survivors
1550–1624	0–1	1059	136	128	1000		137	1000
	1–4	665	48	72	872	46.61	95	863
	5–9	388	14	36	809	(p. 90)	27	781
	10–14	241	10	41	780		19	760
					750			746
1625–1699	0–1	1021	127	124	1000		137	1000
	1–4	684	72	105	876	46.61	95	863
	5–9	413	15	36	784	(p. 90)	27	781
	10–14	271	2	7	756		19	760
					751			746
1700–1774	0–1	1163	172	148	1000		146	1000
	1–4	814	61	75	852	46.38	82	853
	5–9	564	17	30	788		24	783
	10–14	424	11	26	764	(p. 115)	15	764
					744			753
1839–1844	0–1			143	1000		137	1000
	1–4			95	857	46.61	95	863
	5–9			40	776	(p. 90)	27	781
	10–14			30	745		19	760
					723			746

Infant and child mortality rates for the 1839–1844 cohort were not derived from the reconstitution study because of the decline in the comprehensiveness of parochial registration of infant burials. Rather, these rates were calculated from the information presented in the "Eighth Annual Report of the Registrar General." (*P.P.*, 1847–48, xxv) which described the experience of Witham hundred within which Terling is centrally located.
e^0 means life expectancy at birth.

TABLE 8.5
Adult Mortality (MF), Terling

	1575–1624	1625–1699	1700–1774	1775–1851
	Part 1.	Life expectancy at various ages		
25	28.9	28.5	31.9	40.6
30	25.7	25.5	30.0	36.8
35	22.9	23.1	26.9	33.6
40	20.6	20.1	23.9	30.0
45	18.2	17.3	22.1	26.1
50	15.7	14.7	18.8	22.5
55	12.9	13.6	16.0	18.0
60	10.5	11.8	14.3	14.4
65	9.4	11.1	11.7	10.8
70	7.1	9.2	8.8	7.7
75	6.5	6.1	7.1	5.9
80	5.2	5.3	5.5	4.9
85+	3.4	3.4	3.7	3.8
	Part 2.	Survivors at various ages		
25	1000	1000	1000	1000
30	934	928	904	966
35	854	835	847	919
40	753	759	782	878
45	661	676	683	844
50	569	582	627	799
55	487	445	553	779
60	394	346	443	715
65	263	233	369	640
70	186	169	300	518
75	95	130	196	321
80	51	63	113	147
85+	23	28	55	58

9

ILLEGITIMACY: MARRIAGE FRUSTRATED, NOT PROMISCUITY RAMPANT

So far I have discussed the relationship between economic opportunity and family formation without much more than a nod in the direction of premarital sexual activity. To rectify that lapse, in this chapter I consider the relationships among the expectation of marriage, bridal pregnancy, and illegitimacy. It is my contention that premarital sexual activity was governed by the same norms that informed traditional courtship behavior and must be understood in that context. Illegitimacy can be regarded as an unfortunate outcome of the sexual anticipation of marriage. Such anticipation was not confined to a small section of the community but was widespread. From this perspective we can regard illegitimacy as marriage frustrated. Such frustration occurred when uncertainty intervened between courtship and marriage.

In a world we have lost, tradition forced upon most young men and women a period of enforced celibacy at the age when they were most virile or nubile. To the extent that the nuclear family household remained a social ideal, increasing premarital sexuality would not be expected, because the onset of sexual activity would be governed by the expectation of economic independence. The accumulation of enough capital to establish oneself as an independent householder demanded sexual continence because only when one had reached a modest level of economic independence did the possibility of marriage arise. The institutions of service and apprenticeship inhibited one's sexual activity while enabling one eventually to amass sufficient capital (or dowry) to marry.

It is significant that proletarianization reduced this period of enforced waiting. In protoindustry one did not have to wait for a position to become vacant because with this mode of production the number of productive units could be expanded virtually without limit. On the other hand, protoindustry was unpredictable in an altogether new way. Unlike a peasant or artisan whose horizons were both narrow and short, the framework knitter was unable to gauge the local demand for his labor, a demand determined in impersonal and distant markets. Furthermore, the local labor supply was also free of control in that rural industrial villages like Shepshed were usually characterized by weak or nonexistent parochial governments. The demographic importance of these factors is obvious—the decision to marry was made under conditions beyond the betrothed couple's control and/or understanding. Increasing uncertainty would lead to rising levels of illegitimacy.

The position of agricultural laborers, as distinct from those of either peasants or industrial proletarians, was rather more ambivalent. Lack of capital distinguished the agricultural laborer from the peasant, while the nature and conditions of his employment made his social milieu significantly different from that of the industrial worker. Social control and labor discipline were more immediate in an agricultural community than in a protoindustrial village. Moreover, the nature of this social control was such that it governed the local supply of labor. In these circumstances the agricultural laborer's marital decision would not be clouded with the kind of uncertainty that bedeviled the worker in protoindustry. Although the demand for agricultural labor was determined by markets outside the village, the disorganizing effect of this factor was muted because the demand for food, unlike the demand for manufactured products, was relatively inelastic. Thus, for the agricultural laborer the critical independent variable influencing his decision to marry was the harvest. And, in much the same way as the "fantastical folly of fashion" could influence the lives of protoindustrial workers, the weather and the price of grain could intervene in the lives of agricultural laborers.

In the histories of our four villages several phenomena merit attention: the dramatic decline in bastardy in seventeenth century Terling and Bottesford; the rather perverse pattern found in Colyton where the ratio of illegitimate births was higher during the early eighteenth century than either before or afterward; and the fact that the incidence of illegitimacy in Shepshed during the protoindustrial period was almost double that encountered in the three agricultural villages. In this chapter I attempt to explain these variations in terms of a hypothesis linking economic opportunity, family formation, and the sexual anticipation of marriage. Of critical importance is the way social and economic uncertainty intervened between courtship and marriage to frustrate careful planning.

The steep decline in illegitimacy in early seventeenth century Terling occurred within the context of the restructuring of social relationships in the village community.[1] A close examination of the individual cases of illegitimacy at the turn of the seventeenth century reveals that a substantial number resulted from the perpetuation of outdated forms of behavior in a period of adversity. As already described, the sixteenth century in Terling saw the village become socially stratified and economically differentiated. In effect, the peasantry were superseded by tenant farmers and agricultural laborers. At the end of the sixteenth century a series of disastrous harvests reduced the small peasants and laborers to penury. In these circumstances a traditional marriage portion, or dowry, could not easily be accumulated, and engagements were protracted. The sexual dimension of courtship persisted. Not surprisingly, as many as one-third of betrothed women were pregnant at marriage. Others bore illegitimate children.

Many of the bastardbearers could not be identified within the village community. These women were probably servants whose sojourns in Terling were brief. Others, when questioned in the civil and/or ecclesiastical courts, often explained that while they had planned to be married, the hard-times had forced them to postpone the nuptials. Indeed, a number of these bastardbearers later married their children's fathers. Statistical evidence from the family reconstitution study underlines this phenomenon. The fact that unwed mothers in this period were several years older than women who bore their first children within marriage indicates that they were postponing marriage.[2] Moreover, it can be inferred from the observation that so many brides were pregnant that sexual intercourse was a common feature of courtship in this village in Elizabethan and Jacobean times.

The decline in illegitimacy in later seventeenth century Terling has been ascribed to the vigourous supervision and discipline the emerging class of tenant farmers and minor gentry imposed upon their laborers. The social and economic developments of the sixteenth century had replaced an undifferentiated community with one redolent of the stark disparities that

---

[1] A detailed account of the milieu within which illegitimacy flourished in Terling is presented in K. Wrightson and D. Levine, "The Social Context of Illegitimacy in Early Modern England." What follows is, in part, a condensation of that argument and, in part, a development. I should like to take this opportunity to note the debt I owe to Keith Wrightson who has been of great help in every way since I began this research at Cambridge.

[2] Seventeen women who bore illegitimate children between 1575 and 1624 had a (mean) average age of 27.6 years. In contrast, the 77 local brides who married in the parish church were, on average, 24.3 years old.

reverberated in the political and religious credos of the self-proclaimed "better sort." Imbued with a belief in their own righteousness, these puritans set about dismantling the communal agencies of village life—the alehouses and festivities in particular. The Brueghelian world of the peasantry was attacked for its promotion of licentiousness, drunkenness, laziness, and ungodliness. Allied to this ideological opposition was the practical reality that illegitimate children posed a substantial cost to the local ratepayers.

The early boomlet of illegitimacy in Terling occurred at a time of crisis that developed when customary expectations and behavior were undermined by severe economic, social, and demographic disequilibrium. This crisis affected not only the village laborers but also their immediate social superiors, the smaller peasantry, whose dramatic downward mobility was intensified at this time. The problem was resolved by the emergence of a new form of social stability of which hierarchy and deference became the cornerstones. The ideological ramifications of this development were neatly articulated by the ways in which charity was dispensed. The poor had to seem grateful and worthy in order to qualify for consideration. They acquiesced because they had no other choice.

The incidence of illegitimacy in Terling never again approached the level prevailing between 1598 and 1605 when one child in ten was born out of wedlock. In the eighteenth century the level recovered from the intervening nadir, but this recovery was neither sharp nor precipitous. This recovery can, I think, be understood with reference to the increasing confidence and security enjoyed by the village notables and to an unforeseen result of the rigorous supervision of the village poor—their increased freedom from control.

The puritan attack on the disorderly culture of the village community, of which illegitimacy was but one element, occurred in a climate of religious and political unease. This disquiet was compounded by the fact that the disorderly villagers possessed a coherent, vibrant counterculture centering on the alehouse. In the early seventeenth century this counterculture was driven out of existence by a series of legislative onslaughts. An alehouse continued to exist in the village, but its activity was circumscribed by the parish vestry, the local privy council. The alehousekeeper kept his lucrative position only so long as he was able to maintain an orderly tavern which neither permitted drunkenness nor allowed excessive tippling.

In the course of the seventeenth century the village notables became increasingly secure in their positions of authority and grew ever more confident about the stability of their little political world. Security bred toleration, and activity that was not politically threatening was not brought before the official machinery of the law. In a climate of undisputed hegemony, coupled with waning reformist zeal, the authorities became more tolerant of the laboring class's leisure-time pursuits. Indeed, it has been suggested that by promoting some forms of communal recreation the upper class sought to sublimate potential dangers into harmless activities—harmless activities they themselves directed. National studies of this dimension of labor discipline suggest that the eighteenth century provided a respite from the attempts at moral reformation characteristic of Puritan and Victorian England.[3] Discussing this hiatus, E.P. Thompson has noted that in their studied and elaborate hegemonic style, the eighteenth century upper class maintained a high level of visibility that reinforced their position.

> A great part of politics and law is always theater; once a social system has become "set," it does not need to be endorsed daily by exhibitions of power (although occasional punctuations of force will be made to define the limits of the system's tolerance); what matters more is a continuing theatrical style. . . . The theater of the great depended not upon constant, day-to-day attention to responsibilities . . . but upon occasional dramatic interventions. . . . This social lubricant of gestures could only too easily make the mechanisms of power and exploitation revolve more sweetly. The poor, habituated to their irrevocable station, have been often made accessories . . . to their own oppression.[4]

Another way in which the development of economic, social, and political stability promoted greater freedom of action for the eighteenth century laborers was, I believe, largely unintended. The Settlement Laws empowered village officials to set their own balance between a large local supply of labor, low wages, and high poor rates or a restricted supply of labor, higher wages, and low poor rates. In Terling, as in most "closed" landlord-dominated villages, the second course of action was pursued. Rather than taxing themselves with high property assessments, the village officers chose to keep the local supply of labor closely in line with its demand. The effect of the Settlement Laws was to improve the economic position of the laborers by giving them the economic wherewithal to either oppose or ignore the studied application of local benevolence. In late eighteenth century Terling there were always men and women who chose to turn their backs upon the charitable fund because it demanded actions they found repugnant. For many, nonconformity provided an alternative to the hopelessly compromised Anglican Church. The parochial records make it quite clear that whatever their motivations, many of those eligible for charitable disbursements chose to forego this additional source of income.[5] In the seventeenth century such actions would have been far less likely because woolen coats or worsted dresses were more

---

[3] R. W. Malcolmson, *Popular Recreations in English Society, 1700–1850* (Cambridge: Cambridge Univ. Press 1973).

[4] E. P. Thompson, "Patrician Society, Plebian Culture," pp. 389–90.

[5] See, for example, the Terling Churchwarden's Accounts for the period 1780–1805 which include annual listings of those who were awarded a charitable disbursement as well as those who were refused. (E.R.O., D/P 299/5/1.)

valuable. Thus, unintentionally, the village laborers were afforded a "space" free from paternal domination.

In a sense, the sheer isolation of his position allowed the eighteenth century laborer rather more fredom of action than his seventeenth century predecessor. I have already argued that the undisputed hegemony of the eighteenth century propertied class freed the laborers from intrusive supervision of their lives. Courtship was, perhaps, one of the first aspects of their lives to be so affected. In these circumstances couples would again anticipate marriage by enjoying sexual relationships. The rate of bridal pregnancy would rise as would the incidence of illegitimacy now that, once more, unpredictable circumstances could intervene between courtship and marriage. Unpredictability would become more predictable, as it were, to the extent that the local economy was geared to a market outside its control.

Instability in the price of grain became a more pronounced feature of the English economy after 1750 than it had been in the first half of the century. Whenever there was a period of low grain prices, the incidence of illegitimacy in Terling fell. Conversely, during periods of high grain prices the ratio of illegitimate births rose. In the quarter-century between 1760 and 1784, 24 of the 503 children baptized in Terling were illegitimate. During this period there were 11 hungry years.[6] During these years, 6.4% of all births were illegitimate; during the 14 normal harvest years, 3.6% of children were born out of wedlock. From these figures it appears that the laborers of Terling were affected by the state of the harvest more as consumers than as producers. This was to be expected inasmuch as their wages were more or less fixed and the regularity (or semiregularity) of employment was guaranteed by the manipulations of the local labor market permitted by the Settlement Laws.

The relationship between the harvest and illegitimacy changed in the later eighteenth century as the practice of supplementing the income of the village poor become common. Recent research has shown that this practice developed during the Napoleonic Wars in response to recurrent harvest failures.[7] The immediate, deleterious effects of the wage-price scissors were averted, but the institutionalization of this form of relief had the unforeseen result of pauperizing the village laborers by forcing wages down to the subsistence level. It is a matter of controversy whether the Speenhamland system of subsidizing wages from poor law funds was the cause or the consequence of the pauperization of the rural labor force.[8]

---

[6] I am basing this distinction between normal and hungry years on T.S. Ashton's account (*Economic Fluctuations in England, 1700–1800*, p. 36) which was itself derived from the monthly figures in *Gentleman's Magazine*. The hungry years were 1767–69, 1772–75, and 1780–83.

[7] D. A. Baugh, "The Cost of Poor Relief in South-East England, 1790–1834."

[8] Baugh, for instance, argues that the Speenhamland system should be seen as the

No one, however, seriously questions that agricultural laborers suffered severe economic hardship. The subsistence level was itself defined by the parochial officers cum farmers who employed the laborers to work their land. Although this cushioned village laborers from the vagaries of the harvest, it tied them ever tighter to their place of settlement.

The Speenhamland system of poor relief, which subsidized wages out of local taxes, acted in combination with the laws of settlement to produce an underpaid, stable, largely demoralized, and pauperized rural labor force. In this respect it can be argued that the system reinforced the connection between economic opportunity and family formation in an entirely unexpected and unwanted way. Earning their maximum wages at an early age, hoping for no improvement, cushioned from the fluctuations of bread prices, and tied to the parish of their settlement, laborers completely lost the *disincentive* to early marriage. Secure in the knowledge that subsistence would be provided, young couples no longer responded to the material considerations that had previously inhibited marriage. Moreover, the very "security" of their pauperized state may have led to far greater premarital sexual activity. The upshot of this change in the agricultural laborers' socioeconomic situation was that, although their real wages deteriorated and bread prices fluctuated ever more wildly, their level of illegitimacy did not rise. Instead, the incidence of bridal pregnancy jumped. In late eighteenth century Terling 23% (24/105) of all brides were pregnant, in the early nineteenth century the figure was 47% (25/53).

The pauperized state of agricultural laborers did not persist until the end of our period. It was attacked root and branch by the Poor Law Amendment Act of 1834. The intention of this legislation was to render labor relations subject to the law of supply and demand, with no intervening agencies to interfere with its self-regulating mechanisms. It was expected that sheer poverty and lack of employment would lead to the redeployment of labor away from agriculture and into the towns. The rural labor force would be depleted, and wages would consequently reach their "natural level." It was hoped that rural poverty, underemployment, and demoralization would be relieved after a short period of adjustment. Unfortunately, the period of adjustment was neither short nor easy. The 1834 Poor Law Amendment Act, however, significantly changed conditions of rural employment. With wages no longer subsidized laborers began to scramble for available employment, and underemployment gave way to unemployment. This change was reflected in sexual behavior—

"scapegoat" of the New Poor Law Commission. He states that "the Speenhamland system did not matter much at any time, either during and after the war. What mattered was the shape of the poverty problem, and that shape changed" ("The Cost of Poor Relief," p. 67). A contrary viewpoint, which was presented by K. Polanyi (*The Great Transformation*, pp. 75–83), has received the enthusiastic support of E. J. Hobsbawm and Georges Rudé (*Captain Swing*, pp. 27–31).

people continued to anticipate marriage but its economic underpinnings were no longer so steady.[9] Before 1835, 2.4% (24/1001) of all recorded births were illegitimate; after 1840, the figure was 5.2% (10/191). Evidence from the family reconstitution study shows that the women who bore illegitimate children in the 1840s were just over one year younger than those who married, often with child. The (mean) average age of the eight unmarried mothers whose baptism dates could be traced was 19.4. The figure for brides in Terling in the 1840s was 20.7. Marriage frustrated rather than promiscuity rampant? Certainly this suggestion receives strong backing when these women's predicaments are viewed in the context of a bridal pregnancy rate of almost 50%.

Illegitimacy and bridal pregnancy in Bottesford described a pattern similar to that found in Terling: an early period of high illegitimacy and bridal pregnancy was succeeded by a century in which these phenomena were at markedly lower levels, and then, after 1750, both again rose. The explanation for this similarity of experience can be found, I think, in the remarkable similarity of development in the two villages: both grew rapidly in the later sixteenth century, experienced turmoil and then stabilization in the early years of the seventeenth, and from that time forward had stable, secure sociopolitical complexions.[10] Of course, the outside world was not sealed out—neither village was hermetically protected from national trends. In both villages the fluctuation of grain prices after 1750 introduced a new element of instability into the life of the laboring class. In both villages the practices of subsidizing wages and restricting settlement were common and, consequently, the shock of the 1834 Poor Law Amendment Act was severe. In Bottesford the incidence of

---

[9] In a study of the application of the New Poor Law in East Anglia, Anne Digby noted that it was the young, presumably unmarried, who were hardest hit by the changes in the machinery of poor relief. They had to spend the winter in the workhouse. Family men were relieved at home. She states that "the smouldering resentment of the labourers against the farmers who controlled both wages and poor relief flared into active hostility in the rural incendiarism in East Anglia in 1843–4. Many of the incendiarists brought to trial were young men who belonged to the groups with the lowest agricultural wages, the most irregular employment, and the greatest chance of spending the winter months in the workhouse." (A. Digby, "The Labour Market and the Continuity of Social Policy after 1834: The Case of the Eastern Counties," p. 80.)

[10] That turmoil was rife in early seventeenth century Bottesford can be adduced from the fact that this community was shaken by a witchcraft trial involving elements of every social grouping in the village. Recent studies have familiarized us with the seething underworld of the early seventeenth century village community. In his study of witchcraft in Tudor and Stuart Essex, Alan Macfarlane argues that tensions which came to the attention of the courts usually involved the breakdown of communal agencies in times of stress (A. Macfarlane, *Witchcraft in Tudor and Stuart England*). It might not be presumptuous to infer that the Bottesford witchcraft trial was used as a political test case in which charge and countercharge were likely to have been indicative of other, deeper and more generalized antagonisms. The case was resolved when a poor, transient woman was executed after being convicted of practising black magic and directing her malice against the resident nobles, the high and mighty Manners family. (See K. Thomas, *Religion and the Decline of Magic*, pp. 514, 557.)

illegitimacy was higher in the later eighteenth century (3.5%) than in the early nineteenth. In Bottesford, as in Terling, the incidence of illegitimacy jumped after the introduction of the New Poor Law—its incidence was 3.1% before 1835 but 6.4% after 1840.

The incidence of sexual delinquency in Colyton was quite unlike that found in either Terling or Bottesford. With reference to what we know about national trends in illegitimacy, Colyton's experience after 1700 was exceptional. Laslett and Oosterveen found in their national sample that there was an early boomlet in illegitimacy in the late sixteenth and early seventeenth centuries followed by a century in which the level of bastardy was substantially lower. Then, from the middle of the eighteenth century, an upsurge occurred and the earlier level was recovered.[11] In Colyton, the path of illegitimacy between 1561 and 1680 followed the national trend, but thereafter the two separated. The bastardy level in Colyton began rising in the fourth quarter of the seventeenth century and went up more or less continuously until the 1740s, after which it started to decline, slowly and hesistantly at first. By the early nineteenth century, however, the incidence of bastardy was about 50% of what it had been a century earlier. That illegitimacy became three and one-half times more common in the half century after 1700 than in the 50 years before calls for an explanation. Furthermore, the decline in the ratio of illegitimate births after 1750 is also worthy of some comment. Trends in premarital sexuality in Colyton should be discussed with reference to the socioeconomic environment within which they occurred. By linking the course of illegitimacy in Colyton to the shifting structure of industry and agriculture and by further considering the contemporaneous levels of bridal pregnancy and age at marriage, we can begin to explain some of these observable variations.

In the early seventeenth century Colyton, like Terling and Bottesford, underwent a shift in the pattern of premarital sexuality: illegitimacy became less frequent and bridal pregnancy rates almost halved. We saw that a similar phenomenon occurred in Terling under conditions of political, social, and economic stabilization. A new form of equilibrium was established. In Bottesford a readjustment also occurred in an environment of local political tension and socioeconomic realignment. A similar explanation, stressing social disequilibrium and the emergence of a new form of stability, can be advanced in discussing the restriction of premarital sexual activity in Colyton in the early seventeenth century.

The transformation of the woolen industry in the west country made itself felt at the individual level in Colyton by influencing the factors affecting the expectation of marriage among a substantial section of the

---

[11] P. Laslett and K. Oosterveen, "Long-Term Trends in Bastardy in England." I would like to acknowledge Miss Oosterveen's generosity in allowing me to use her material on the bastardbearers in Colyton. Tables 9.1, 9.2, and 9.3 are based wholly on her researches.

village population. As the "New Draperies" became established, the relocation of weaving reduced the possibility of supporting a family with the *combined* income from agriculture and industry. For this reason the expectation of marriage would be deferred, marriage itself postponed. The sexual anticipation of marriage would not arise. As the reorganization of the Devonshire cloth industry progressed, leaving Colyton high and dry, many young people deferred marriage or, more commonly, left the village to find better prospects elsewhere. After 1610 many potential marriages were frustrated, and young men and women were forced to move elsewhere to find an economic environment in which they could marry and raise families within their modest expectations.[12] Such a period of constriction hit the poor hardest—those who relied on by-employment to supplement the meager livings they derived from their small holdings. For many, the deindustrialization outlined in Chapter 7 removed the essential prop from their fragile household economies. Those who remained adjusted their behavior to meet their straitened circumstances.

For women the situation was rather different, they were able to replace one kind of by-employment, spinning, with another, lacemaking. In this way they may even have gained a degree of independence from male-dominated household economies. I argued earlier that the rising age at marriage for women which accompanied deindustrialization should be viewed in terms of changing marital strategies. The age of brides increased after 1650, but the age of unwed mothers did not. Although our sample is regretably small, some similarities can be found in the patterns of the age at marriage and of the age of unwed mothers. The rise in the age of unwed mothers, however, was not nearly so great as that in the age of brides. Unlike unwed mothers in Terling and other seventeenth century English communities, these bastardbearers were younger than women who married. Moreover, in Colyton the age gap increased in the later seventeenth century so that unwed mothers of that time were 3.6 years younger than brides. After 1700 this gap progressively narrowed, so that by the first half of the nineteenth century brides were only 0.8 years older

---

[12] This suggestion is supported by a brief consideration of the long-term trend in the annual totals of marriages celebrated in Colyton. From an annual average of about seven or eight per year in the 1560s, the curve moves upwards until it peaks in about 1610 when there was an average of about 18 marriages per year in the village. From 1610 the trend moves downwards, slowly at first, but then with an abrupt decline in the mid 1640s, after which it persists at a substantially lower level. The period that is of greatest interest from our present point of view is the early years of the seventeenth century when a long-term upwards trend was reversed. In many ways the absolute levels do not accurately reflect this demographic turnaround, because they do not take into account the number of marriages that one would expect to occur if the long-term trend persisted. When a population is rapidly growing, the base of its age pyramid expands, and the size of each succeeding cohort is substantially larger. The implication of this phenomenon for our discussion of Colyton in the early seventeenth century is that, not only was 1610 the absolute end of the period of expansion, it was, to a much greater extent, the relative end.

TABLE 9.1
Mean Age at First Marriage and at Bastardbearing, Colyton

Brides			Unwed mothers	
N	Age		Age	N
124	26.9	1550–99	24.9	15
199	27.3	1600–49	26.2	25
89	29.4	1650–99	25.8	13
67	28.7	1700–49	26.1	32
110	26.2	1750–99	24.9	34
141	23.9	1800–49	23.1	30

than unwed mothers. The movements of the (mean) age at first marriage and the (mean) age of bastardbearing are presented in Table 9.1.

One of the most interesting comments in Laslett and Oosterveen's essay is the suggestion that repetitive bastardbearing became more common in times of high illegitimacy ratios.[13] Although they give some information regarding this phenomenon in Colyton, they select cohort groups structured to lend support to their overall arguments. Reorganizing these data in such a way that they correspond to the secular trend in Colyton's illegitimacy curve yields some interesting results. In particular, the high tide of bastardy in early eighteenth century Colyton is quite apparent, and yet both the proportion of all illegitimates born to repetitive bastardbearers and the proportion of such "repeaters" rose even more dramatically. See Tables 9.2 and 9.3.

These phenomena—rising levels of illegitimacy and increasing rates of repetitive bastardbearing—are closely linked with the changes in Colyton's socioeconomic complexion that took place at the end of the seventeenth century. More particularly, I contend that these phenomena must be seen in the context of an increase in independent *women's work*. The spread of lacemaking in Colyton was probably crucially important in freeing women from the strict confines of family economies. It gave them a form of independence that enabled them to amass dowries more quickly and, therefore, at earlier ages than their mothers had. In this way the spread of this female-oriented handicraft reduced the *disincentive* to early courtship and early marriage. And, just as surely, it increased the expectation of marriage on the part of women while, at the same time, not doing so for their prospective husbands.

This peculiar, somewhat contradictory state of affairs seems to have receded in the course of the eighteenth century, and yet the incidence of illegitimacy still remained relatively high and repetitive bastardbearing persisted. To explain this continuity an essentially different set of argu-

---

[13] P. Laslett and K. Oosterveen, "Long-Term Trends in Bastardy in England," pp. 282, 284.

TABLE 9.2
Repetitive Bastardbearing, Colyton, by Children

	All bastards	Children of "repeaters"	%
1540–1589	54	19	35.2
1590–1639	90	20	22.2
1640–1689	49	2	4.1
1690–1739	112	45	40.0
1740–1789	125	55	44.0
1790–1839	118	34	28.8

ments can tentatively be advanced. The persistence of high levels of illegitimacy may have been related to increasing uncertainties about the harvests, as was the case in Terling. The perpetuation of repetitive bastardbearing may have been connected with the stricter enforcement of the Settlement Laws which made it more difficult for bastardbearers to be shunted from village to village by anxious ratepayers.

After 1790 the incidence of illegitimacy fell as did the role played by repetitive bastardbearers, not only in Colyton but also in Terling and Bottesford. As I have argued, this decline may be related to the application of the Old Poor Law which tended to remove the element of uncertainty that often intervened between courtship and marriage. In Colyton, as in Terling and Bottesford, the incidence of bridal pregnancy was markedly higher in the early nineteenth century than before. In Colyton after 1800, 43.1% of brides were pregnant, an increase from 32.8% in the later eighteenth century. Although in Terling and Bottesford the years after the introduction of the New Poor Law witnessed a doubling in the illegitimacy ratio, in Colyton this did not occur. Indeed, the illegitimacy ratio in the early 1840s, 2.1%, was less than half what it had been in the days of the Old Poor Law.

In their article on illegitimacy, Laslett and Oosterveen do not draw the reader's attention to the many ways in which Colyton's experiences di-

TABLE 9.3
Repetitive Bastardbearing, Colyton, by Mothers

	All unwed mothers	Bearing more than one	%
1540–1589	44	9	20.5
1590–1639	79	9	11.4
1640–1689	48	1	2.1
1690–1739	87	20	23.0
1740–1789	92	22	23.9
1790–1839	99	15	15.2

verged from the national pattern they claim to have discovered. It is curious and somewhat fortuitous that the first English village chosen for intensive study by historical demographers proved to be so surprizing, interesting, and, in so many ways, unique in its demographic behavior. It is on this point—the uniqueness and individuality of Colyton's experience—that my argument has focused.

During the century after 1750 Shepshed seems to exemplify the type of community in which the experience of protoindustrialization undermined traditional patterns of courtship and marriage. Before 1750 the incidence of bastardy and bridal pregnancy was low; fewer than 1.5% of all children were born to unmarried mothers, and just one bride in eight was pregnant. In the course of the following century, during the full-scale protoindustrialization of Shepshed, the level of illegitimacy rose more than fivefold, to 7.5% after 1800, while the incidence of bridal pregnancy also jumped dramatically.[14] The reconstituted results suggest that 33% of brides in the later eighteenth century and 36% in the early nineteenth were pregnant: However, the lengthening interval between birth and baptism that developed in this era undermines the accuracy of this set of reconstituted figures, and there is no way of knowing the actual proportion of pregnant brides after 1800. It would not be unreasonable to put it at over 40% since this level was found in the other studies.

The rising levels of illegitimacy that the cohort measures identify should not divert our attention from the fact that much of this activity was concentrated into three distinct periods: 1752–1758; 1791–1821, peaking in 1814; and 1834–1849. During these 54 years the average incidence of illegitimacy was 8.0% while during the other 46 years the figure was 4.0%. Within each of these three periods of widespread illegitimacy there were several years which stood out because of unusually high levels: 1755 (12.1%), 1756 (12.9%), and 1758 (11.1%) during the first period; 1804 (20.7%), and 1814 (16.5%) during the second; and 1834 (12.0%), 1840 (11.3%), 1842 (10.8%), 1846 (12.2%), 1847 (14.1%), and 1848 (11.5%) during the third. In contrast to these years, it is of interest to note that the illegitimacy level during the 46 "normal" years, 4.0%, was roughly the same as that prevailing in the rural communities already discussed. In Shepshed, therefore, the impact of protoindustrialization upon the sexual anticipation of marriage did not proceed uniformly over time.

The variations in the incidence of illegitimacy in protoindustrial Shepshed after 1750 can be explained only with reference to the recurrent fluctuations in the prosperity of framework knitting, on which an ever increasing section of the community became dependent. The initial peak in the illegitimacy curve coincides with the demographic takeoff. In the

---

[14] This development would be even more striking if I could describe the changes in illegitimacy rates. My inability to construct rates of illegitimacy stems from the fact that there is no way of knowing how many women were at risk, or for how long.

later 1750s the number of marriages celebrated in Shepshed doubled, and age at marriage began to fall. Clearly, expectations were severely jolted as the demographically unsettling influence of protoindustrial employment made itself felt. Could it be that the loosening of traditional constraints on marriage was accompanied by a more ready anticipation of marriage? In addition, the availability of employment would have attracted a number of immigrants who would be likely to swell the local pool of unmarried eligibles. The catalyst that joined these two factors together into a socially explosive formula would have been the seasonality of employment in protoindustry. Thus, an element of uncertainty would intervene between courtship and marriage and, in several cases, have unfortunate and unforeseen results. This factor could explain the high levels of illegitimacy in 1755 and 1756, but one expects that the element of seasonal underemployment would quickly become integrated into the popular consciousness. Unpredictability and seasonality would become predictable. The remaining year in which a markedly higher level of illegitimacy obtained, 1758, was a time of hunger and rising prices. In this instance the traditionally unsettling effect of a bad harvest may have been of real importance.

E.P. Thompson has noted that the socially dynamic influence of the harvest declined at the end of the eighteenth century and was replaced by an alternative form of economic pressure—the pressure on wages.[15] In Shepshed this transition seems to have occurred earlier. After 1758, the harvest apparently did not play an independent role, nor did the uncertanty posed by changing prices have any noticeable effect on marital decisions in Shepshed. After 1760, in the wake of 15 hungry years, the illegitimacy ratio was 4%, whereas in the 25 years of normal prices, 4.3% of all births were illegitimate.[16]

While the impact of the harvest on illegitimacy was seemingly unimportant, the population's response to industrial depression affecting their wages was not unambiguous. In the eighteenth century, the years of the American Revolution, 1775–1783, stand out because of the serious consequences that the war had for the trade in knitted products. As we have seen earlier, during these years there was a fall in the number both of marriages celebrated in Shepshed and of baptisms recorded in the parish register. But depression, dislocation, and mass suffering among the framework knitters did not result in an upsurge of premarital sexuality. Instead, the incidence of illegitimacy was at a low level, 2.7%. From this finding it probably should be inferred that the sexual anticipation of marriage was predicated on the expectation of marriage. Some support for this inference can be found in the fact that in 1786, a boom year by any

---

[15] E. P. Thompson, "The Moral Economy of the English Crowd in the Eighteenth Century," p. 128.
[16] The definition of "hungry" and "normal" years was derived from T. S. Ashton, *Economic Fluctuations*, p. 36.

standards, there was a sharp jump in the number of illegitimate births to 9.1%. In the succeeding five years the ratio of illegitimacy slumped back to its previous low level. The fact that these years, 1787–91, were similarly prosperous suggests that prosperity alone is not enough to explain variations in the incidence of illegitimacy. The critical factor, as I suggested, may have been uncertainty—uncertainty intervening between the initiation of sexual intercourse and marriage.

The following two decades, from 1791 to 1821, were a time of turmoil. Foreign wars, gigantic mobilization of armed forces, economic blockades, exceedingly deficient harvests, and systematic political repression marked these years. Among the framework knitters, these national dislocations struck with particular force because they affected a naturally outward looking protoindustry. Markets, foreign markets in particular, were of great importance and the Continental Blockade hit hard. On the other hand, the large and increasingly permanent armed forces supplied a ready market for mass produced textiles. So, the final result was ambiguous. Ambiguity breeds instability, and this uncertainty was critical because it meant that courtship took place against a backdrop of quickly changing fortunes. In these circumstances decisions would perforce become reversible. In this one protoindustrial village the reverberations of international diplomacy and its natural extension, war, were felt at the most personal level.

With the cessation of hostilities in 1815 the frenetic activity of the war years was replaced by an era of prolonged depression in the hosiery industry. Wages fell, the village practically stood still. The level of illegitimacy also dropped after 1815 as the expectation of marriage receded and young people began to emigrate. It also became increasingly common for the poor law fund to subsidize wages. Pauperization ensued but, on another level, the framework knitters were freed from economic uncertainty. An unequal trade, to be sure, but one with demographic repercussions in protoindustrial Shepshed similar to those occurring in Bottesford, Colyton, and Terling—lower levels of illegitimacy allied with higher rates of bridal pregnancy. During the period after 1834 the Old Poor Law was dismantled, and framework knitters were once again exposed to the uncertainties of reliance on an export-oriented industry whose foreign markets were being taken away by cheaper German products. Once again, the level of illegitimacy rose.

Let us now turn from the secular trends in illegitimacy in Shepshed to an analysis of the cohort measures which enable us to compare the age at which unmarried women bore bastards with the age at marriage. To begin with, these measures show that the age at which women in protoindustrial Shepshed bore illegitimates was rather higher than the age at marriage. In the last half of the eighteenth century 38 bastardbearers had an average (median) age of 22.0 while 114 unwed mothers traced after 1800 averaged

21.5. Brides, many of whom were pregnant, were 23.6 before 1800 and 22.3 afterward. It is of further interest to note that the age gap between unwed mothers and brides halved after 1800—whereas bastardbearers had been 1.6 years younger before 1800, they were 0.8 years younger after 1800. This finding does not support an argument ascribing the upsurge in illegitimacy to a lowering in the age of sexual activity. Instead, if anything, it suggests that illegitimacy became more closely linked to the expectation of marriage as protoindustrialization took hold. Once again, the onset of economic disequilibrium may initially have created socially unsettling conditions, but in the course of time the effect of these conditions moderated as the population adjusted its behavior to meet new circumstances.

Nevertheless, the fact remains that the relationship between illegitimacy and marriage found in protoindustrial Shepshed seems to have been quite different from that prevailing in the seventeenth century. At that time, as we saw in the case of Terling, unmarried mothers were, on average, somewhat older than the brides whose age at marriage could be determined. In Shepshed, unwed mothers were younger than brides. We can explain this reversal partly, I think, with reference to the changing occupational bases of the groups under investigation. Some of the women who bore illegitimate children in Elizabethan and early Stuart Terling were the daughters of a declining peasantry or of an emergent rural proletariat. Their expectations about marriage and dowry were likely to be informed by the preconceptions of a traditional society. As I have argued, illegitimacy in late sixteenth and early seventeenth century Terling should be viewed in the context of the passing of a normative world whose inhabitants were only dimly aware of the change. In a time of economic crisis the disjunction between preconception and reality became apparent, but people persisted in their traditional forms of behavior—forms of behavior no longer relevant or effective. Marriage was postponed but the sexual dimension of courtship persisted and illegitimate births ensued. In contrast, the population of protoindustrial Shepshed was proletarianized and increasingly conscious of its predicament. I have argued that after the 1750s their behavior was largely governed by their wages—which were neither certain nor secure. For these protoindustrial workers the life cycle was quite different from that of their predecessors. In a sense it was simpler, because there was no hiatus between adolescence and economic maturity. With the breakdown of the traditional methods of control over the framework knitting trade, apprenticeship became a formality, usually a form of poor relief, rather than a method of initiation into a closed corporate world. The openness of the new protoindustrial order was based on the abolition of this period of testing. The onset of economic maturity was reduced to a cash nexus. To say this, however, is not to deny that new traditions grew up to celebrate the *rites de passage* but it is rather to insist that this factor was crucial in distinguishing the preindustrial order from the protoindustrial one. As a demographic result of this change marriage took place earlier, much earlier. Furthermore, the expectation of marriage was not deferred by the knowledge that economic independence, its necessary precondition, was governed by social rules or economic constraints.

For Shepshed, some evidence was found to suggest that repetitive bastardbearers become increasingly common with the onset of protoindustrialization. Before 1750 just two women gave birth to more than one illegitimate child, and they made up 4.7% of all unwed mothers. After 1750 there were 62 women who bore more than one illegitimate child. They made up 17.9% of all unwed mothers, but they accounted for 35.1% of all bastards. This impressive total underlines the observation of Laslett and Oosterveen that these women were of disproportionate importance at times of increasing illegitimacy. Before accepting Laslett and Oosterveen's proposition without qualification, however, we should see how the experiences of Colyton and Shepshed compare with those of the two rural villages, Bottesford and Terling. In these two purely agricultural villages, in which paying jobs for women were almost totally unknown, repetitive bastardbearing was comparatively infrequent. In Bottesford and Terling about one bastard in six was born to a "repeater," while in the two other villages the figure was higher than one in three. In Bottesford and Terling "repeaters" accounted for about one unwed mother in twelve, in Colyton and Shepshed they accounted for one in six. Repetitive bastardbearing, then, was about twice as important in Colyton and Shepshed as in Bottesford and Terling. One wonders if it was accidental that in the two villages where women could find work outside the household repetitive bastardbearing was comparatively common. Perhaps these unwed mothers were younger than contemporaries who bore their first children after marriage because their illegitimate children were born in consensual unions, common-law marriages. Still, marriage seems to be the state toward which these women (and their men) aspired—many of these couples subsequently married.

The changing relationship between age at marriage and the age of unwed mothers has been remarked upon at several points in this chapter. It may be worthwhile to devote some attention to this development because it is of great importance. In a survey of nine seventeenth-century English villages it was found that the average age of bastardbearers was about one year higher than that of brides.[17] All the information presented in this chapter, however, shows that in the period after 1750 the relative ages were reversed. In protoindustrial Shepshed, in rural Bottesford and Terling, and in Colyton evidence underlined the relative precocity of unwed

---

[17] K. E. Wrightson and D. Levine, "The Social Context of Illegitimacy in Early Modern England."

mothers after 1750. This statistical evidence suggests that, insofar as earlier bastardbearing can be linked to the emergence of common-law marriage, this was not solely an urban phenomenon. This line of argument queries that proposed by Scott, Tilly, and Cohen who ascribe these developments to urbanization.[18] Although I grant that the anonymity of the urban milieu, in contrast to the lack of privacy in the village community, would probably promote the kind of culture of poverty in which consensual unions are common, the role of capitalism—both urban and rural, industrial and agricultural—was much more important in undermining traditional forms of behavior and creating social conditions within which new ones could develop. The example of Colyton, I think, proves my point. In this village, earlier than in the others, the dynamic mixture of economic opportunities acted like a solvent on traditional forms of courtship. Throughout the whole period of the study women in Colyton could find employment in activities which tied them to a larger, extralocal economy. Throughout the whole period of the study Colyton women who bore illegitimate children were younger than those who married in the parish church. In other villages this extralocal economic integration occurred at a later date, and at that later date the age of unmarried mothers dropped below that of married ones.[19]

In discussing the changing incidence of illegitimacy in these four English villages between the sixteenth and nineteenth centuries, we have seen no convincing evidence that changing sexual attitudes occurred independent of material conditions.[20] In fact, the point of my presentation

---

[18] "Our explanation of urban illegitimacy involves the notion of a sub-culture like the one advanced by Laslett and Oosterveen. In this case it is a working class subculture in which alternative marriage—the free or consensual union—was common long before the mid–eighteenth century. Unions of this type preceded legal marriage by a period of years, sometimes they replaced legal marriage for a couple's entire period of cohabitation. The source of this practice was economic. Whereas young people from artisan and peasant families insured the transmission of skill and property by marrying legally, the children of the poor had not such resources to protect. Their jobs were their only security, no contract could protect those." It should be pointed out that this paper is somewhat misleadingly titled, since it largely refers to French examples and French experiences. (J. Scott, L. Tilly, and M. Cohen, "Women's Work and European Fertility Patterns," University of Michigan Center for Research on Social Organization, Working Paper 95, p. 24. A revised version of this paper appears in the *Journal of Interdisciplinary History*, 6, 3 (1976) pp. 447–476.)

[19] In Terling, of course, this economic integration was in train in the early seventeenth century, but the period after 1625 was characterized by such low levels of illegitimacy that it was impossible to discover reliably whether these few unwed mothers were younger or older than the married women. In Bottesford, the same situation prevailed after 1650 as the village's agrarian economy was reorganized to bring it into line with the national division of agrarian production then emerging.

[20] E. Shorter has proposed that "female emancipation" from the control of the traditional male-dominated family resulted in a new attitude towards sex and sexuality on the part of a great many European women after 1750. This liberated mentality, which Shorter attributes to

has been to stress how sexual attitudes were conditioned by the circumstances of these four sets of villagers. Courtship behavior, sexual activity, and the expectation of marriage occurred within a circumscribed perimeter which was itself constantly changing. It is this dialectic of change, the interaction of personal experience and material trends, that must be consulted when we examine the social context of illegitimacy.

---

the modernization of consciousness consequent upon socioeconomic development, is thought to account for a switch from instrumental to expressive sexuality. For his latest statement of his position on this issue, see E. Shorter, *The Making of the Modern Family*.

10

CONCLUSION

In concluding I should like to discuss some of the ways future research into demographic change and family life in the age of nascent capitalism can build on the results of these four reconstitution studies. This "agenda" will be as much a reflection of what has been left out of my research through the relative niggardliness of English data as it will be an attempt to focus the reader's attention on points that I believe have not been conclusively proven. In contradistinction to the tentative nature of much that follows it will perhaps be helpful if I first summarize the main points of my argument and then proceed to expose the chinks or hollow spaces in its construction.

When I began my research, I was primarily concerned to discover whether the birth rate or the death rate was the dynamic variable in the demographic disequilibrium accompanying the Industrial Revolution. I wanted to join the controversy over this perennial problem in English economic history. However, the particular problems of record survival, on the one hand, and a manageable data base, on the other, made it necessary for me to move further back into history and look at the long period of time preceding the exponential rises in production and urbanization that accompanied the classic Industrial Revolution. However, it has since become apparent to me that I was originally mistaken about the crucial question. It is now my belief that the critical factors in promoting rapid demographic growth were the proletarianization of the mass of producers, peasants, and artisans and their integration into an extralocal commercial system. The Industrial Revolution was merely the last stage, albeit a crucial one, in this transformation.

Proletarianization was accompanied by a reduction in age at marriage and, to a lesser extent, by rising fertility—both within and before marriage. I have tried to show that this rising birth rate was of substantially greater importance than the falling death rate. Changes in mortality appear to have affected population growth less than many earlier commentators have argued. To be sure, there was a noticeable reduction in crisis mortality after the middle of the eighteenth century, but the improvement in life expectancy at birth observable in a rural parish like Bottesford was not found in a semiurban one like Shepshed. To the extent that the distribution of the population changed as it became more urban and less rural, this finding is of some significance, particularly if we view the deteriorating health of infants in Shepshed alongside the improved life expectancy of their parents. To the extent that Shepshed represents the conditions of the urban, industrial environment in which a growing proportion of the population lived, its experience underlines my point about the unpredictability of the death rate in response to changing material conditions. Although the elimination of famine and epidemic disease apparently was of great importance in lowering the short-term death rate by ending periodic sieges of crisis mortality, it seems likely that this blessing was not equally shared—children born into an urban or semiurban environment were even more likely to encounter death at an early age. High infant mortality in urban areas can be linked to diseases thriving on poor sanitation and high population density. In contrast with the crisis mortality of earlier periods this mortality, although both heavy and continuous, was not spectacular. Furthermore, the exchange was not equal because an ever greater proportion of children were born into urban conditions. Even so, the effect of a rising birth rate was so significant that it not only completely overwhelmed the sharp deterioration in life expectancy at birth—by as much as 12 years in protoindustrial Shepshed—but also contributed to a massive rise in population as well. Moreover, my research revealed that, in any event, the impact of a falling death rate in rural, agricultural communities like Terling, Bottesford, and Colyton was of no greater importance than that of the rising birth rate. Indeed, even in these communities the rising birth rate was more important.

The main finding of this study, then, is that undermining a traditional economy and replacing it with one where capitalist agriculture or protoindustry held sway had identifiable demographic implications. The main effect of the proletarianization of labor was to reduce age at marriage. In arguing this point I have taken pains to avoid a mechanistic, reductionist explanation and have mentioned the various ways in which this effect came about. I have argued that the proletarianization of labor did not, ipso facto, lead to a lower age at marriage. The timing of this decline in the age at marriage was crucially influenced by the way the larger world impinged upon the demand for labor at the village level. Under conditions of a rising local demand for labor, the effect of a crumbling *disincentive* to early marriage made itself felt.

Of course, wage labor was not a new phenomenon. It was encountered on thirteenth century manors, and sixteenth century justices of the peace made it their business to assess wage rates. In such instances of simple wage labor, the achievement of maximum earning power came early. An unskilled farm laborer, for instance, had reached it at the age of 20, at the latest. However, in precapitalist England such men did not marry until their later 20s, and it appears that a sizable fraction never married at all. The reason for this phenomenon of postponed marriage is, I believe, to be found in the social solidarity of the peasant community. Individuals who transgressed the "moral economy" were subject to public humiliation—one of the ways in which an inward-looking, seemingly changeless society governed behavior and projected its normative precepts. The demographic implication of this traditional *mentalité* lies in the way this "moral economy" played a role in asserting the primacy of group norms over individual action. In a society which equated social maturity with economic independence, which regarded laborers as unfree, and which subjected laborers cum servants to patriarchal household discipline, the age at marriage for such men (and women) was kept high. Only when one gained independence by filling a vacant position in the village economy could one consider marriage. Through the use of formal and informal constraints like "charivaris," "rough music," or "skimmington rides" the people of the village community enforced the strategies of family formation they had themselves created to promote a form of stability, an optimization of the demoeconomic balance so far as the group was concerned.

Capitalist relations of production enlarged the proportion of permanently proletarianized laborers. Just as the material foundations of the traditional economy were undermined by the advent of capitalism, so too were the modes of behavior that were essential props of this sytem. Thereafter, the decision to marry could be made with reference to individual needs and not communal motivations. In this way the advent of capitalism undercut the social controls which previously buttressed a system of late marriage. Moreover, an increase in the proportion of the population who were proletarianized further lowered the age at marriage since early marrying groups became proportionately more important. And, finally, the advent of capitalism as a system, meant that for the village laborer the period of wage dependency stretched to encompass his whole life. For the rural lower class, wage labor became a lifelong condition, not just a phase in the life cycle. In the capitalist political economy the need for patriarchal discipline waned, the institution of service passed away, and a new set of social norms took its place. Thus, the argument I have consistently advanced has stressed the dynamic demographic potential unleashed when the village laborer was no longer governed by the "prudential check" of late marriage.

As I see it, a major difficulty with the research program I undertook arose from the fact that English parish registers only rarely give detailed information concerning occupation. The upshot of this deficiency is that my arguments are susceptible to the so-called "ecological fallacy" which occurs when one generalizes from aggregated evidence to the behavior of one of the groups which composed the aggregation. Only for the last period, after 1825 in Shepshed, was it possible to get around this problem. We saw that at that time the aggregated results were a weighted compromise between the earlier marriage, lower fertility, and higher mortality of the framework knitters and the somewhat later marriage, higher fertility, and lower mortality of the agricultural laborers and village artisans who composed the rest of the population. In the light of this example, it is necessary to treat my other generalizations with some caution. On the other hand, I think that experience will serve as a lesson for those who follow, since they should be at pains not to fall into this trap. For this reason I should like to see further research programs which utilize detailed records so that it will be possible to have a multidimensional approach to the issues of early capitalism, protoindustrialization, and demographic change. Ideally it will be necessary to select for study a large community where there were several sectors—peasant farming, capitalist farming, agricultural labor, and protoindustry. By making such a selection one could address a plethora of questions that had to be bypassed in this study. Perhaps it will be useful if I indicate a few of them.

The first, most obvious questions are those concerning demographic variations along occupational lines. If peasants and traditional village artisans (blacksmith, butcher, baker, etc.) followed a pattern of impartible inheritance in which their entire estates descended to their oldest sons, did the advent of wage labor in protoindustry change their fertility strategies? Did the opportunities it created change the prospects of later children (e.g., second sons, third daughters)? How, in fact, did the coexistence of traditional and capitalist economies in the same economic space affect the demographic relationships of each group? In what ways, if at all, was the maintenance of a traditional social structure among the peasantry buttressed, supported, and nurtured by the parallel protoindustrial system? Did the recruitment pattern of protoindustry involve the younger children of wealthier peasants, or was it confined to the submerged mass at the bottom of peasant society? How did the creation of a new system of economic opportunity affect the life cycles of the prosperous peasantry, on the one hand, and the masses subsisting at the base of the village community, on the other? Did the institution of service die out as the children of cottagers and laborers found, in protoindustry, a life style more attractive than the patriarchal one that Peter Laslett has dubbed "extra-familial secondary socialization"? Finally, protoindustrialists could be divided along lines suggested by their own division of labor so as to determine whether, say, spinners or weavers had different demographic experiences from those of the fledgling capitalists who worked as middlemen, mediating between the putters-out and the domestic workers. Similarly, it might be possible to understand the recruitment of these two distinct strata among the protoindustrialists. Examination of such questions within a single community, or indeed, within the experience of a single family, would address many issues only hinted at (or sometimes sidestepped) in the course of this study.

Besides the questions of demography and social structure already mentioned, a researcher could open a whole new prospect by combining a family reconstitution study with material detailing household structure. The existence of periodic informal censuses and surveys, particularly in parts of continental Europe, should open this avenue to future research. The problem, it seems to me, is to integrate questions of family size and domestic arrangements into a broader scheme emphasizing the material factors governing these phenomena.

In this study, it was possible to examine household structure and domestic organization only at the very end of the period, in 1851. The fact that this issue could be reviewed only for this one year is particularly unfortunate, since in Shepshed this year marked the end of a period of industrial involution that had persisted for a full 35 years following the end of the Napoleonic Wars in 1815. This factor made it difficult to determine whether the particular propensity of framework knitters to live in complex households was a response to an immediate crisis or an adjustment to the exigencies of the protoindustrial family economy. This important point deserves further consideration. It would be helpful to determine how the existence of wage labor *within* the household economy changed the relationships among the members of the domestic group. In this vein, it would be important to discover the nature of the protoindustrial family economy in terms of its income-earning potential. A great deal has been written on the rationality of the peasant economy and the ways peasant income and consumption were regulated by various stages in the life cycle. For the protoindustrial family economy, similar questions need to be considered. Thus, did the presence of nonfamily members in the household fluctuate in conjunction with the dependency ratio of the household head's family? If so, when, precisely, were there lodgers? Were kin relationships as strong in a rural, protoindustrial community as Michael Anderson has suggested they were in an urban factory town? If the protoindustrial family broke its ties with such social conventions as "extra-familial secondary socialization," what was the status of late adolescent and unmarried youths? Did they stay at home until they married?

Was the pattern the same for men and women? How strong were ties between parents and their married children? Did the elderly, in many cases widowed, parents live with their children and help in production and in such household chores as childminding? Or was the protoindustrial laborer's household, like that of the agricultural laborer, streamlined to include only the nuclear family?

These questions about the domestic organization of the protoindustrial family look backward from my vantage point in 1851 to an earlier stage in the development of the framework knitting industry. In a sense, this perspective does not include the view in the other direction. What would we see if we looked forward, as it were, toward the transition from domestic to factory manufacturing? What was the impact on the family of the complete severance of the house from the workplace? The first complex of questions that need consideration deals with the demographic repercussions of this change. Did an early age at marriage persist among men and women factory workers from the period of domestic industrialization? Were their fertility strategies also similar? Did high levels of mortality continue? A second set of questions concerns the social solidarity of factory workers and their communities. Did they intermarry with the same frequency as the protoindustrialists of Shepshed? Did they live the kind of residentially stable lives that distinguished framework knitters from other social groups in Shepshed? Was the recruitment of the factory labor force determined by familial ties or past experiences with protoindustry? Finally, a study of the switch-over from domestic to factory industry would focus on questions of household structure and composition. For instance, how representative was the differentiated household division of labor? Was a differentiated production process replicated by transferring the domestic division of labor into a new workplace? Were factory workers' households characterized by the presence of extra, coresident wage earners? Did a strategy of family formation persist characterized by early marriage, high fertility in the first years of marriage, and a preference for coresidential living in these early years? Some of these questions have already been addressed by other historians but not, to the best of my knowledge, in relation to the continuity between the protoindustrial period and the age of mechanized factory production. Many of the centers of the Industrial Revolution, in England was well as on the Continent, were erected on a foundation laid in the age of nascent capitalism.

To date, work published in historical demography has revised a number of beliefs commonly held about the English experience in the age of nascent capitalism. Recent research is making it clear that age at marriage in traditional, precapitalist society was relatively high, fertility was not at its maximum—indeed, evidence suggests that fertility restriction was not unknown—and mortality was comparatively low but surprisingly variable. Other findings have shown that the average household was small, the extended family household was rarely found, illegitimacy was quite infrequent, and literacy was relatively widespread. This list of revisions to accepted beliefs is impressive, but the work that produced it has been conducted with little reference to the socioeconomic conditions under which the population studied was living—J. D. Chambers' studies of eighteenth century Nottinghamshire and Michael Anderson's work on mid–nineteenth century Preston being notable exceptions to this statement. In contrast, my deliberate intention here was to choose communities for examination where revolutionary changes in economic activity and social structure were occurring. This book has been an attempt to explain the interplay between socioeconomic change and demographic behavior and to test the adequacy of that explanation with reference to empirical data.

APPENDIX:
THE RELIABILITY OF
PAROCHIAL REGISTRATION AND
THE REPRESENTATIVENESS OF
FAMILY RECONSTITUTION

Family reconstitution involves the reassembly of family units from recorded baptisms, burials, and marriages from parochial records. Therefore, the data found in a parish register must be both reliable and complete. If there are serious gaps in registration data, it is difficult to place much confidence in results derived from a source of information. The first part of this appendix will present evidence from which we can determine the variations in comprehensiveness of parochial birth registration and the implications of such variations for a family reconstitution study. A method of compensating for the resulting deficiencies by using the 1851 census to "re-reconstitute" the population married after 1825 will be discussed.

Assessing the credibility of results derived from family reconstitution studies requires as much confidence in the representativeness of these results as in the reliability of the data on which they are based. To be sure that the results derived from family reconstitution are based on complete evidence it is necessary to create various conditions to which the evidence must conform before it is included in any calculations. However, limiting the number of examples to those which conform to these safeguards creates a possibility that the results will be based on an unrepresentative sample of the population. In the second part of this appendix, evidence will be presented to test whether the fertility and nuptiality of the "reconstitutable minority" was broadly representative of the general population.

In the third section, I will analyze the changes that occurred in burial registration. It has been argued that the use of private cemeteries, which

mushroomed at the end of the eighteenth century, had serious consequences for parochial registration of deaths. In some places this problem was
compounded by the fact that a lengthy interval between birth and baptism
meant that many children died unbaptized. In order to remedy this problem, historical demographers "manufacture" birth dates: that is, a child
who died unbaptized is assumed to have died on the day he was born
unless his age was noted when his burial was recorded. To determine the
adequacy of this method of compensating for registration deficiencies
and, more important, to assess the reliability of burial registration and the
representativeness of mortality rates derived from a family reconstitution
study, I have compared the reconstituted mortality rates with a set of
figures derived from the Registrar-General's 1839–44 annual totals of
births and deaths.

Shepshed, on whose registration records most of the following discussion is based, was the most intensively industrialized village in
Leicestershire—its population roughly quadrupled between 1750 and
1850. It was also a stronghold of dissenting religion, the only village in
Leicestershire to have five separate nonconformist congregations. For
these reasons, Shepshed provides us with a microcosm of the changes
occurring during the Industrial Revolution that are thought to be at the
root of the declining adequacy of English parochial registration. In contrast, the three other villages (Bottesford, Colyton, and Terling) were rural
and agricultural, with little or no trace of manufacturing activity.

The conventions of data linkage used in family reconstitution were first
formulated for exploring French parochial records.[1] When this methodology was adapted to English registers, allowance had to be made for the fact
that vital events were not described in the English records in as much
detail as was common in France.[2] For example, when a child was baptized
in a French parish, it was usual for the *curé* to record the dates of the
child's birth and baptism, his full name, his father's full name, residence,
and occupation, and, in addition, his mother's Christian and maiden
names. Moreover, in some registers one can find the maternal grandfa-
ther's name, residence, and occupation. Godparents are often noted. Rather
than this wealth of information, English registers typically record only the
child's name, his date of baptism, and his father's and mother's names.
Father's occupation and place of residence are rarely noted, and the
mother's maiden name or her father's name, residence, and occupation are
almost never mentioned, nor are godparents. While English registers may

---

[1] M. Fleury and L. Henry, *Nouveau Manuel de dépouillement et d'exploitation de l'état civil
ancien.*
[2] The second chapter of Fleury and Henry's pioneering study of a Norman village, Crulai,
describes the amount of information that one can expect to find in a good French register. (M.
Fleury and L. Henry, *La Population de Crulai.*) E. A. Wrigley has written on the difficulties
that arise from the relative deficiency of information in English parish registers. (E. A.
Wrigley, "Some problems of family reconstitution using English parish register material: The
example of Colyton.")

at times yield complete information, this is by no means characteristic, and they vary a great deal depending on the degree of commitment or inclination of the parish clerk. This inadequacy of information can make allocating events to their proper family contexts uncertain. Matching events with families becomes particularly difficult when the number of surnames is limited and a great many people of the same name further confuse the picture.

In anticipation, one would expect the relative paucity of detail in an English register to create overwhelming problems, but in actuality it does not cause as much difficulty for a family reconstitution study as the villagers' propensity to migrate or to leave observation for short periods. Except for a few brief periods, Shepshed did not possess exceptionally detailed registers, yet the process of reconstituting families was not particularly difficult, nor was a residue of doubt left in many cases after an allocation had been made.[3] Only when several branches of a family lived in the community at the same time was the exact identity of an individual in question, and this confusion was almost wholly restricted to the burial register. The Alt family, for example, had several active branches in Shepshed in the middle of the eighteenth century, and some of their numbers spread vertically through two or three generations. Thus, had the register noted merely that John Alt was buried on May 21, 1757, it would have been impossible to determine which of eight John Alts of various ages was meant. By a process of elimination based on later burials, three John Alts could be accounted for, leaving five other possibilities. However, in this case and others like it, the clerks gave other pieces of information, realizing, no doubt, the confusion that so bold a statement could create. To the entry recording that John Alt was buried on May 21, 1757 the clerk added that he was 81 years old and a husbandman. This extra information made it relatively simple to match his burial with the proper baptism.

Historians have claimed that after 1790 the Anglican system of parochial registration broke down in many areas where population growth outstripped the Anglican Church's ability to perform its role as a state agency.[4] Another factor that caused deterioration of parochial registration is thought to be the growth of dissenting religious congregations, some of which objected to the religious role of the Anglican Church so strenuously that they disavowed it as a civil institution as well. Foremost among these dissenters were the Baptists. They not only refused to have their children baptized according to Anglican ritual but they also declined to be buried in consecrated ground and actively opened their own cemeteries. Moreover, the Baptists, whose doctrines differed, discouraged their

---

[3] In this study, over 25,000 entries from the Shepshed parish register were used, yet there were very few occasions (fewer than 1% of all events) when one was in doubt about the individual to whom a particular event referred.

[4] The major recent proponent of this argument has been J. T. Krause. His various articles are summarized in "The Changing Adequacy of English Registration, 1690–1837."

neighbors' from observing the Anglican rubric that children be baptized within two weeks of birth, so that in areas where Baptists were well represented there was "a dramatic increase in the numbers of children of the same family being baptized [in the Anglican Church] at the same time."[5]

Because Shepshed suffered from many of the growing pains that characterized early industrial England, it will be helpful to analyze the changing comprehensiveness of its parochial registration system. This can be done by crossmatching the population enumerated in the 1851 census with entries in the parish register.[6] In this way we can not only judge how much confidence to place in calculations derived from Shepshed's parish register but also scrutinize some of the more general arguments about the changing adequacy of parochial registration. Of particular interest in this regard is the degree to which the registration of that minority of the population eligible for some of the more precise measurements derived from the family reconstitution study differed from that of the general population. We shall see that, for the selective purposes of family reconstitution, much of the deterioration in parochial registration was unimportant, as it hardly affected those people who qualified for inclusion in these calculations.

The crossmatching exercise described in this study is based on an alphabetical sample of the 1851 census population of Shepshed. Initially, all people whose surnames began with A, B, or C were crossmatched, but since children and adolescents made up a disproportionate share of this population, it was necessary to expand the scope of the sample for the adults. For convenience, and to remove a possible source of error, married women were omitted from these calculations. The final structure of the sample was as follows:

Age in 1851	Surname Groups
0–19	A–C
20–29	A–E
30–39	A–H
40–49	A–M
50+	A–Z

The alphabetical sample ensured an element of randomness in the selection of individuals whose registrations were crossmatched. Moreover, the fact that this sample consists of individuals whose sur-

---

[5] J. T. Krause, "Changing Adequacy," pp. 390–91. On the prevalence of baptism in the East Midlands and its impact on parochial registration, see T. H. Hollingsworth, *Historical Demography*, p. 155. The widespread practice of delayed, group baptism in Shepshed meant that 14.6% of all children baptized in the early nineteenth century were over one year old.

[6] P. E. Razzell has done a pilot study of crossmatching. ("The Evaluation of Baptism as a Form of Birth Registration through Cross-Matching Census and Parish Register Data: A Study in Methodology.") His method has been to identify individuals separately, outside their family units.

names began with at least three different letters makes it highly probable that it is representative of the population from which it was drawn.[7]

When individuals who told the 1851 census enumerators that they were born in Shepshed were linked with entries in the Anglican and Baptist registers, it was found that a relatively constant proportion of those born after 1780 (about one in five) either were recorded in the Baptist register or, although unrecorded, could be assumed to have been Baptists because of strong family connections with the congregation.[8] Although the Shepshed Particular Baptist congregation's register of births started in 1754 and continued until 1837, it was effective for only a short time at the end of the eighteenth century.[9] Its protracted demise, however, did not send the congregation back to the Anglican registration system but rather encouraged them to remain outside both systems. Thus, just five of 28 presumed Baptists, alive in 1851 and born between 1825 and 1837, were actually recorded in this register. And, what is more, all five belonged to the same family.

Families which entered their children's births in the Baptist register did not avoid all future contact with the Anglican register. It was not completely unknown for families to wander between the two registration systems, although such cases were not common. The registration experience of Edward Atkin's family provides a good example. Edward Atkin was baptized in 1766, and his marriage was celebrated in the parish church in 1787. His first two children, Mary and Joseph, were baptized according to the rites of the Anglican Church and their baptisms duly recorded in the parish register. Joseph's birth was also recorded in the Baptist register. Edward's third, fourth, and fifth children (William, Hannah, and John) were registered with the Anglican Church. The burial of the sixth child (Edward), an unbaptized, day-old infant, was recorded in

---

[7] M. Livi Bacci, "Some problems in nominal record linkage in Tuscany, 17th–18th centuries." In this article Livi Bacci shows that in the use of an alphabetical sample there could be a distortion or bias. In seventeenth and eighteenth century Tuscany a disproportionate number of surnames beginning with certain letters belonged to lower social classes, were of foundling origin, or were Jewish. This objection to an alphabetical sample has been taken into consideration, although in my case such an objection is less cogent since the probability of this kind of bias being common to a group of individuals whose surnames begin with three consecutive letters is very slight indeed.

[8] Apart from the Particular Baptists there were four other nonconformist congregations in nineteenth century Shepshed. (1829 Return of Dissenters, Leicestershire County Record Office, Q.S. 95/2/1/88.) Unfortunately, no register survives for these other groups, so we have had to assume that all non-Baptists were Anglicans. This point should be borne in mind by the reader when we talk about the registration experiences of "presumed Anglicans."

[9] This register is held in the Public Record Office. (RG 4/1456 No. 47, Vol. 1.) From 1754 to 1777 only two or three births per year were recorded in this register, but during the 1780s there appears to have been an increase in the size of the congregation and a tremendous rise in the annual number of recorded births, which reached a high point of 24 in 1790. In the 1780s and 1790s, about 15 births were registered each year, but after 1800 the Baptists' registration system became less effective and the numbers recording their children's births fell so rapidly that by the 1810s only about six births were recorded annually. The register continued to operate until 1837, but numbers never regained their previous levels: in the 1830s, there were only 26 recorded births.

TABLE A.1
The Comprehensiveness of Parochial Registration in Shepshed

Age in 1851	Birth date	Baptism registered	Baptism not registered	Presumed Baptists	N
0–5	1846–1851	38.5%	45.0%	16.5%	122
6–9	1841–1845	43.0	35.5	21.5	79
10–19	1831–1840	70.5	25.5	14.0	153
20–29	1821–1830	59.0	25.5	15.5	90
30–39	1811–1820	55.0	25.0	20.0	91
40–49	1801–1810	59.0	21.6	19.5	97
50–59	1791–1800	62.5	21.0	16.5	96
60–69	1781–1790	71.0	9.0	20.0	45
70+	Before 1780	83.3	6.7	10.0	30

the parish register. The births of the two last children (Thomas and Elizabeth) were recorded in the Baptist register but not in the Anglican. This family pattern of burial registration was likewise inconsistent: the burial of Edward's wife was noted in the parish register, but so were the burials of two of the children (Joseph and Elizabeth) whose births were recorded in the Baptist register. In fact, all three of the children entered in the Baptist register died before 1851, but Thomas' death had to be inferred from the fact that his widow remarried.

Family of Edward Atkin

		Date of baptism	Date of birth	Date of burial	Date of marriage
Husband	Edward Atkin	6 Jan 1766			
Wife	Mary Start		16 Aug 1770*	16 Feb 1816	18 Nov 1787
Children	Mary	13 Apr 1789			3 Jul 1809
	Joseph	13 Jun 1790	6 Jun 1790	18 May 1802	
	William	26 Aug 1792			7 Feb 1821
	Hannah	17 May 1795			15 Nov 1815
	John	19 Apr 1799			28 Feb 1822
	Edward		27 May 1804*	27 May 1804	
	Thomas		20 Aug 1805	21 Nov 1839*	1 Oct 1829
	Elizabeth		11 Apr 1809	29 Jul 1838	25 Dec 1828

Dates followed by an asterisk are either "manufactured" or extrapolated from other information.

For the Atkins family the distinction between the doctrines of the two contending churches was obviously nonexistent; their migration from one registration system to another indicates little concern for religious scruples. However, such lack of discrimination between the two opposing systems of registration was rare. Indeed, almost all such nondiscrimination was confined to the last two decades of the eighteenth and the first decade of the nineteenth century.

After 1780, the Baptists accounted for a relatively constant proportion of the unregistered vital statistics in Shepshed. Among the rest of the population, the presumed Anglicans, there was a marked deterioration in the comprehensiveness of parochial registration beginning in the last decade of the eighteenth century. Whereas about one in ten of the presumed Anglicans born in Shepshed before 1790 went unregistered, more than one in four of those born between 1790 and 1840 were unrecorded. Moreover, about one-half of the children born after 1840 into these families went unrecorded in the Anglican register. However, in view of the widespread practice of delayed baptism it is probable that many of these children were registered after the end of our period of observation.[10] The registration frequency of these presumed Anglicans is presented separately in Table A.2.

TABLE A.2
The Comprehensiveness of Parochial Registration among "Presumed Anglicans"

Age in 1851	Birth date	Baptism registered	Baptism not in register	N
0–5	1846–1851	46.0%	54.0%	102
6–9	1841–1845	55.0	45.0	62
10–19	1831–1840	70.4	29.6	132
20–29	1821–1830	69.5	30.5	76
30–39	1811–1820	68.5	31.5	73
40–49	1801–1810	73.0	27.0	78
50–59	1791–1800	75.0	25.0	80
60–69	1781–1790	88.9	11.1	36
70+	Before 1780	92.5	7.5	27

Among these "presumed Anglicans" are included members of other nonconformist congregations (four in all) which either did not keep separate registers or whose registers have since been lost.

An examination of the pattern of registration among three generations of the Bramley family will be most illuminating, and it will convey the impression that any family reconstitution study based solely on a single parish is likely to be deficient, in that a parish is, to some extent, an artificial entity with respect to the reality of people's lives. William Norman Bramley I was born in 1758 into a family of husbandmen and yeomen who had lived in Shepshed since the early seventeenth century. Members of the family were often churchwardens and were conscientious in recording their vital events in the parish register. The marriage of William Norman Bramley I, however, took place in 1782 in the parish church of his bride. In the Shepshed register there is no record of this event, nor of the baptisms of any of William's children until 1786. A record of the baptisms

---

[10] In nineteenth century Shepshed about one child in seven was over one year old when baptized, and many of these children were over five.

of his two oldest children was eventually located in the register of Belton, the parish where he was married. His first child was baptized in 1782, and his eldest son, William Norman Bramley II, in 1784. This evidence suggests that William Norman Bramley I spent several years in Belton but, some time between 1784 and 1786, brought his family back to Shepshed. Thereafter we have a full record of their activities in that parish register.

Family of William Norman Bramley I

		Date of baptism	Date of birth	Date of burial	Date of marriage
Husband	William Norman Bramley I	28 Apr 1758		20 Oct 1824	
					(11 Jul 1782)
Wife	Sarah Jones		18 Sep 1761*	18 Mar 1828	
Children	Elizabeth	(29 Oct 1782)			
	William Norman II	(28 Apr 1784)			(13 Jun 1810)
	George	14 Mar 1786		12 Sep 1834	25 Aug 1810
	Mary Ann	31 Dec 1787			
	Thomas	2 Oct 1791			
	Ann	25 Aug 1793			18 Sep 1821
	Sarah	24 Jun 1797		22 Jun 1821	
	Maria	1 Jul 1800		9 Mar 1804	
	Jane	8 Jul 1803			5 May 1835

Dates in parentheses were recorded in the parish register of Belton. Dates followed by an asterisk are either "manufactured" or extrapolated from other information.

Family of William Norman Bramley II

		Date of baptism	Date of birth	Date of burial	Date of marriage
Husband	William Norman Bramley II	(28 Apr 1784)			(13 Jun 1810)
Wife	Mary Skermer	(16 Jun 1789)		10 Feb 1847	
Children	William Norman III	(16 Jun 1811)			24 Oct 1848
	Hannah	4 Jul 1813			15 Dec 1835
	John	(16 Jun 1816)			26 Jan 1847
	George	28 Aug 1817			
	Charles	2 Feb 1819			
	Mary Ann		1 Apr 1823*		1 Oct 1850
	Jane		7 Oct 1825*		
	Richard Norman		23 Apr 1828*	23 Apr 1828	
	Louisa		22 Aug 1829*	22 Feb 1831	
	Elizabeth	14 Jun 1831			

Dates in parentheses were recorded in the parish register of Belton. Dates followed by an asterisk are either "manufactured" or extrapolated from other information.

William Norman Bramley II probably spent his youth in Shepshed, moving there from Belton when he was under two years old. He returned to Belton to marry in 1810 and was living there in 1811 when his first child, William Norman Bramley III, was baptized. By 1813, he was again living in Shepshed where his daughter Hannah was baptized. Between 1813 and 1819 the family remained in Shepsed. The second son, John, was baptized in Belton in 1816, but the Belton register notes that the family resided in Shepshed. The fourth and fifth children were baptized in Shepshed in 1817 and 1819. From 1819 until 1828 there is no mention of William Norman Bramley II's family in either the Shepshed or the Belton registers, suggesting that they were living elsewhere in the neighborhood. In 1828, an entry in the Shepshed burial register noted that Richard Norman Bramley, an infant, was buried, and again in 1831, another infant, Louisa, was buried. For neither of these children was an appropriate record of baptism found. Then, in 1831, another child, Elizabeth, was baptized in Shepshed. The Shepshed marriage register informs us that another daughter, Mary Ann, was 27 when she married in 1850. The 1851 census reveals that yet another daughter, Jane, was born in 1825. Thus, between 1819 and 1831, at least four children were born to William Norman Bramely II but not registered in either Shepshed or Belton. However, it would be unwise to infer from the absence of records that William withdrew from the registration system of the Anglican Church. His observed lack of loyalty to any particular parish church leads one, rather, to believe that these children were baptized wherever William was living when they were born. In the 1851 census, William Norman Bramley II and his eldest son, William Norman Bramley III, were both substantial farmers, working 190 and 152 acres respectively. Members of their class were known for their mobility. They were not peasants but capitalists who worked the land. Their place of residence was determined not by habit or custom but by the location of the best available financial opportunities. Thus, it is not surprising to observe that they moved with relative frequency. Their mobility does not necessarily imply that they withdrew from the Anglican registration system, but rather that they used different parishes with frustratingly little concern for future historical demographers.

In order to determine whether the registration experience of the Bramleys was unique or relatively commonplace, families from the 1851 census were compared with those reconstituted from the parish register. Because late baptism was so widespread in Shepshed, with the result that a majority of children under six were not registered by 1851, it was decided to consider only children stated to be aged six or over in the census. Looking at the pattern of registration among those aged six or over should be most suggestive because the level of registration was relatively constant from 1790 to 1845 and the rate of omission fluctuated between 22.5% and 30.5%. Such a rate could seriously, if not grievously, impair the results derived from a reconstitution study based on these data if the omissions were randomly distributed. Thus it is of greatest importance for us to ascertain whether most families registered their children in a haphazard fashion or whether omissions were clustered in a small group of families whose children went systematically unrecorded. Comparison of reconstituted families with those found in the 1851 census would, therefore, give a clearer impression of the vagaries of Anglican registration in the first half of the nineteenth century and the implications of any deficiencies for family reconstitution.

Families containing children six and over whose surnames began with A, B, or C were compared with those reconstituted from the parish register. Slightly more than 25% of families (199 of 785) were inspected, which gave a sufficiently large group to ensure that the findings were representative. Of 199 families checked, 93 were not suitable for a variety of reasons: either children were under six or children six or over were born in other parishes; the couple was childless or their children had left home by 1851; the family contained only a single or widowed person without children. Thus, for 106 cases we were able to compare the census family with its reconstitution, and in only 48 cases were all the children's baptisms recorded in the parish register. This completion rate of 45.3% gives the impression that the registration system was so defective that it would be unwise to place any confidence in results based on it. However, a closer examination of the 58 incomplete families shows that, although gaps do exist, they are not so serious as might initially be expected. In addition, it is necessary to bear in mind that, in most reconstitution studies, only a fraction of the families can be used for some tabulations which are governed by strict conventions concerning the acceptability of data. All 106 families were divided into four categories according to the registration status of the head. It was found that 41 family heads were born in Shepshed and their baptisms recorded in the parish register, 21 were Baptists, and 14, although stated to have been born in Shepshed, were not found in either register. The remaining 30 families were headed by people born elsewhere who had settled in Shepshed at some earlier time and had children born in the parish before 1845. Families in each of these four categories were subdivided into four other categories according to the registration experience of their children. As noted above, in 48 cases all children were recorded in the parish register, in a further 24 cases some children were registered but others were not. Of the remaining 34 families, 18 were Baptists, leaving 16 families with children completely unrecorded in either register. Data crosstabulating both sets of four categories are presented in Table A.3.

Although the children's registration experiences tended to reflect those of their parents, this was by no means a matter of course. Family heads baptized and registered in the Anglican Church were most likely to have

TABLE A.3
Matched Families by Registration Status of Father

Father	Children				
	All in the Anglican register	Some in the register	None in the register	Baptists	Total
In the Anglican register	22	10[a]	7	2	41
Baptist	5	2	—	14	21
Not in register	7	3	4	—	14
Born elsewhere	14	9	5	2	30
Total	48	24	16	18	106

[a]One mother in Baptist register.

their children baptized and registered, but a large proportion of this group did not do so conscientiously. Of the families whose heads were listed in the Anglican register, 46.5% had either none or only some of their children baptized by 1851. Baptist family heads were more likely to retain their affiliations with the nonconformist congregation, and 66.7% (14 of 21) of these families made no use of the Anglican registration system. The other two groups, families with heads born outside Shepshed and those with heads born in Shepshed but entered in neither register, were about evenly divided between families that regularly used the Church register and families that did so only occasionally or not at all.

For the purpose of our family reconstitution study, the most important finding has been that a relatively large number of the families considered had a mixed registration experience; some of their children were recorded but others were not. As noted above, our results will be unaffected as long as these people were systematically recorded or unrecorded, but when an element of haphazardness was present, problems will emerge. For this reason it will be informative to discuss more thoroughly those families in which some, but not all, children were recorded in the parish register. In analyzing these families, it was decided initially to see in how many instances there was evidence that they had connections with another parish and to discover the frequency of complete breakdowns in registration after one or more children had been baptized. In only eight of the 24 families with patterns of mixed registration were all family members stated to have been born in Shepshed. In 12 families at least one parent was born elsewhere, but all children were born in Shepshed. In the four other families, at least one parent was born elsewhere and at least one of the children was also nonnative. Leaving the four families thought to have Baptist affiliations, we found that in only 40% (eight of 20) of the families with mixed registration experiences can we rule out the possibility that the "missing" children were baptized and registered elsewhere. The experience of the Bramley family recounted above suggests that other families may also have had children baptized in parishes where they previously lived. Moreover, the example of the Bramleys also shows that such baptisms could be interspersed with others occurring in their place of residence. For a family reconstitution study, the greatest difficulty arises when baptisms are haphazardly either forgotten or recorded elsewhere. The families were reexamined to see how frequently this occurred. Three new categories were created: the first included families with two children of whom only one was registered; the second, families with several children of whom the first one or two or even three were registered but the remainder unrecorded; the final case included families with three or more children but no pattern in the way that some of them went unrecorded. These categories have been crosstabulated with the information about place of birth given in the census, and the results are presented in Table A.4.

The most important finding to emerge from this exercise was that, in six of eight cases involving native Shepshed families that had a propensity for leaving some of their children unbaptized, these omissions occurred in a haphazard manner. There was no recognizable pattern to which these omissions conformed. The family of John Bexon provides a good example. From the parish register, we learn that the marriage of John Bexon and Mary Bramley took place on August 12, 1821. Both were stated to be residents of Shepshed, but neither was recorded in the baptism register.

TABLE A.4
Families with "Mixed" Registration Experience

	Registration experience			
Birthplace	2 children, 1 not in register	Clean break, first child(ren) registered, the rest not	Mixed, some registered, others not	Total
All born in Shepshed	—	2	6	8
Parent/parents born elsewhere; children born in Shepshed	5	5	2	12
Parent/parents born elsewhere; some children born elsewhere	1	3	—	4
Total	6	10	8	24

In the four years between their marriage and August 31, 1825, they had four children baptized. In the next 20 years, three more baptisms were registered: in 1832, 1840, and 1845, when Nathaniel was registered and the clerk noted that he was nine months old. From the 1851 census, however, we learn that this couple had six more children. After interpolating these missing children's birth dates, then, we can re-reconstitute this family and have far greater confidence that the final picture is substantially accurate.[11] The results of the combined reconstitution from the register and the census are shown in tabular form below.

Family of John Bexon

		Date of baptism	Date of birth	Date of burial	Date of marriage
Husband	John Bexon		7 Oct 1798*		
					12 Aug 1821
Wife	Mary Bramley		7 Oct 1802*		
Children	Thomas	7 Nov 1821			
	Thomas	5 Mar 1823			
	Ann	2 Feb 1824			23 Jun 1824
	Joseph	31 Aug 1825			5 Apr 1849
	Mary		7 Oct 1827*		
	John		7 Oct 1829*		
	William	12 Jul 1832			
	Hannah		7 Oct 1834*		
	Henry		7 Oct 1835*		
	Elizabeth		7 Oct 1838*		
	George	23 Sep 1840			
	Nathaniel	17 Mar 1845	3 May 1844*	9 Apr 1845	
	Thomas		7 Oct 1845*		

Dates followed by an asterisk are either "manufactured" or extrapolated from other information.

Another example of how the 1851 census can help us to re-reconstitute the families initially reconstructed from the parish register is supplied by the registration experience of John Burn's family. John Burn married Catherine Bailey on August 24, 1829. In this case, it was possible to locate records not only of the baptisms of both bride and bride-groom but also of the burial of Catherine Burn in 1849. Their first four children were also

[11] The criteria for eligibility in a reconstitution analysis of marital fertility are a date of the birth (baptism) of the mother, a date of marriage, and further evidence that the family remains in observation after marriage. So, strictly speaking, the Bexon family would not be included in an analysis of marital fertility because the mother's date of birth was extrapolated from her age as recorded in the 1851 census. But, for our present purposes, the Bexon family's registration experience has been included in the discussion because it provides a good example of "mixed" registration and the way in which a "re-reconstitution" can remedy this problem.

baptized, but one child (Joseph) obviously was baptized a considerable time after his birth so that it was necessary to relocate his birth date at the midpoint between his immediately younger and older brothers' baptism dates. From 1836 to 1848, only two of six known children were baptized (John and Ann). From the census we learn of the existence of three of these children (Jane, Sarah, and William) but the fourth (Eliza) is mentioned only in the burial register. The combined results of the reconstitution and the re-reconstitution of this family are presented in tabular form below.

Family of John Burn

		Date of baptism	Date of birth	Date of burial	Date of marriage
Husband	John Burn	22 Jul 1810			
					24 Aug 1829
Wife	Catherine Bailey	11 Dec 1810		28 Mar 1849	
Children	Thomas	7 Sep 1829			
	William	12 Dec 1831		21 Nov 1834	
	Joseph	26 Mar 1836	10 Feb 1834*		
	John	19 May 1836			
	Jane		7 Oct 1837*		
	Ann	22 Dec 1840			
	Sarah		7 Oct 1842*		
	William		7 Oct 1846*		
	Eliza		1 Jun 1847*	16 Oct 1847	
	Isaac	25 Sep 1848		1 Oct 1848	

Dates followed by an asterisk are either "manufactured" or extrapolated from other information.

At this point it will be useful to determine whether families eligible to contribute to fertility calculations were as lax as the general population in registering their children's births. To do this, we have calculated quinquennial changes after 1825 in the registration frequency of the re-reconstituted families. The results are presented in Table A.5. These figures show that families eligible for reconstitution displayed a much higher frequency of registration than the general population. The figures for the general population's registration frequency differ from those presented above in the crossmatching exercise in that only registered baptisms and births have been included in the column "Anglican." In the crossmatching exercise, children *assumed* to have been born into Baptist families were counted, and as a result the proportion unregistered was lower. In fact, only five of the 28 presumed Baptist births thought to have occurred between 1825 and 1837 were actually recorded in the Baptist register. In view of this, and also because the "general population" contains those people who were eligible for reconstitution, the figures in

TABLE A.5
Registration Frequency of the "Reconstitutable Minority"

General population				"Reconstitutable minority"		
All births	Anglican	Anglican (%)		All births	Anglican	Anglican (%)
90	60	66.7	1825–1829	66	52	78.8
153	98	64.1	1830–1834	135	105	77.8
153	98	64.1	1835–1839	199	155	77.9
79	34	43.0	1840–1844	262	185	70.6
122	47	38.5	1845–1849	399	199	49.9

Table A.5 suggest that the non-Baptist families in the "reconstitutable minority" were conscientious in registering their children's births. This, in turn, makes it plausible to suggest that the deficiencies in Shepshed's registration system were not so serious as they first appeared—a great deal of the leakage occurred among families which, for the purpose of family reconstitution, can be regarded as nonessential.

In concluding this section on the reliability of the parochial registration system during the Industrial Revolution, it will be useful to consider briefly the registration experiences of three rural, nonindustrial nineteenth century villages: Bottesford, Colyton, and Terling.

In Bottesford, the dukes of Rutland exerted uncontested influence, and their family seat at Belvoir Castle—overlooking Bottesford from its hilltop position three miles away—dominated the community, physically, socially, and economically. The results of a crossmatching exercise for Bottesford are presented in Table A.6. Of 255 children born in the decade before the 1851 census, the baptisms of 38 could not be located in the parish register. Nine of these 38 were under a year old in 1851 and another 15 had at least one parent not a native of Bottesford. This leaves just 14 children (5.5%) about whom there is little doubt that their births went unrecorded (later or elsewhere) in the parochial registration system.

A similar kind of crossmatching exercise was carried out for Colyton by E. A. Wrigley. He found that 79.1% of those stating in the 1851 census that they were born in Colyton were recorded in the Anglican parish register, 6.3% were recorded in the two Colyton nonconformist chapels, a further 7.5% were registered in neighboring Anglican parishes. This left just 7.2% of the enumerated 1851 population for whom no baptism (or birth) entry was found in any local source.[12] Wrigley goes on to note that the general picture conceals an important change in the completeness of registration that coincided with the beginning of civil registration. Among the 1851 population, the proportion *not found* in any register was 10.9% for

---

[12] E. A. Wrigley, "Baptism Coverage in Early Nineteenth-Century England: The Colyton Area," pp. 307–08.

TABLE A.6
The Comprehensiveness of Parochial Registration in Bottesford

Age in 1851	Birthdate	Baptism registered (%)	Baptism not registered (%)	N
0–9	1841–1851	85.0	15.0	255
10–19	1831–1840	96.8	3.2	199
20–29	1821–1830	90.0	10.0	100
30–39	1811–1820	90.7	9.3	65
40–49	1801–1810	92.0	8.0	50
50–59	1791–1800	91.5	8.5	47
60+	Before 1790	96.5	3.5	28

those under ten but 5.1% for those over ten years of age.[13] Summarizing his discussion of this subject, Wrigley states that "Anglican registration held up well in Colyton and probably in its vicinity. Before civil registration began, very few children who survived infancy failed to be recorded in a baptism register."[14]

In Terling, nonconformity played a role in weakening the comprehensiveness of the parochial registration system. Among persons claiming to be natives of Terling, about one in eight enumerated in 1851 was either identified in the local nonconformist register or else thought to be a member of one of the local nonconformist families. Leaving aside these Congregationalists and focusing on the presumed Anglicans, we find that the incidence of successful crossmatching deteriorated gravely after the onset of civil registration. After 1840, just 76.1% of these children were recorded in the Terling Anglican register, whereas before 1840 registration frequency of the presumed Anglicans was 90.7%.[15]

For both Bottesford and Terling, as in Shepshed, a re-reconstitution was undertaken incorporating those births recorded in nonconformist registers as well as others extrapolated from the 1851 census. The Colyton data have not, to my knowledge, been treated in this way. This difference should be borne in mind in considering the results of the four reconstitution studies presented in this book.

The main question about the representativeness of the results of a family reconstitution study concerns the identity of the reconstituted population. Who are actually being considered? R. S. Schofield has argued that there is no single "reconstitutable minority" because "different calculations impose different periods of observation, and as a result rest upon

[13] E. A. Wrigley, "Baptism Coverage," pp. 308–09.
[14] E. A. Wrigley, "Baptism Coverage," p. 316.
[15] These figures are not quite parallel to those derived by Wrigley for Colyton in that no search of the neighboring parish registers was undertaken.

very different proportions of the events recorded in the register."[16] Whereas almost all children are included in the calculation of infant mortality rates, the conditions for the calculation of age-specific fertility are so stringent that only a small number of families are considered. Schofield noted: "It is in this context of the measurement of fertility that the greatest doubts have been expressed about the representativeness of family reconstitution, especially in the form of fears that the fertility of migrant women who have been excluded from the calculations, may have differed in some way from the fertility of the less mobile women on whose experience the fertility rates are based."[17] In order to deal with this most vexing problem, I have attempted a comparison between the fertility of the "reconstitutable minority" and that of another group of women who were married in Shepshed but whose birth dates, found in neither the Anglican nor Baptist registers, were extrapolated from the information given in the 1851 census. From this comparison I hope to be able to judge whether the use of the limited sample demanded by the strict conventions of family reconstitution prejudices the results derived from this method of investigation.

TABLE A.7
A Comparison of Fertility between the Reconstitutable Minority and a Group of Other Women

Reconstitutable minority				Nonnatives		
Years lived	Children born	Fertility rate per 1000	Age	Years lived	Children born	Fertility rate per 1000
615	265	431	under 25	514	221	430
631	219	347	25–29	500	177	354
472	140	297	30–34	426	132	310
252	59	234	35–39	310	73	235
146	17	116	40–44	166	21	127
68	1	15	45–49	52	1	19

In Table A.7 are presented sets of age-specific fertility rates for women married in Shepshed after 1825. In this table "nonnative" refers to the women whose birthdates were unknown from the reconstitution study but were extrapolated from the 1851 census. The tabulations include registered baptisms and also births deduced from the 1851 census in accordance with the methods described above. These results attest to the representativeness of the "reconstitutable minority": there was no significant difference between the fertility of native and nonnative women.

Further evidence suggesting the representativeness of the "reconstitut-

---

[16] R. S. Schofield, "Representativeness and Family Reconstitution," p. 121.
[17] R. S. Schofield, "Representativeness and Family Reconstitution," p. 122.

able minority'' was forthcoming when the distributions of age at marriage of these two groups of women were compared. In this case information about age taken from the 1851 census was utilized to determine the nonnatives' ages at marriage. These women were between 20 and 60 at the time. For this reason there is probably some inaccuracy about these results, since it is impossible that they all knew their ages exactly. Moreover, the method of calculating backward from census day, 1851, to these women's supposed dates of birth introduces more uncertainty about the precise outline of the distribution of nonnatives' ages at marriage. For example, if we want to derive the age at marriage of a woman who said she was 47 at the time of the census and who married on October 16, 1826, we must first try to determine her birthdate. To do this, we substract 47.5 years from the census date: in this case the woman's supposed birthdate is October 7, 1803, give or take six months. Thus, her age at marriage was 23 although there is an almost equal chance that she was only 22 because she could have been born in the half-year between October 17, 1803 and April 6, 1804. With these caveats in mind, it can be seen from the figures presented in Table A.8 that marriage among the two groups of women occurred at very similar ages.

In terms of both their ages at marriage and their fertility, it appears that the behavior of these nonnative women, whose experiences were recovered from the 1851 census, was practically identical to the behavior of the "reconstitutable minority." This evidence suggests that family reconstitution does yield an accurate approximation of fertility and nuptiality, despite the fact that its carefully defined observational rules restrict the analysis to a minority of the population.

TABLE A.8

A Comparison of Age at Marriage between the Reconstitutable Minority and a Group of Other Women

Part 1		
Reconstitutable minority		Nonnatives
21.60	Mean	22.40
4.15	Standard deviation	6.32
20.14	Lower quartile	19.53
22.10	Median	21.77
24.33	Upper quartile	24.33
4.19	Interquartile range	4.80
234	Number	184

Part 2 Cumulative frequency of age at marriage

Age	15	16	17	18	19	20	21	22	23	24	25	26	27	28	29	30+
Natives (%)	0	0	4	12	23	38	49	62	74	78	81	86	90	94	95	100
Nonnatives (%)	0	1	8	19	30	43	52	65	73	79	83	84	86	88	89	100

I would now like to discuss briefly the reliability of burial registration and the representativeness of the reconstituted mortality figures.

Some time in the later eighteenth century, the Shepshed Particular Baptist congregation opened its own private cemetery. The only information we possess about the extent to which this cemetery was used comes from the Particular Baptists' register which for a short period recorded burials in the "Sheepshead Burying Ground." Between 1786 and 1794, the nine years for which this register gives complete information, there were 59 burials or an average of 6.5 per year. Not one of these 59 Baptists had ever been acknowledged in the Anglican registration system. Nevertheless, it would be unwise to generalize from these cases that the two registration systems were not mutually exclusive. As we have seen, they were not.

Burial, unlike baptism, was unlikely to be celebrated twice, and we must necessarily remain uncertain that all the people observed passing through an age group were still alive at the end of it just because their burials were not recorded. This problem of unrecorded burials creates particular difficulties in calculating mortality rates for children because the conventions of family reconstitution assume that burial registration was comprehensive during the period under observation. This assumption is evident from E. A. Wrigley's statement on the subject: "The risk that an infant death does not give rise to an entry in the burial register is greatest for very young babies before baptism. Once a child has been baptized, it is unlikely that its subsequent death would go unregistered."[18] We must, therefore, try to discover whether the results derived from this particular reconstitution study understate the true mortality level of children. On the other hand, the prevalence of a lengthy interval between birth and baptism would have the contrary effect of inflating infant mortality rates because some older children, aged over one year at burial, will be included in our calculations. The only children whose true ages we know are the minority for whom both birth and baptism dates were registered, and the somewhat larger number whose ages were mentioned when their burials were recorded. Such cases were not unusual, but a degree of uncertainty still remains whether our description of the number of deaths occurring in the first year is accurate.

Children who died before baptism are given "manufactured" birth-dates. That is, they are assumed to have died on the days they were born, unless their ages were noted when their burials were registered. In order to illustrate the deleterious effect of the lengthening interval between birth and baptism, we compared the distribution of deaths occurring within the first year for two groups: one includes children with manufactured birth

---

[18] E. A. Wrigley, "Mortality in Pre-Industrial England: The Example of Colyton, Devon, Over Three Centuries," pp. 564–66.

TABLE A.9
Distribution of Infant Deaths (MF), 1750–1849

Registered		Registered and Manufactured		
N	%	Age in days	%	N
4	0.8	0	22.0	179
94	17.9	1–6	14.2	115
108	20.6	7–29	15.9	129
206	39.3	0–29	52.1	423
45	8.6	30–59	7.1	58
43	8.2	60–89	6.2	50
84	16.0	90–179	12.3	100
146	27.9	180–365	22.3	181
524	100.0	0–365	100.0	812

dates, while the other excludes them. From the evidence, presented in Table A.9, we can see how the lengthy interval between birth and baptism affected our figures describing infant mortality. For children born after 1750, just 64.5% of all recorded infant deaths referred to children whose baptisms were also registered. In contrast, the figure for children born before 1750 in Shepshed was 84.5%. The rate of omission was more than twice as high for the later cohort.[19] In this way the influence of the Baptists' doctrinal aversion to infant baptism has serious implications for the calculation of mortality rates based on parochial registration. Thus, for obvious reasons, it is necessary to use the experiences of those children whose birthdates were manufactured when calculating infant mortality rates.

In order to test the adequacy of this method of deriving infant mortality rates, I have compared the reconstituted population with the rural-industrial Registration District of Loughborough, in which Shepshed was located, and the urban Registration District of Leicester. In the *Eighth Annual Report of the Registrar-General* there are annual totals of the births and infant deaths occurring between 1839 and 1844 in each registration district.[20] By dividing infant deaths into births we can produce an approximation to the infant mortality rate in each of these registration districts. These figures, together with those of the reconstituted 1825–49 cohort from Shepshed, are presented in Table A.10.

The mortality rates derived from the reconstitution study are in broad agreement with those derived from civil registration. It is significant that

---

[19] Another point should be noted: the use of "manufactured" birthdates produces a more "normal" distribution of infant deaths. That is, demographers have observed that endogenous mortality (deaths occurring within the first month and largely due to problems arising from the child's delivery or to stillbirth) usually accounts for about 50% of all infant deaths. The second distribution in Table A.9 (which includes children who died unbaptized) more closely conforms to this pattern than does the first distribution.

[20] *P.P.*, 1847–48, XXV, 204–05.

TABLE A.10
Infant Mortality (MF), 1839–1844

	Births	Deaths	Rate/000
Leicester R.D. (1839–44)	12,023	2374	197
Loughborough R.D. (1839–44)	8,594	1521	177
Shepshed (1825–49)	832	173	208

The Shepshed results are based on a cohort who, unless they died, were all "in observation" for at least one full year.

Shepshed's infant mortality was comparable to that of the urban population, because it is unlikely that the sanitary and housing conditions in an overgrown industrial village like Shepshed were much different from those in a city like Leicester. Industrialization meant that Shepshed became a quite densely populated village with jerrybuilt housing to accommodate its mushrooming population: "mean cottages, low and narrow, badly lit, fronting on the street or around common yards, and often built in odd shapes to squeeze into odd pieces of land. They were cheaply built and badly maintained."[21] In this squalid environment, inadequate sanitary arrangements made cholera, typhus, and other "urban" diseases common. For example, there was a severe outbreak of cholera from November 1831 to January 1832, and there were three outbreaks of typhus in the 18 months between July 1839 and December 1840. In addition, smallpox was endemic in this area.

This general agreement between the reconstituted results and those derived from the registrar general's figures provides some confidence in the reliability and representativeness of the reconstituted results.

As was noted earlier, the most interesting questions about the interaction between economic and demographic change concern parishes like Shepshed, where the registration system suffered a partial breakdown at the end of the eighteenth century. If we are to use the parish registers of such places to examine the demographic implications of industrialization, then it is necessary to determine the extent of underregistration and to find methods of compensating for this diminishing comprehensiveness. In this study, we have seen that in Shepshed the "reconstitutable minority" was quite conscientious in registering its children's births. However, some members of the group displayed a haphazard registration behavior, recording some births but omitting others in no set order. It was found that by supplementing the family reconstitution with information from the 1851 census we could re-reconstitute the families of people married after

---

[21] A. Bécherand, "The Poor and the English Poor Laws in the Loughborough Union of Parishes, 1837–1860," p. 116.

1825 and compensate for most of the deficiencies caused by the declining comprehensiveness of parochial registration. Another benefit of re-reconstitution was that it incorporated a larger number by expanding the "reconstitutable minority" to include both women married in the village but born elsewhere and those whose births were unrecorded, groups which would otherwise have been left out of a reconstitution study because we did not have enough information about them. A comparison of the fertility and nuptiality experiences of the "reconstitutable minority" and the "re-reconstitutable minority" showed that the use of the strict conventions to restrict the sample does not seem to prejudice the results. This finding is important because it allays fears that the results of family reconstitution studies, and more particularly the measurement of fertility, are based on unrepresentative samples of the population.

REFERENCES

MANUSCRIPT SOURCES

Leicestershire County Record Office

Probate Records

1600–1750	Wills
1600–1711	Inventories

Parochial Records

Shepshed

D.E. 610/1–18, 20, 27	Parish Registers
D.E. 394/38	Settlement Certificates
D.E. 394/39	Settlement Examinations
D.E. 394/40	Settlement Bonds
D.E. 394/42	Removal Orders
D.E. 394/43	Quarter Sessions Orders (re: Settlement and Removal)
D.E. 394/44	Apprenticeship Indentures
D.E. 394/45	Orders Discharging Apprentices
D.E. 394/46	Bastardy Orders
D.E. 394/47	Bastardy Bonds
D.E. 394/48	Bastardy Examinations
D.E. 394/49–52, 57	Poor Relief
D.E. 394/67	1841 Census Return

Bottesford

D.E. 829/1–10, 12–14	Parish Registers
D.E. 829/98	Apprenticeship Indentures
D.E. 829/100	Settlement Certificates
D.E. 829/101	Settlement Bonds

D.E. 829/102	Settlement Paper
D.E. 829/103	Removal Orders
D.E. 829/105	Bastardy Examination
D.E. 829/106	Bastardy Bonds
D.E. 829/107	Bastardy Order
D.E. 829/78	Churchwardens' Accounts, 1783–1850
D.E. 829/114	Ecclesiastical Census, undated

Quarter Sessions

Q.S. 93/2/C 24/4	Poor rate returns, Bottesford, 1801–17
Q.S. 93/2/C 24/186	Poor rate returns, Shepshed, 1801–17
Q.S. 62/269/1–55	Land Tax, Shepshed, 1775–79, 1781–1832
Q.S. 62/47/1–47	Land Tax, Bottesford, 1777–79, 1781–1832
Q.S. 95/2/1/88	1829 Return of Dissenters
Q.S. 44/3/1	Licensed Dissenting Congregations

LEICESTER CITY MUSEUM AND RECORD OFFICE

21/D/60	Diary of Jon Alt, 1791–1818
1 D41/2 601–06	Shepshed Glebe Terrier, 1638, 1674, 1690, 1694, 1700, 1724

PUBLIC RECORD OFFICE

E 179 240/279	Hearth Tax, 1670
E 179 251/4	Hearth Tax, Michaelmas 1664
E 179 251/8	Hearth Tax, Lady Day 1665
E 179 251/9	Hearth Tax, Lady Day 1666
E 179 134/322	Hearth Tax, undated
RG 4/1456 No. 47, vol. 1	Shepshed Particular Baptist Register
HO 107 2085 284–505	1851 Census, Shepshed
HO 107 2102 360–405	1851 Census, Bottesford

ESSEX COUNTY RECORD OFFICE

Parochial Records

Terling

T/R 60	Terling Parish Register, Microfilm of Transcript
D/P 299/11	1715 Rates
D/P 299/18	1775, 1778 Lists of Labouring Population
D/P 299/5/1	Churchwardens' Accounts, 1780–1805
D/P 299/5/1A	Churchwardens' Loose Papers, 1668–1719
D/P 299/5/1B	Churchwardens' Accounts, 1720
D/P 299/12/0, OA, OB, 1, 1A, 2–8	Overseers' Accounts and Penny Rate, 1694–1849 (not continuous)
D/P 299/13/1A	Register of Settlement Certificates
D/P 299/13/1B	Certificates of Legal Settlement
D/P 299/13/2	Removal Orders from Terling
D/P 299/13/3	Removal Orders to Terling
D/P 299/13/4	Settlement Examinations

PRINTED SOURCES

PARLIAMENTARY PAPERS

Censuses

1801–02, VI, VII	1801 Census
1812, XI	1811 Census
1822, XV, XXI	1821 Census
1833, XXXVI, XXXVII, XXXVIII	1831 Census
1843, XXII, XXIII	1841 Census
1844, XXVII	1841 Census
1852–53, LXXXV, LXXXVI, LXXXVIII	1851 Census

Annual Reports of Registrar-General

1839, XVI	First Report
1840, XVII	Second Report
1841, VII	Third Report
1842, XIX	Fourth Report
1843, XXI	Fifth Report
1844, XIX	Sixth Report
1846, XIX	Seventh Report
1847–48, XXV	Eighth Report
1847–48, XXV	Ninth Report
1849, XXI	Tenth Report
1850, XX	Eleventh Report
1851, XXII	Twelfth Report
1852, XVIII	Thirteenth Report

Poor Law

1803–04, XIII	Poor Rate Returns, 1776, 1783–85, 1803
1822, V	Poor Rate Returns, 1816–21
1825, IV	Poor Rate Returns, 1822–24
1830–31, XI	Poor Rate Returns, 1825–29
1834, XXVII	Poor Law Report
1835, XLVII	Poor Rate Returns, 1830–34
1837–38, XXXVIII	Second Report for Poor Law Commissioner
1838, XVIII	Select Committee, Poor Law Amendment Act

Industrial Relations

1845, XV	Framework Knitters, Commissioners' Reports and Minutes of Evidence
1854–55, XIV	Select Committee on Stoppage of Wages (Hosiery)
1871, XXXVI	Truck System, Commissioners' Report and Minutes of Evidence

BOOKS, ARTICLES, AND UNPUBLISHED MATERIAL

Anderson, M.
 1967 "Family Structure in Nineteenth Century Lancashire." Ph.D. dissertation, Cambridge University.
 1971 "Family, Household and the Industrial Revolution." In *Sociology of the Family*, edited by M. Anderson, pp. 78–96. Harmondsworth: Penguin Books.
 1972 "The Study of Family Structure." In *The Study of Nineteenth Century Society*, edited by E.A. Wrigley, pp. 47–81. Cambridge: Cambridge University Press.
   "Standard tabulation procedures for the census enumerators' books 1851–1891." In *The Study of Nineteenth Century Society*, edited by E.A. Wrigley, pp. 134–145. Cambridge: Cambridge University Press.
   Family Structure in Nineteenth Century Lancashire. Cambridge: Cambridge University Press.

Appleby, A.B.
 1973 "Disease or Famine? Mortality in Cumberland and Westmoreland, 1580–1640." *Economic History Review*, 2nd ser., XXVI, 2: 403–431.
 1975 "Nutrition and Disease: The Case of London, 1550–1750." *Journal of Interdisciplinary History*, 6, 1: 1–22.
   "Agrarian Capitalism or Seigneurial Reaction?" *American Historical Review*, 80, 3: 574–594.

Armstrong, W.A.
 1966 "Social Structure from the Early Census Returns." In *An Introduction to English Historical Demography*, edited by E.A. Wrigley, pp. 209–237. London: Weidenfeld & Nicolson.
 1966 "The interpretation of the census enumerators' books for Victorian towns." In *The Study of Urban History*, edited by H.J. Dyos, pp. 67–76. London: Edward Arnold.

Ashton, T.S.
 1959 *Economic Fluctuations in England, 1700–1800*. Oxford: Oxford University Press.

Auty, R.M.
 1943 *The Land of Britain*. London: Geographical Publications.

Bateman, J.
 1879 *The Landowners of Great Britain and Ireland*. London.

Baugh, D.A.
 1975 "The Cost of Poor Relief in South-East England, 1790–1834." *Economic History Review*, 2nd ser., XXVIII, 1: 50–68.

Beaver, M.W.
 1973 "Population, Infant Mortality and Milk." *Population Studies*, 27, 2: 243–254.

Bécherand, A.
 1972 "The Poor and the English Poor Laws in the Loughborough Union of Parishes, 1837–1860." Mémoire presenté pour l'obtention de la Maîtrise-es-lettres, Université de Nancy.

Berkner, L.
 1972 "The Stem Family and the Development Cycle of the Peasant Household." *American Historical Review*, 77, 2: 398–418.

Blackner, J.
 1815 *The History of Nottingham*. Nottingham.

Blagg, T.M. and Wadsworth, F.A., eds.
 1930 *Abstracts of Nottinghamshire Marriage Licenses*. London.

Boserup, E.
 1965 *The Conditions of Agricultural Growth*. London: George Allen & Unwin.

Bowden, P.J.
    1962   *The Wool Trade in Tudor and Stuart England.* London: Macmillan.
    1967   "Agricultural Prices, Farm Profits, and Rents." In *The Agrarian History of England and Wales, 1500–1640,* edited by J. Thirsk, pp. 593–695. Cambridge: Cambridge University Press.
Branca, P.
    1975   "A New Perspective on Women's Work: A Comparative Typology." *Journal of Social History,* 9, 2: 129–153.
Braun, R.
    1966   "The Impact of Cottage Industry on an Agricultural Population." In *The Rise of Capitalism,* edited by D.S. Landes, pp. 53–64. New York: Macmillan.
Buer, M.C.
    1926   *Health, Wealth and Population in the Early Days of the Industrial Revolution.* London: Routledge.
Burley, K.H.
    1957   "The Economic Development of Essex in the Later Seventeenth and Early Eighteenth Centuries." Ph.D. dissertation, Cambridge University.
Bythell, D.
    1968   *The Handloom Weavers.* Cambridge: Cambridge University Press.
Chambers, J.D.
    1929   "The Worshipful Company of Framework Knitters." *Economica,* 27: 296–329.
    1957   *The Vale of Trent.* Economic History Review Supplement, 3. Cambridge: Cambridge University Press.
    1965   "Enclosure and the Labour Supply in the Industrial Revolution." In *Population in History,* edited by D.V. Glass and D.E.C. Eversley, pp. 308–326. London: Edward Arnold.
           "Population Change in a Provincial Town: Nottingham, 1700–1800." In *Population in History,* edited by D.V. Glass and D.E.C. Eversley, pp. 334–353. London: Edward Arnold.
           "The Rural Domestic Industries during the Period of Transition to the Factory System with special reference to the Midland Counties of England." In *Communications, Second International Conference of Economic History, 1962,* pp. 429–455. Paris: Mouton.
    1966   *Nottinghamshire in the Eighteenth Century.* 2nd ed. London: Frank Cass.
    1969   "Some Aspects of E.A. Wrigley's *Population and History.*" *Local Population Studies,* 3: 18–28.
    1972   *Population, Economy and Society in Pre-Industrial England.* Oxford: Oxford University Press, Oxford University Paperback Series.
Chapman, S.D.
    1967   *The Early Factory Masters.* Newton Abbott: David and Charles.
    1972   *The Cotton Industry in the Industrial Revolution.* Studies in Economic History. London: Macmillan.
           "The Genesis of the British Hosiery Industry 1600–1750." *Textile History,* 3: 7–50.
    1973   "Industrial Capital before the Industrial Revolution." In *Textile History and Economic History,* edited by N.B. Harte and K.G. Ponting, pp. 113–137. Manchester: Manchester University Press.
    1974   "A Textile Factory before Arkwright: A Typology of Factory Development." *Business History Review,* XLVIII, 4: 451–478.
Church, R.A.
    1966   *Economic and Social Change in a Midland Town 1815–1900: Victorian Nottingham.* London: Frank Cass.

Church, R.A. and Chapman, S.D.
  1967 "Gravenor Henson and the Making of the English Working Class." In *Land, Labour and Population in the Industrial Revolution*, edited by E.L. Jones and G.E. Mingay, pp. 131–161. London: Edward Arnold.
Clark, C. and Haswell, M.
  1969 *The Economics of Subsistence Agriculture*. London: Macmillan.
Clarke, A.B., ed.
  n.d.   *An Index to Some Leicestershire Clandestine Marriages*. Leicester.
Clay, C.G.A.
  1966 "Two Families and their Estates: the Grimsons and the Cowpers from c.1650 to c.1815." Ph.D. dissertation, Cambridge University.
Coleman, D.C.
  1969 "An Innovation and its Diffusion: The 'New Draperies'." *Economic History Review*, 2nd ser., XXII, 3: 417–429.
  1973 "Textile Growth." In *Textile History and Economic History*, edited by N.B. Harte and K.G. Ponting, pp. 1–21. Manchester: Manchester University Press.
Defoe, D.
  1928 *A Tour Through England and Wales, 1724–26*. London: Everyman.
Deprez, P.
  1965 "The Demographic Development of Flanders in the Eighteenth Century." In *Population in History*, edited by D.V. Glass and D.E.C. Eversley, pp. 608–630. London: Edward Arnold.
  1970 (Ed.) *Population and Economics*. Winnipeg: University of Manitoba Press.
Digby, A.
  1975 "The Labour Market and the Continuity of Social Policy after 1834: The Case of the Eastern Counties." *Economic History Review*, 2nd ser., XXVIII, 1: 69–83.
Dobson, T. and Roberts, D.F.
  1971 "Historical Population Movement and Gene Flow in Northumberland Parishes." *Journal of Biosocial Science*, 3, 2: 193–208.
Drake, M.
  1962 "An Elementary Exercise in Parish Register Demography." *Economic History Review*, 2nd ser., XIV, 3: 427–445.
  1969 *Population and Society in Norway, 1735–1865*. Cambridge: Cambridge University Press.
         (Ed.) *Population in Industrialization*. London: Methuen, University Paperbacks.
  1972 "Fertility Controls in Pre-Industrial Norway." In *Population and Social Change*, edited by D.V. Glass and R. Revelle, pp. 185–198. London: Edward Arnold.
Dunlop, J.C.
  1914 "The Fertility of Marriage in Scotland." *Journal of the Royal Statistical Society*, LXXVII: 259–288.
Eden, F.M.
  1797 *The State of the Poor*. London.
Erickson, C.
  1959 *British Industrialists: Steel and Hosiery 1850–1950*. Cambridge: Cambridge University Press.
Everitt, A.
  1972 "The Grass-Roots of History." *Times Literary Supplement*, July 28: 889–891.
  1972 *The Pattern of Rural Dissent*. Department of English Local History, Occasional Papers, second series, Number 4. Leicester: Leicester University Press.
Eversley, D.E.C.
  1965 "Population Economy and Society." In *Population in History*, edited by D.V. Glass and D.E.C. Eversley, pp. 23–69. London: Edward Arnold.

1967 "The Home Market and Economic Growth in England, 1750–80." In *Land, Labour and Population in the Industrial Revolution*, edited by E.L. Jones and G.E. Mingay, pp. 206–259. London: Edward Arnold.

Felkin, W.

1867 *A History of Machine-Wrought Hosiery and Lace Manufactures*. London.

Fischer, W.

1973 "Rural Industrialization and Population Change." *Comparative Studies in Society and History*, 15, 2: 158–170.

Fletcher, W.G.D.

1888 "A Religious Census of Leicestershire in 1676." *Transactions of the Leicestershire Archaeological Society*, vi.

Fleury, M. and Henry, L.

1956 *Nouveau Manuel de dépouillement et d'exploitation de l'état civil ancien*. Paris: Presses Universitaires de France.

1958 *La Population de Crulai*. Paris: Presses Universitaires de France.

Flinn, M.W.

1970 *British Population Growth 1700–1850*. Studies in Economic History. London: Macmillan, 1970.

1974 "The Stabilization of Mortality in Pre-Industrial Europe." *Journal of European Economic History*, 3, 2: 285–318.

Foster, J.O.

1967 "Capitalism and Class Consciousness in Earlier 19th Century Oldham." Ph.D. dissertation, Cambridge University.

1974 *Class Struggle and the Industrial Revolution*. London: Weidenfeld & Nicolson.

Fox, H.S.A.

1975 "The Chronology of Enclosure and Economic Development in Medieval Devon." *Economic History Review*, 2nd ser., XXVIII, 2: 181–202.

Freudenberger, H. and Redlich, F.

1964 "The Industrial Development of Europe: Reality, Symbols, Images." *Kyklos*, XVII, 2: 372–403.

Friedlander, D.

1969 "Demographic Responses and Population Change." *Demography*, 6,4: 359–381.

Fussell, G.E.

1949 "Four Centuries of Leicestershire Farming." In *Studies in Leicestershire Agrarian History*, edited by W.G. Hoskins, pp. 154–176. Leicester: The Leicestershire Archaeological Society.

Geertz, C.

1963 *Agricultural Involution: The Processes of Ecological Change in Indonesia*. Berkeley and Los Angeles: University of California Press.

Glass, D.V.

1953 (Editor) *Introduction to Malthus*. London: Watts.

1965 "Gregory King and the population of England and Wales at the end of the seventeenth century." In *Population in History*, edited by D.V. Glass and D.E.C. Eversley, pp. 167–183. London: Edward Arnold.

"Gregory King estimate of the population of England and Wales, 1695." In *Population in History*, edited by D.V. Glass and D.E.C. Eversley, pp. 183–216. London: Edward Arnold.

"Population and Population Movements in England and Wales, 1700–1850." In *Population in History*, edited by D.V. Glass and D.E.C. Eversley, pp. 221–246. London: Edward Arnold.

Glass, D.V., and Eversley, D.E.C., eds.

1965 *Population in History*. London: Edward Arnold.

Gooder, A.
   1972 "The Population Crisis of 1727–30 in Warwickshire." *Midland History*, 1, 4: 1–22.
Gottfried, R.
   1976 "Epidemic Disease in Fifteenth-Century England." *Journal of Economic History*, XXXVI, 1: 267–270.
Goubert, P.
   1968 *Cent Mille Provinciaux au XVIIe Siècle*. Paris: Flammarion.
Greven, P.
   1971 *Four Generations*. Ithaca, New York: Cornell University Press.
Griffith, G.T.
   1926 *Population Problems of the Age of Malthus*. Cambridge: Cambridge University Press.
Habbakuk, H.J.
   1955 "Family Structure and Economic Change in Nineteenth-Century Europe." *Journal of Economic History*, XV, 1: 1–12.
   1963 "Population Problems and European Economic Development in the Late Eighteenth and Nineteenth Centuries." *American Economic Review*, LIII, 2: 607–618.
   1965 "The Economic History of Modern Britain." In *Population in History*, edited by D.V. Glass and D.E.C. Eversley, pp. 147–158. London: Edward Arnold.
        "English Population in the Eighteenth Century." In *Population in History*, edited by D.V. Glass and D.E.C. Eversley, pp. 269–284. London: Edward Arnold.
        "La Disparition du Paysan Anglais." *Annales, E.S.C.*, XX, 4: 649–663.
   1971 *Population Growth and Economic Development*. Leicester: Leicester University Press.
Hajnal, J.
   1965 "European Marriage Patterns in Perspective." In *Population in History*, edited by D.V. Glass and D.E.C. Eversley, pp. 101–143. London: Edward Arnold.
Hareven, T.
   1974 "The Family as Process: The Historical Study of the Family Cycle." *Journal of Social History*, 7, 3: 322–329.
Hartopp, H., ed.
   1902 *Calendar of Wills and Administrations, proved and granted in the Archdeaconry Court of Leicester, 1495–1649*. London: The Index Library.
   1910 *Leicestershire Marriage Licenses, 1570–1729*. London: The Index Library.
   1920 *Index to the Wills and Administrations, proved and granted in the Archdeaconry Court of Leicester, 1660–1750*. London: The Index Library.
   1927 *Register of the Freemen of Leicester*. Leicester.
Hartwell, R.M.
   1969 "Economic Growth in England before the Industrial Revolution." *Journal of Economic History*, XXIX, 1: 13–31.
Hawthorn, G.
   1970 *The Sociology of Fertility*. London: Collier-Macmillan.
Hay, D.
   1975 "Property, Authority and the Criminal Law." In *Albion's Fatal Tree*, edited by D. Hay, P. Linebaugh, and E.P. Thompson, pp. 17–64. New York: Pantheon.
Head, P.
   1961–62 "Putting Out in the Leicester Hosiery Industry in the Middle of the Nineteenth Century." *Transactions of the Leicestershire Archaeological Society*, 37.

Helleiner, K.F.
    1965   "The Vital Revolution Reconsidered." In *Population in History*, edited by D.V. Glass and D.E.C. Eversley, pp. 79–86. London: Edward Arnold.

Henson, G.
    1830   *A History of the Framework Knitters.* Nottingham.

Hey, D.G.
    1969   "A Dual Economy in South Yorkshire." *Agricultural History Review*, 17, 2: 108–119.
    1972   *The Rural Metalworkers of the Sheffield Region.* Department of English Local History, Occasional Papers second series, Number 5. Leicester: Leicester University Press.

Hobsbawm, E.J.
    1952   "The Machine Breakers." *Past and Present*, 1 (1952): 57–70.

Hobsbawm, E.J. and Rudé, G.
    1969   *Captain Swing.* London: Lawrence and Wishart.

Holderness, B.A.
    1972   " 'Open' and 'Close' Parishes in England in the Eighteenth and Nineteenth Centuries." *Agricultural History Review*, 20, 2: 126–139.

Hollingsworth, T.H.
    1965   "A Demographic Study of the British Ducal Families." In *Population in History*, edited by D.V. Glass and D.E.C. Eversley, pp. 354–378. London: Edward Arnold.
    1968   "The Importance of the Quality of the Data in Historical Demography." *Daedulus*, 97 (1968): 415–432.
    1969   *Historical Demography.* London: Hodder and Stoughton.

Homans, G.C.
    1970   *English Villagers of the Thirteenth Century.* New York: Harper & Row.

Hopkins, S.V. and Phelps-Brown, E.H.
    1956   "Seven Centuries of the Prices of Consumables Compared with Builders' Wage-Rates." *Economica*, new ser., 23: 296–314.
    1957   "Wage-rates and prices: evidence for population pressure in the sixteenth century." *Economica*, new ser., 24: 289–306.

Horn, P.L.R.
    1968   "Agricultural Labourers' Unions in Four Midland Counties." Ph.D. dissertation, Leicester University.
    1974   "Child Workers in the Pillow Lace and Straw Plait Trades of Victorian Buckinghamshire and Bedfordshire." *Historical Journal*, XVII, 4: 779–796.

Hoskins, W.G.
    1929   "The Rise and Decline of the Serge Industry in the South-West of England, with Special Reference to the Eighteenth Century." M.Sc. dissertation, University of London.
    1949   (Ed.) *Studies in Leicestershire Agrarian History.* Leicester: The Leicestershire Archaeological Society.
    1950   *Essays in Leicestershire History.* Liverpool: Liverpool University Press.

Hoskins, W.G. and McKinley, R.A., eds.
 1954–55   *A History of the County of Leicester.* Vols. II and III. In *The Victoria County History of the Counties of England*, edited by R.B. Pugh. London.
    1957   *The Midland Peasant.* London: Macmillan.
    1963   *Provincial England.* London: Macmillan.

Howell, C.
    1975   "Stability and Change 1300–1700. The Socio-Economic Context of the Self-Perpetuating Family Farm in England." *Journal of Peasant Studies*, 2, 4: 468–482.

Hull, F.
   1950   "Agriculture and Rural Society in Essex 1560–1640." Ph.D. dissertation, University of London.
Hundert, E.J.
   1969   "The Conception of Work and the Worker in Early Industrial England." Ph.D. dissertation, University of Rochester.
Hunt, H.G.
   1957   "The Chronology of Parliamentary Enclosure in Leicestershire." *Economic History Review*, 2nd ser., X, 2: 265–272.
   1959   "Landownership and Enclosure, 1750–1830." *Economic History Review*, 2nd ser., XI, 3: 497–504.
Hunt, W.A.
   1974   "The Godly and the Vulgar: Puritanism and Social Change in Seventeenth Century Essex, England." Ph.D. dissertation, Harvard University.
Huzel, J.P.
   1969   "Malthus, the Poor Law, and Population in Early Nineteenth-Century England." *Economic History Review*, 2nd ser., XXII, 3: 430–452.
Innes, J.W.
   1938   *Class Fertility Trends in England and Wales, 1876–1934.* Princeton, New Jersey: Princeton University Press.
Innocent, G.A.G.
   1969   "Aspects of the Practical Working of the New Poor Law in Leicester and Leicestershire, 1834–1871." M.A. dissertation, Leicester University, Victorian Studies Centre.
Jones, E.L.
   1968   "The Agricultural Origins of Industry." *Past and Present*, 40: 58–71.
Jones, E.L. and Mingay, G.E., eds.
   1967   *Land, Labour and Population in the Industrial Revolution.* London: Edward Arnold.
Jones, R.E.
   1968   "Population and Agrarian Change in an Eighteenth Century Shropshire Parish." *Local Population Studies*, 1: 6–29.
Kerridge, E.
   1967   *The Agricultural Revolution.* London: Allen and Unwin.
Klima, A.
   1974   "The Role of Rural Domestic Industry in Bohemia in the Eighteenth Century." *Economic History Review*, 2nd ser., XXVII, 1: 48–56.
Knodel, J.
   1967   "Law, Marriage and Illegitimacy in Nineteenth-Century Germany." *Population Studies*, 20, 3: 279–294.
   1968   "Infant Mortality and Fertility in Three Bavarian Villages: An Analysis of Family Histories from the 19th Century." *Population Studies*, 22, 3: 297–318.
   1970   "Two and a Half Centuries of Demographic History in a Bavarian Village." *Population Studies*, 24, 3: 353–376.
   1974   "The Influence of Child Mortality on Fertility in European Populations." Mimeographed. Brown University, Providence, Rhode Island.
Koellmann, W.
   1965   "The Population of Barmen before and during the Period of Industrialization." In *Population in History*, edited by D.V. Glass and D.E.C. Eversley, pp. 588–607. London: Edward Arnold.

1970 "Population and Labour Force Potential in Germany, 1815–1865." In *Population and Economics*, edited by P. Deprez, pp. 11–32. Winnipeg: University of Manitoba Press.

Krause, J.T.

1958 "Changes in English Fertility and Mortality, 1781–1850." *Economic History Review*, 2nd ser., XI, 1: 52–70.

1959 "Some Implications of Recent Work in Historical Demography." *Comparative Studies in Society and History*, 1, 2: 164–188.

1965 "The Changing Adequacy of English Registration, 1690–1837." In *Population in History*, edited by D.V. Glass and D.E.C. Eversley, 379–393. London: Edward Arnold.

1967 "Some Aspects of Population Change, 1690–1790." In *Land, Labour and Population in the Industrial Revolution*, edited by E.L. Jones and G.E. Mingay, pp. 187–205. London: Edward Arnold.

1969 "Some Neglected Factors in the English Industrial Revolution." In *Population in Industrialization*, edited by M. Drake, pp. 103–117. London: Methuen, University Paperbacks.

"English Population Movements Between 1700 and 1850." In *Population in Industrialization*, edited by M. Drake, pp. 118–127. London: Methuen, University Paperbacks.

Krier, D.F.

1969 "Population Movements in England, 1650–1812: A Family Reconstitution Study of Three Eighteenth-Century Lancashire Parishes." Ph.D. dissertation, Boston College.

Krier, D.F., and Loschky, D.J.

1969 "Income and Family Size in Three Eighteenth Century Lancashire Parishes." *Journal of Economic History*, XXIX, 3: 429–448.

Kuczynski, R.P.

1938 "British Demographer's Opinions on Fertility, 1660–1760." In *Political Arithmetic*, edited by L. Hogben, pp. 278–322. London: Allen & Unwin.

Langer, W.

1975 "American Foods and Europe's Population Growth 1750–1850." *Journal of Social History*, 8, 2: 51–66.

Laslett, P. and Harrison, J.

1963 "Clayworth and Cogenhoe." In *Historical Essays Presented to David Ogg*, edited by H.E. Bell and R.L. Ollard, pp. 157–184. New York: Barnes & Noble.

Laslett, P.

1965 *The World we have lost*. London: Methuen, University Paperbacks.

1966 "The Numerical Study of English Society." In *An Introduction to English Historical Demography*, edited by E.A. Wrigley, pp. 1–13. London: Weidenfeld & Nicolson.

"Social Structure from Listings of Inhabitants." In *An Introduction to English Historical Demography*, edited by E.A. Wrigley, pp. 160–208. London: Weidenfeld & Nicolson.

1969 "Size and Structure of the Household in England over Three Centuries." *Population Studies*, 23, 2: 199–224.

1970 "The Comparative History of the Household and Family." *Journal of Social History*, 4, 2: 75–87.

1976 "The family and industrialization: a 'strong theory'." Mimeographed. Cambridge Group for the History of Population and Social Structure, Cambridge.

Laslett, P. and Oosterveen, K.O.

1973 "Long-Term Trends in Bastardy in England." *Population Studies*, 27, 2: 255–286.

Laslett, P. and Wall, R., eds.
    1972 *Household and Family in Past Times*. Cambridge: Cambridge University Press.
Ledermann, S.
    1969 *Nouvelles Tables-Types de Mortalité*. Paris: Presses Universitaires de France.
Lee, R.
    1973 "Population in Pre-Industrial England, an Econometric Analysis." *Quarterly Journal of Economics*, LXXXVII: 581–607.
    1974 "Estimating Series of Vital Rates and Age Structures from Baptisms and Burials: A New Technique, with Applications to Pre-Industrial England." *Population Studies*, 28, 3: 495–512.
Lee, W.
    1849 *Report to the General Board of Health on a preliminary inquiry into the sewerage, drainage and supply of water and the sanitary conditions of the inhabitants of the parish of Loughborough*. London.
Leibenstein, H.
    1957 *Economic Backwardness and Economic Growth*. New York: Wiley.
    1974 "An Interpretation of the Economic Theory of Fertility: Promising Path or Blind Alley?" *Journal of Economic Literature*, 12, 2: 457–479.
Lestaeghe, R.
    1971 "Nuptiality and Population Growth." *Population Studies*, 25, 3: 415–433.
Livi Bacci, M.
    1972 "Some problems in nominal record linkage in Tuscany, 17th–18th centuries." *Annales de Démographie historique*, 323–334.
Lorimer, F.
    1954 *Culture and Human Fertility*. New York: Unesco.
Macfarlane, A.
    1970 *Witchcraft in Tudor and Stuart England*. London: Routledge.
          The Family Life of Ralph Josselin: An Essay in Historical Anthropology. Cambridge: Cambridge University Press.
McKeown, T. and Brown, R.G.
    1965 "Medical Evidence Related to English Population Changes in the Eighteenth Century." In *Population in History*, edited by D.V. Glass and D.E.C. Eversley, pp. 285–307. London: Edward Arnold.
Mantoux, P.
    1965 *The Industrial Revolution in the Eighteenth Century*. New York: Harper & Row.
Martin, J.M.
    1967 "The Parliamentary Enclosure Movement and Rural Society in Warwickshire." *Agricultural History Review*, 15, 1: 19–39.
Marx, K.
    1961 *Capital*. Moscow.
Medick, H.
    1976 "The proto-industrial family economy: The structural function of household and family during the transition from peasant society to industrial capitalism." *Social History*, 3: 291–315.
Medick, H., Kriedte, P., Schlumbohm, J. et al.
    1977 *Industrialisierung vor der Industrialisierung: Gewerbliche Warenproduktion auf dem Land in der Formationsperiode des Kapitalismus*. Göttingen: Vandenhoek & Ruprecht.
Mendels, F.
    1970 "Industrialization and Population Pressure in Eighteenth Century Flanders." Ph.D. dissertation, University of Wisconsin.
          "Industry and Marriages in Flanders before the Industrial Revolution." In

Population and Economics, edited by P. Deprez, pp. 81–93. Winnipeg: University of Manitoba Press.

1972 "Proto-Industrialization: The First Phase of Industrialization." *Journal of Economic History*, XXXII, 1: 241–261.

Mills, D.

1963 "Landownership and Rural Population." Ph.D. dissertation, Leicester University.

1965 "English Villages in the Eighteenth and Nineteenth Centuries: A Sociological Approach." *Amateur Historian*, VI and VII.

1973 (Ed.) *English Rural Communities*. London: Macmillan.

Mingay, G.E.

1968 *Enclosure and the Small Farmer in the Age of the Industrial Revolution*. Studies in Economic History. London: Macmillan.

Monk, J.

1794 *General View of Agriculture of the County of Leicester*. London.

Moxon, C.J.M.

1971 "Ashby-de-la-Zouch—a social and economic survey of a market town—1570–1720." D.Phil. dissertation, Oxford University.

Nichols, J.

1795 *The History and Antiquities of the County of Leicester*. Vol. II, part i and Vol. III, part ii. London.

Ogle, W.

1890 "On Marriage-Rates and Marriage-Ages with Special Reference to the Growth of Population." *Journal of the Royal Statistical Society*, LIII: 253–280.

Ohlin, P.G.

1955 "The Positive and the Preventative Check: A Study of the Rate of Growth of Pre-Industrial Population." Ph.D. dissertation, Harvard University.

1961 "Mortality, Marriage, and Growth in Pre-Industrial Populations." *Population Studies*, 14, 3: 190–197.

Paterson, A. T.

1954 *Radical Leicester*. Leicester: Leicester University Press.

Pentland, H.C.

1972 "Population and Labour Supply: England in the Eighteenth Century." In *Communications, Third International Conference of Economic History, 1965*, pp. 157–189. Paris: Mouton.

Perry, P.J.

1969 "Working-Class Isolation and Mobility in Rural Dorset, 1837–1936: A Study of Marriage Distances." *Transactions of the Institute of British Geographers*, 46: 121–139.

Phillimore, W.P.W. et al., eds.

1906–22 *Derbyshire Parish Registers, Marriages*. Vols. 1–15. London.

1908–14 *Leicestershire Parish Registers, Marriages*. Vols. 1–12. London.

1905–21 *Lincolnshire Parish Registers, Marriages*. Vols. 1–11. London.

1898–39 *Nottinghamshire Parish Registers, Marriages*. Vols. 1–22. London.

Philpot, G.

1975 "Enclosure and Population Growth in Eighteenth Century England." *Explorations in Economic History*, 2nd ser., 12, 1: 29–46.

Pickering, A.J.

1940 *The Cradle of the Hosiery Trade 1640–1940*. Hinckley: W. Pickering & Sons.

Polanyi, K.

1944 *The Great Transformation*. Boston: Beacon.

Pollard, S.
    1968   *The Genesis of Modern Management*. Harmondsworth: Penguin Books.
    1973   "Industrialization and the European Economy." *Economic History Review*, 2nd
            ser., XXVI, 4: 636–648.
Post, J.D.
    1976   "Famine Mortality and Epidemic Disease in the Process of Modernization."
            Economic History Review, 2nd ser., XXIX, 1: 14–37.
Postan, M.M.
    1950   "Some Evidence of the Declining Population in the Later Middle Ages."
            Economic History Review, 2nd ser., 11, 3: 221–246.
Rawstron, E.M.
    1958   "Some Aspects of the Location of Hosiery and Lace Manufacture in Great
            Britain." *East Midland Geographer*, 9: 16–28.
Razzell, P.E.
    1967   "Population Growth and Economic Change in Eighteenth- and Early
            Nineteenth-Century England and Ireland." In *Land, Labour and Population in the
            Industrial Revolution,* edited by E.L. Jones and G.E. Mingay, pp. 260–281.
            London: Edward Arnold.
    1969   "Population Change in Eighteenth Century England: A Re-Appraisal." In *Popu-
            lation in Industrialization,* edited by M. Drake, pp. 128–156. London: Methuen,
            University Paperbacks.
    1972   "The Evaluation of Baptism as a Form of Birth Registration through Cross-
            Matching Census and Parish Register Data: A Study in Methodology." *Popula-
            tion Studies*, 26, 1: 121–146.
Saville, J.
    1969   "Primitive Accumulation and Early Industrialization in Britain." In *The Socialist
            Register, 1969,* pp. 247–271. New York: Monthly Review Press.
Schofield, R.S.
    1970   "Age-Specific Mobility in an Eighteenth Century Rural English Parish." *An-
            nales de Démographie historique*, 261–274.
    1972   "Representativeness and Family Reconstitution." *Annales de Démographie his-
            torique* (1972): 121–126.
    1973   "Dimensions of Illiteracy, 1750–1850." *Explorations in Economic History*, 2nd
            ser., 10, 4 (1973): 437–454.
    1976   "The Pre-Industrial Population and its Economic Space." Mimeographed.
            Cambridge Group for the History of Population and Social Structure, Cam-
            bridge.
Schumpeter, E.B.
    1960   *English Overseas Trade Statistics 1697–1808*. Oxford: Oxford University Press.
Scott, J. and Tilly, L.
    1975   "Women's Work and the Family in Nineteenth-Century Europe." *Comparative
            Studies in Society and History*, 17, 1: 36–64.
Scott, J., Tilly, L., and Cohen, M.
    1976   "Women's Work and European Fertility Patterns." *Journal of Interdisciplinary
            History*, 6, 3: 447–476.
Seward, D.
    1970   "The Devonshire Cloth Industry in the Early Seventeenth Century." In *Industry
            and Society in the South-West*, edited by R. Burt, pp. 31–50. Exeter Papers in
            Economic History, Vol. 3. Exeter: Exeter University Press.
Shorter, E.
    1971   "Illegitimacy, Sexual Revolution and Social Change in Modern Europe." *Journal
            of Interdisciplinary History*, 2, 2: 237–272.

1973   "Female Emancipation, Birth Control and Fertility in European History."
        American Historical Review, 78, 3: 605–640.

1976   *The Making of the Modern Family*. New York: Basic Books.

Shrimpton, C.

1966   "Landed Society and the Farming Community in Essex in the Late 18th and
        Early 19th Centuries." Ph.D. dissertation, Cambridge University.

Skinner, A.J.P., ed.

1928   *The Register of Colyton, Devon, 1538–1837*. Exeter.

Smith, D.S.

1976   "A Homeostatic Demographic Regime. Patterns in West European Family Re-
        constitution Studies." Mimeographed. University of Illinois, Chicago.

Smith, R.

1968   "The Social-Structure of Nottingham and Adjacent Districts in the Mid–
        Nineteenth Century: An Essay in Quantitative Social History." Ph.D. disserta-
        tion, Nottingham University.

Spenceley, G.F.R.

1973   "The Origins of the English Pillow Lace Industry." *Agricultural History Review*,
        21, 2: 81–93.

Spengler, J.J.

1961   "Population Change: Cause, Effect, Indicator." *Economic Development and Cul-
        tural Change*, IX, 3: 249–266.

Stephens, W.B.

1958   *Seventeenth Century Exeter*. Exeter: Exeter University Press.

Tawney, R.H.

1966   *Land and Labour in China*. Boston: Beacon.

1967   *The Agrarian Problem in the Sixteenth Century*. New York: Harper & Row.

Thirsk, J.

1961   "Industries in the Countryside." In *Essays in the Economic and Social History of
        Tudor and Stuart England*, edited by F.J. Fisher, pp. 70–88. Cambridge: Cam-
        bridge University Press.

1967   (Editor) *The Agrarian History of England and Wales*. Cambridge: Cambridge Univ.
        Press.

1973   "The Fantastical Folly of Fashion: The English Stocking Knitting Industry,
        1500–1700." In *Textile History and Economic History*, edited by N.B. Harte and
        K.G. Ponting, pp. 50–73. Manchester: Manchester University Press.

Thomas, K.

1971   *Religion and the Decline of Magic*. London: Weidenfeld & Nicolson.

Thomis, M.

1969   *Politics and Society in Nottingham, 1785–1835*. Oxford: Oxford University Press.

1970   *The Luddites*. Newton Abbott: David and Charles.

Thompson, D.M.

1969   "The Churches and Society in Leicestershire 1851–1881." Ph.D. dissertation,
        Cambridge University.

Thompson, E.P.

1963   *The Making of the English Working Class*. New York: Pantheon.

1965   "The Peculiarities of the English." In *The Socialist Register, 1965*, pp. 311–362.
        New York: Monthly Review Press.

1967   "Time, Work Discipline and Industrial Capitalism." *Past and Present*, 38: 56–97.

1971   "The Moral Economy of the English Crowd in the Eighteenth Century." *Past
        and Present*, 50: 76–136.

1972   " 'Rough Music': Le Charivari anglais." *Annales, E.S.C.*, XXVII, 2: 285–312.

1974   "Patrician Society, Plebian Culture." *Journal of Social History*, 7, 4: 382–405.

Tilly, C.
    1964   *The Vendée*. Cambridge, Mass.: Harvard University Press.
Titow, J.Z.
    1961   "Some Evidence of the Thirteenth Century Population Increase." *Economic History Review*, 2nd ser., XIV, 2: 218–222.
Tranter, N.L.
    1966   "Demographic Change in Bedfordshire from 1670–1800." Ph.D. dissertation, Nottingham University.
    1967   "Population and Social Structure in a Bedfordshire Parish." *Population Studies*, 21, 2: 261–282.
Tucker, G.S.L.
    1963   "English Pre-Industrial Population Trends." *Economic History Review*, 2nd ser., XVI, 2: 205–218.
Vancouver, C.
    1808   *A General View of the Agriculture of the County of Devon*. London.
Wall, R.
    1976   "Reconstitution and census: Colytonians in parish register and enumerator's book." Mimeographed. Cambridge Group for the History of Population and Social Structure, Cambridge.
Wallerstein, I.
    1974   *The Modern World-System*. New York: Academic Press.
Wells, F.A.
    1972   *The British Hosiery and Knitwear Industry*. 2nd ed. Newton Abbott: David and Charles.
West, F.
    1966   "The Social and Economic History of the East Fen Village of Wrangle, 1603–1837." Ph.D. dissertation, Leicester University.
White, W.
    1846   *History, Gazetteer, and Directory of Leicestershire*. Sheffield.
Wolff, K.
    1963   "Stages in Industrial Organization." *Explorations in Entrepreneurial History*, 2nd ser., 1, 1: 125–144.
Wrigley, E.A.
    1966   (Editor) *An Introduction to English Historical Demography*. London: Weidenfeld & Nicolson.
    1967   "A Simple Model of London's Importance in Changing English Society and Economy 1650–1750." *Past and Present*, 37: 44–70.
    1968   "Mortality in Pre-Industrial England: The Example of Colyton, Devon, Over Three Centuries." *Daedalus*, 97: 546–580.
    1969   "Family Limitation in Pre-Industrial England." In *Population in Industrialization*, edited by M. Drake, pp. 157–194. London: Methuen, University Paperbacks. *Population and History*. London: World University Library.
    1972   "Some problems of family reconstitution using English parish register material: The example of Colyton." In *Communications, Third International Conference of Economic History, 1965*, pp. 199–221. Paris: Mouton.
            (Editor) *The Study of Nineteenth Century Society*. Cambridge: Cambridge University Press.
            "The Process of Modernization and the Industrial Revolution in England." *Journal of Interdisciplinary History*, 3, 2: 225–259.
    1975   "Baptism Coverage in Early Nineteenth-Century England: The Colyton Area." *Population Studies*, 29, 2: 299–316.
            "Fertility Strategy for the Individual and the Group." Mimeographed. Cam-

bridge Group for the History of Population and Social Structure, Cambridge, 1975.

1976   "The changing occupational structure of Colyton over two centuries." *Local Population Studies,* in press.

Wrightson, K.E.
   1975   "Terling and the Courts." Mimeographed. University of St Andrews, St Andrews.

Wrightson, K.E., and Levine, D.
   1977   "The Social Context of Illegitimacy in Early Modern England." In *Bastardy and Its Comparative History,* edited by P. Laslett and R. Smith. London: Edward Arnold. In press.

Yelling, J.A.
   1968   "Common Land and Enclosure in East Worcestershire, 1540–1870." *Transactions of the Institute of British Geographers,* 43: 157–168.

   1973   "The Combination and Rotation of Crops in East Worcestershire, 1540–1660." *Agricultural History Review,* 17, 1: 24–43.
      "Changes in Crop Production in East Worcestershire 1540–1867." *Agricultural History Review,* 21, 1: 18–33.

INDEX

A
B   7
C   8
D   9
E   0
F   1
G   2
H   3
I   4
J   5